OLDE LEEKE.

LEEK OLD TOWN HALL

A. Mosley

CONTENTS.

xvi   CONTENTS.

LIST OF ILLUSTRATIONS.

OLDE LEEKE.

The Old Town Hall.

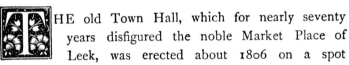

HE old Town Hall, which for nearly seventy years disfigured the noble Market Place of Leek, was erected about 1806 on a spot where once stood an old stone cross, which cross, shortly before the hall was built, was removed to land belonging to the parish on Compton, and it now stands a somewhat prominent object in the Cemetery. Round this cross the country people used, on market days, to stand with butter and eggs for sale as they do in the immediate neighbourhood of the fountain, which, thanks to the generosity of Mr. Challinor, now adorns the bottom end of the **Market Place.**

Towards the cost of the building the then Earl of Macclesfield gave a donation of twenty guineas, and the sum of £160 was allowed by the county out of the rates. The residue was raised by subscription in shares, which were afterwards bought up by the trustees of the Town Lands.

The edifice was designed and built by Mr. Joseph Radford (maternal grandfather of Mr. Samuel Travis), who kept the Black's Head Inn.   As constable or head-borough, he was connected, in company with Mr. William Lowndes, butcher, of Cawdry, in the apprehension of George Fearne, of Bottom House, who was, with others of the gang, hung at Stafford, for forging bank notes.

In the basement of the building were two cells or lock-ups, in which, before the erection of the present police office, prisoners were temporarily incarcerated. The ground floor was originally left open for the use of the market people, the upper room (supported on stone pillars) was occasionally used by the magistrates, also by the managers of the Savings Bank, and generally by the inhabitants for the public purposes of the town.   In course of time, the open portion of the building on the ground floor being found dark and inconvenient, was deserted by the market people, and was by most persons deemed a nuisance.

About the year 1817, certain gentlemen of the town who, it is said, used to meet to read the newspapers at the Queen's Head or in some room in Custard street (now Stanley street), determined, by subscription, to convert the ground floor into a news-room by putting in sash windows and building up the space between the pillars.   This was done, and the room was occupied principally as a news-room until June, 1871.

In June, 1848, at the freeholders' annual meeting a committee was appointed to inquire into, and report generally on the state of the property known as the Leek Town Lands.   In the course of inquiries made by this committee, it was ascertained that the sum of more than £800 had been paid out of the freeholders' fund towards the erection of the Town Hall, including £400 for the repayment of loans, £288 for interest, and £54 odd for alterations.

About this time, the freeholders finding the building had been paid for, chiefly from their funds, passed a resolution that application should be made to the managers of the Savings Bank for payment of £6, being a charge for the use of the room for one year: this sum was paid. A resolution was also passed unanimously, that application should be made to the occupants of the news-room for a similar sum of £6, being a year's rent for the use of the room. Repeated applications were made, but the members, for certain reasons, declined to pay, and the room continued to be occupied rent free.

As no rent was paid for the room, and as the Trustees of the Town Lands had all died, the freeholders at a meeting held in 1851, deemed it right that no further time should be lost in obtaining the appointment of new trustees, and authorised the committee to take the needful steps thereto, by applying to the Court of Chancery, and also as to their right to charge rent for the news-room. This was resisted by the occupiers of the room, and in consequence a considerable sum was spent in litigation, but before judgment was given proceedings were stayed.

At the freeholders' meeting held at the Town Hall in June, 1870, the Trustees of the Town Lands and other freeholders present were unanimous in expressing their opinion that, as the building was a dirty, unsightly,

and an almost useless erection, it would be very desirable
if it were taken down and entirely swept away.   Fortunately, the members of the news-room generally—with
the exception of some three or four—signed a document
agreeing to leave the room at the end of June, 1871.

As a public building, it had long become almost
useless, having for public purposes been superseded by
larger and more convenient buildings.   Whatever may
have been thought of it as an architectural ornament
at the time of its erection, it had long ceased to have
any attractions, but was rather considered a disfigurement, and by some a disgrace to the inhabitants that
they should allow it to continue so long to deface
their otherwise handsome Market Square.

On June 24th, 1871, after the annual meeting of
the Town Lands Trustees, over which the late Mr.
Joshua Nicholson presided, his friend and partner, the
late Mr. Joshua Brough, moved "That in the opinion
of this meeting the Leek Town Hall is, as a central
public building, a disfigurement and of little use to the
inhabitants."   The motion was seconded by the late
Mr. Samuel Haynes and carried *nem. con.*   Mr. H. L.
Johnson then moved, and Mr. E. Pickford seconded
—"That the building at the bottom of the Market
Place, called the 'Town Hall,' be handed over to the
Improvement Comissioners, to be by them, as soon as
convenient, taken down and disposed of as they may
think best, for the benefit of the ratepayers."   Upon
the Chairman putting the resolution to the meeting it
was declared to be carried unanimously.

A handbill was issued about this time by "A Free-
holder," who expressed his opinion in the following

vigorous fashion :—" It is reported that there are a few miserable, old-fashioned persons who, from selfish or other reasons, think that the old building should not be disturbed, and who intend to oppose its being taken down—and if any resolution is passed at the meeting in favour of sweeping it away, they talk about applying to the Court of Chancery for an injunction to stop it. When the old hall was first built—at a time when a great portion of the houses in Leek were covered with thatch—when there was not a steam engine in the town —and when the population only numbered a little over 3,000, it might be sufficient for the wants of the inhabitants. But at the present day to allow the little dirty building to stand in your Market Place, and to call it a Town Hall, is simply a disgrace to you. What do you call it ?—A Town Hall ! Faugh !—Call it a Magpie Cage, and remove it out of sight at once."

The strange gift was accepted by the Commissioners, and on December 29th, 1871, the Board determined to sell by auction the materials forming the condemned edifice, and accordingly advertisements were inserted in the *Leek Times* fixing the sale for January 15th, 1872. On the day named the Market Place presented an animated appearance, a large crowd of Commissioners and tradesmen surrounding the rostrum of the late Mr. William Michael Hilliard, who had undertaken to sell the building without cost to the ratepayers. Having read the death warrant, the auctioneer remarked that during his long practice he had never before had the honour and pleasure of submitting a town hall to public competition. The block—or rather, as he said, stumbling-block, they had long been ashamed to call a town hall,

so unsuitable was it for the public purposes of a large
town like Leek. The first bid was £10 by Mr.
Thomas Hulme, and slowly the amount rose to £75.
Then the bidding appeared to have ceased, and the
auctioneer appealed, for some time in vain, for an
advance, stating that it would be a disgrace to Leek
to knock the building down for such a paltry sum.
Ultimately the whole of the materials were sold to
Mr. Joseph Flower, of Westwood Terrace, for £85, and
was afterwards removed to Rosebank, and now forms
part of Portland House, where he resides. On the
motion of Mr. Hilliard, seconded by Mr. John Ward,
a vote of thanks was unanimously passed to Mr. Joshua
Brough, through whose instrumentality the removal of
the "unsightly excrescence" had been mainly effected.

From the Nicholson Institute.

Graphic Sketch of Leek.

PEAKING on November 17th, 1881, in acknow-
ledgment of the presentation of his portrait,
which now adorns the Improvement Commissioners' Board-room at the Town Hall, the late
Mr. Joshua Brough said that about 1811, when first he
came to the school now conducted by Mr. Sykes, the
Rev. Richard Bentley, the vicar of Leek, was the master.
He recollected very well Mr. Bentley writing the men-
suration table in his account book and giving him some
needful instructions. After remaining at the school some
time he was removed to a school taught by a Mr.
Hobson, where he remained until the latter end of the
year 1815. His father had then entered into partnership
with a gentleman in the silk trade, with whom he (the
speaker) had to serve a five years' apprenticeship. The
partnership was dissolved in the year 1821, and he had
then to take the sole charge of the business, and turn
out at the age of 18 with a bag and some patterns
as a commercial traveller. This occupation he found
uphill work for sometime, for even then competition was
strong and prejudice great. However, he persevered
and by degrees the trade increased and a fair living-
profit was the result. Going back to his early years
to describe the town of Leek with respect to its

buildings, it contained some very good houses (as there were now) interspersed with a great number of thatched houses and cottages, many of which were of mean appearance, and were low and uncomfortable dwellings. The main streets, however, were then, as they are described in some of the old histories, wide, well-paved, and clean. At that time there were no lights or lamps in the streets, and the inhabitants on dark nights, had to carry a lanthorn, or grope their way as best they could. He need not say to-day that a very different state of affairs exists: the streets are all well lighted with brilliant gas, thanks to Mr. John Ward, who, with others, had on the whole, managed the gas very well. Formerly, most of the footpaths were narrow and unflagged; now they are generally of good width and well-flagged. Formerly dirt and filth were allowed to accumulate; now the streets, roads, ash-pits, etc., are regularly cleared by a staff of scavengers and carters. Formerly safety and order were attended to by one solitary constable in the day-time, and by three or four old watchmen (or "Charleys" as they were called) by night, who used to cry out the hour and state of the weather; now by a body of clever, able, and well-appointed policemen. Formerly a great number of the houses and cottages were covered with thatch; now all the buildings in the town were covered with tiles or slates. Formerly the streets were not labelled or the houses numbered; now all the streets were labelled with cast iron labels and the houses numbered. Formerly the lower part of Stockwell Street was narrow and quite in a valley; now the road had been raised and levelled, and the footpaths flagged and channels paved.

Joshua Brough

Formerly the road leading from the bottom of Stockwell Street to Ballhaye Green was very narrow and without footpaths; now the road was much widened and improved. Formerly the entrance to the town from Newcastle, the wharf, and the railway station, was narrow, steep and dirty; now the road from the station had been very much widened and a good flagged footpath made, and a part of the road from the bottom of St. Edward Street, as they all knew, is now in the course of being further widened and improved. Formerly the lower part of Brook Street (then called Workhouse Lane) was very narrow, not being sufficiently wide for two carriages to pass abreast, and on one side of the street there were several old, dirty-looking, and dilapidated houses; now these houses, after much tedious negotiation with the owner, had been taken down and clean swept away, and the street made thirty-six feet wide. Formerly the entrance from Mill Street to West Street (or as it was then called Barn Gates) was by a narrow inconvenient passage; now, by the purchase of land and building from various persons and societies, and by the permission of the county authorities to reduce the size of the police station yard, and the kindness of Mr. Stephen Goodwin in taking away some land in front of his mill, the street had been much enlarged, and is now wide and well paved. He ought here to say that Mr. Robinson, of Westwood, contributed a very considerable sum towards the expense, and he (Mr. Brough) and others contributed smaller sums. Formerly cattle, both horses, horned cattle, and sheep were exposed for sale on fair days in the leading streets, and on the footpaths, much to the inconvenience and discomfort of the inhabitants, and by the dirt and filth thus occasioned, the air was so polluted as to render it injurious to health; now, by the new central and extensive cattle market in Haywood Street, the site for which the Commissioners obtained on very reasonable terms, all the unpleasantness was avoided, and the dealers in cattle had every reasonable accommodation for transacting their business—and which he believed gave very general satisfaction. Formerly the business of the Savings Bank was transacted with depositors every other Monday, in a small inconvenient room at the old Town Hall; now by the aid of a few friends who advanced a portion of the funds required, a new and substantial building had been erected in an excellent situation, at the corner of Russell Street, in Derby Street, and was open to depositors every Monday. The Mechanics' Institution, established by himself and a few friends in the year 1837, was at first held in a small low room in Russell Street. Some cottage property being on sale, where the institution now stands, he bought the property on his own responsibility, and immediately re-sold it at cost price to trustees for a site on which to build the present institution, which as they all knew is a handsome, lofty, and convenient building, containing a spacious reading room, sundry committee rooms and an excellent library stored with books, which for extent and value would bear comparision with any mechanics' library in the county, and the building was out of debt. Formerly there stood at the bottom of the Market Place, a small insignificant building, the upper room of which was approached by a flight of stone steps on the ouiside of the building, opposite to Mr. Andrew's shop.

At his instance and with the unanimous consent of the trustees and the Improvement Commissioners, the building was taken down and the space on which it stood was thrown open to the Market Place. Another eligible site has been purchased on which at some future time a town hall, a covered market, Commissioners' offices, and other public buildings may be erected. On the space thus thrown open to the Market Place their friend, Mr. Challinor, had, with a munificence not often shown to the ratepayers in Leek, purchased at considerable expense and presented to the town a beautiful drinking fountain, a specimen of art designed by the late Mr. Durham, R.A., and which as a work of art when exhibited in London called forth the admiration of a considerable number of art critics and persons of taste. Mr. Brough urged strongly the necessity of the erection of a covered market and public offices, believing that although they were now in a most commodious place it would be better to be in a building of their own.

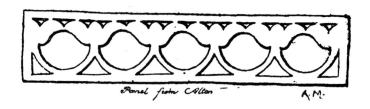

Panel from Alton — A.M.

The Leek Theatre.

NEARLY one hundred years ago, the now disused theatre behind the Swan Hotel, was the scene of some of the early triumphs of Miss Harriot Mellon, who married Mr. Coutts, the great London banker, and subsequently became Duchess of St. Albans. She was then only eighteen years of age, but had already attracted a good deal of notice, her talent being of an undoubtedly high order and her beauty very remarkable. She came to Leek whilst a new theatre was being built at Stafford, and she must have resided in the town for upwards of twelve months. Her father was a Mr. Entwistle, and whilst he was in Leek he appears to have endeavoured to add to his slender income by teaching the violin and piano. The theatre was open only three nights a week, and Mr. Entwistle's tuition of the young ladies of the town brought upon him the jealous violence of his wife, who was a perfect virago, and upon Harriot fell all the discomforts of a miserable home. She returned to Stafford to open the new theatre in 1792, and three years later she appeared at Drury Lane, London, and Leek knew her no more. We have before us an old playbill bearing date April 4th, 1796, Theatre Royal, Drury Lane, announcing that their Majesties'

servants will act a comedy, called *The School for
Scandal*, with full caste, and a new pantomime called
Harlequin Captine, or The Magic Fire, and among
the names of the principal lady actors is to found
that of Miss Mellon. Her last appearance on the
stage was on February 7th, 1815, and at the end of
the same month she married her friend and benefactor,
Mr. Coutts, and was presented at Court. Her husband
died on March 2nd, 1822, and on June 16th, 1826,
she married the Duke of St. Albans.

We have also before us an old playbill, printed on
white satin by Messrs. Hilliard and Son (who in 1760
introduced printing into Leek), of a performance in the
Theatre, Leek, of Morton's comedy, *The School of
Reform; or How to Rule a Husband*. The occasion
is described as the "seventh fashionable evening," the
prices of admission being two shillings to the pit, and
one shilling to the gallery. The caste included Messrs.
Davenport, Copeland, Bickerton, Howard, Bonsall (manager), Bell, Fishwick, and Mesdames Davenport, Bickerton,
Berriman, and Miss Bickerton. As an interlude, Mr.
Fishwick sang a comic song, by particular desire; and
Mr. Fishwick gave "the admired song, called 'Nice
Young Maidens'"; the performance closing with a laughable farce, *The Lying Valet*.

A second playbill, also on white satin, which was
"presented to R. Gaunt, Esq.," is in our possession,
giving details of probably the first performance in Leek
of *The Rivals*. The principal performers were Messrs.
Manly, Pearce, H. Benwell, C. Thornhill ("Bob Acres"),
St. Clair, Thornhill, Braint; Miss Hilton ("Lydia
Languish"), Mrs. Thornhill ("Mrs. Malaprop"), and the

Misses Thornhill and E. Thornhill. After a laughable interlude called *The Rendevouz*, the farce of *The Spoil'd Child*, was played, Miss Hilton enacting "Little Pickle" —the character Miss Mellon essayed when making her *debut* at Ulverstone in 1787.

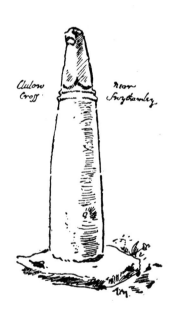

Execution of John Naden.

THE MURDER.

JOHN NADEN, the unhappy author of the following most wicked act, was born at Hore's Clough, near Leek, in the County of Stafford, of poor but honest parents, who, so far as their slender capacity would admit, bestowed what learning they could upon him, insomuch that he attained a competent knowledge in reading and writing, promising in the blossom of his youth, a fair prospect of a happy and comfortable life in his riper years. But, alas! how unstable and unfixed are the minds of most youths; for, coming home, having acquired what learning was thought by his parents most convenient for him, was placed some time after in quality of hired servant to one Mr. Robt. Brough, grazier, of White Lea, with whom he behaved himself faithful in every respect, till by the sweet allurements of his mistress, who with wanton dalliances, and fair promises, drew him into a fatal snare, and proved the death of her husband and the untimely end of her servant, and 'tis hoped herself will share the same fate as the latter. . . . The said John Naden had not been long in service, but his mistress several times importuned him to murder her husband, that thereby they might have the freer access together, without suspicion; and by so doing he should become master of his store. He seemed at first unwilling, but by her daily persuasions consented, and soon after perfected both their designs.

THE TRIAL.

When he was apprehended and carried before Thomas Palmer, coroner, and examined concerning the murder, he denied the fact; but the evidence appearing plain against him, he was committed to Stafford gaol, on Saturday, 25th June, 1731, in order to take his trial at the Assizes following.

The committing magistrate was Thomas Hollinshead, Esq., of Ashenhurst, and the *Gentleman's Magazine* had it that Naden "first knocked Brough down, then cut a great gash under his nose, and another on his wrist, and having almost separated his head from his body, left him."

On Thursday, 19th August, 1731, the Assizes began at Stafford, and the charge against him being read, and several questions propounded by the judge concerning the murder, he again denied the fact, pleading "not guilty."

It seems that his mistress had advised him beforehand to swear against one William Wardle, a prisoner then in the said gaol, as the chief person who committed the murder: but a great number of credible persons appearing in the said Wardle's behalf, and giving him a character suitable to his deserts, he was acquitted; nay, even John Naden himself afterwards cleared him, by affirming his innocence in open court, and heartily begged his pardon.

Naden was then tried for the murder and found guilty, and the Judge proceeded to pronounce sentence against him, viz.:—That on Tuesday, the 31st August, he should be brought to his master's door, where he committed the fact, and there hanged till he was dead, and afterwards conveyed to Gun Common, near Danebridge, and there hanged in chains.

THE CONFESSION.

On August 25th, 1731, Naden made the following confession whilst lying in Stafford gaol, under sentence of death:—"I, John Naden, do confess (not having the fear of God before my eyes, but spurred on by the instigation of the devil), that I am guilty of the murder of my master, Robert Brough, by cutting my said master's throat with his own knife. I cannot reflect upon the abominable fact but with the greatest horror and abhorrence, and therefore must own the justice of my sentence, most willingly submitting myself to undergo the same; hoping by sincere repentance, for pardon and remission of this most heinous sin, and all other my grievous sins, through the merits of my dear Redeemer, Jesus Christ. Now, what prompted me to do this most wicked fact, was that unlawful familiarity I had with my mistress, the wife of my said master, Robert Brough: I had never attempted such familiarity, had she not first made me offers of the same. Soon after this, about three or four years ago, she gave me a ring, and expressed her love to me, and said if anything happened to my master she should be very happy with me. In the procedure of our acquaintance, she continued often making suchlike professions, but

towards the last she solicited me to murder him, or
to have him murdered, adding, that if I would not do
it, she would have it done.   After her frequent persuasions to this bloody fact, I went out to meet my
master, about a fortnight before he was murdered, on
his return from Congleton market; but being then
disappointed, at my coming home she expressed a great
deal of anger, and asked me why I had not done it,
meaning why I had not murdered my said master.
Upon the morning of that fatal day whereon the murder
was committed, . . . I concluded with her to murder
my master, he my said master having determined to
part with me from his service.   I accordingly followed
him to Leek, and on his return home, I, being much
heated with liquor, did way-lay and did also take away
his life, as before stated.   Soon after I came to my
master's house, and in a little time acquainted her with
what I had done.   Afterwards, when the family were
gone to bed, she went out to the place where my
master lay murdered, rifled his pockets, and threw the
knife (the unfortunate instrument wherewith I committed
the murder) over the hedge.   She, my said mistress,
called me up about three o'clock in the morning, and
told me this, and bid me say that I saw William
Wardle, an innocent person, do the murder.   By her
wicked persuasions I accused the said Wardle upon
oath, for which enormous crime I heartily beg pardon,
and wish it was in my power to make him satisfaction.
In the meantime, I beg forgiveness from all I have
injured, and do declare and solemnly affirm this my
confession to be exactly true, as I am a dying man,
and expect in a few days to appear before the tribunal

of the Great God of Heaven: as witness my hand
this 27th day of August, 1731.—JOHN NADEN."

THE EXECUTION.

The 31st August, 1731, was a hot and sultry day.
The sun rose in a clear blue sky, there being not the
slightest appearance of a cloud in the firmanent to hide
its bright and life-giving light from the earth.

"To die on such a day as this," said Naden, as
he gazed through the window in one of the upper
rooms of the Cock Inn, Leek, "is hard, and yet 'tis just,
for could I die a dozen times I could not wipe out the
heinous sin I have committed," and as he spoke
large tears rolled down his cheek.

"I am glad to see that thou art in such a frame
of mind," said one of the clergymen who had been
keeping vigils with him, "for it is only by true
penitence that thou can'st be prepared to meet thy
Maker."

"I do repent me of all my sins," sobbed the
culprit, "but God's mercy is very great, or there
would be no mercy for me, and though I have been
a vile wretch, I hope for pardon through the merits
of Jesus Christ."

Shortly after the Rev. Mr. Corn, and the other
clergyman from Leek, administered the sacrament to
the wretched man, and also gave him such other
consolation as they deemed necessary to prepare him
for his doom.

That had been an awful night in Leek. Most of
the public-houses were kept open all night, and whilst
Naden was preparing himself for his fate with his

spiritual advisers, in the other rooms of the Cock Inn and the various public-houses of the town, scenes of a different kind and of a more repulsive nature were transpiring. Hundreds of persons who had come on the previous night, with many of the inhabitants of the town itself, spent the night in revel. In any one of the inns and taverns groups of men of all ages and conditions, and women, too, were drinking draughts of the home-brewed beer for which Leek was famous, and more fiery spirituous liquors, some discussing the crime for which Naden had to suffer, and others debauching themselves, as if their only object was to besot themselves and thus deaden their sensibilities, to enable them all the better to witness the sad sight with which they were waiting to satisfy their morbid passions.

Long before the time appointed for the procession to start many of them were helplessly drunk, and a more shocking spectacle than was subsequently presented can scarcely be imagined.

About nine o'clock in the morning the choirs from Leek, Bosley, and Wincle Churches met outside the Cock Inn, and sang a funeral hymn, and about the same time the public-houses disgorged their contents, and the sickening sight that was presented in the Market-place and Stockwell Street cannot be described. There were some present whose faces bespoke sympathy and sorrow, others seemed impressed with the solemnity of the occasion, and expressed their feelings in a demonstrative manner, but the majority were a drunken rabble, whose coarse jests and occasional vulgar ditties only too truly showed that they were there from feelings of morbid curiosity more than anything else.

Presently Naden was led from the inn, his head resting upon his breast, his hands clasped, and his eyes fixed upon the ground. As he proceeded slowly from the house, in a nervous and most pitiable condition, he muttered words scarcely audible, as if he were already communicating with the dead. A clergyman walked on either side of him, whispering words of consolation and hope in his ears. Mr. Thomas Hollinshead, one of the committing magistrates, was also present to conduct the execution, and he walked in front of the procession, carrying the warrant for the execution. The halter was already round Naden's neck, the end of it being borne by the hangman, who walked immediately behind him, and attending this official were also several officers, one of whom carried the heavy chains in which the murderer had to be hanged on Gun-Common. After them walked the three choirs already mentioned, and then followed the motley rabble. Thus formed, the procession started on its awful errand, the choirs singing appropriate hymns and psalms, and many of the others who followed acting in a coarse and unseemly manner. Arriving at White Lea the clergyman again asked Naden if he was fully prepared to die, when he said in a low voice that he was, and added that he would not live longer if he could do so. The hangman then reared a lander against a branch of the tree in front of Brough's house, and after the funeral service had been read by the clergyman, the choirs sang the 51st psalm.

Naden was then ordered to mount the ladder, and as he did so, he lifted up his hands and shook his head sorrowfully, wishing his friends good-bye, and begging of them to take warning from his terrible end. He particularly begged of Wardle to forgive him, and then lifting up his eyes towards heaven, he fervently exclaimed, "O Lord, be merciful to me, John Naden, and show the greatness of Thy mercy, in pardoning a great and notorious offender. Amen."

In another moment the rope, which had been fastened to the tree, was adjusted on his neck, and the ladder was removed, leaving the body suspended in the air. As this was done a thrill of horror ran through the crowd, some of the women shrieked and fainted, and the most hardened and callous-hearted men quaked at the terrible sight as they beheld the wretched man dangling from the tree. When the ladder was removed the body gave several violent spasmodic jerks, a gurgling noise was heard in the throat, the legs and arms worked convulsively for some minutes, the chest heaved heavily, the face became black as suffocation became more intense, the eyes almost burst from their sockets, and blood began to ooze from the mouth, nostrils, and ears of the unfortunate man. Then all was over. He died a hard and violent death. After the body had hung from the tree three-quarters of an hour it was cut down. The cavalcade was then re-formed, and the corpse was borne to a place called Danebridge, or Gun Common, and there hanged in chains to a gallows erected for the purpose, and it is said that the body hung there until one limb fell from another.

A portion of the gallows-tree, utilized as a gate-post, remained until very recently; and people still living remember the irons heavily swinging from its cross-arm in the winter's blast.

The Grub Street Journal, of September 16th, 1731, said :—"Stafford, August 30. This day John Naden who murdered his master, Mr. Brough, was carried on a horse having his legs ty'd and hand cuft, to Leek. The next morning he was carried to the highest hill on Gun Heath, within a quarter of a mile of his master's house, where in the presence of some thousands of spectators he confessed the facts for which he died. The gibbet is 21 feet high, and may be seen 5 miles round the country. The chains which were made by one of Birmingham, are made in so curious a manner, that they will keep his bones together till they turn to powder, if the iron will last so long."

TRADITIONS OF NADEN.

Traditions concerning John Naden, collected from oral accounts preserved by various respectable persons long resident in Leekfrith :—

1. John Naden was a handsome, and, at first, an amiable young man. Prior to his adulterous connection with Mrs. Brough he was attached to his master, and had saved him from death by drowning.

2. When Mr. Brough was returning from Congleton market, Naden went out to meet him, and tried to crush his master to death between a gate and its post. Brough subsequently remarked to a person that his man had thus tried to murder him. But no attention was paid to the remark, as it was believed to be a jest.

3. On the night of the murder Naden, as he stated in his confession, followed his master to Leek. As they returned Mr. Brough stayed to drink at the Abbey Green public house. Naden knew this, and

hastened on to the gate situated, as an old song says—
"Within a call of the Hollin Hall." Against this gate he
placed a stone, so that when his master came up, he
must necessarily stoop to remove it. By-and-bye Mr.
Brough arrived; and whilst bending to move the stone
Naden struck him and afterwards cut his throat.

4. As the murderer travelled through Danebridge
he called at a house to get a drink. The girl who
supplied him, noticed that he took the cup with his
left hand, and at the same time blood was seen upon
him, and this led to his conviction.

5. When being led to the place of execution, as
he arrived at Gun Gate, the crowd on either side was
so dense as to appear like a living wall. Naden,
viewing the concourse, remarked, "Take all the women
out of my sight."

6. The ladder used was borrowed from the Hulmes
of Wetwood. When taken back they would not again
use it, but took it and made a stile of it on the road
between Wetwood and Burnt Oak Hollins. This stile
has but recently been taken up.

7. On the day he was hanged Meerbrook public
house was "sold out," and Barber, the landlord, "wished
a man was hung every day."

8. After Naden had been gibbetted some time his
brothers took him down and buried him in a stone
pit near, but the inhabitants of the country round
dragged him out, and again hung him up.

9. Mrs. Brough died a truly wretched death at
either Peck's house, or Cloud House, in Rushton.

10. Some time during this century Mr. John Hulme
took down the gibbet post and made it into two gate

posts, and a post to stop the gate from opening **too**
far.   The western gate post, and also the stop post
were burned at the great fire on Gun in 1855-6.   One
stout oaken post still remains standing, about twenty
yards south-west of the place of execution.

Cistercian Monk Ploughing.

Ancient Poor Law Administration.

FROM an account book, kept by George Lomas "overseer of the poor," in 1698, we are able to give some details of the way in which the poor were relieved in those ancient times. The places included in Lomas's authority were Leekfrith, Tittesworth, Heaton, Rushton (spelt Ruston) Spencer, Rushton James, and Leek, and at a meeting held on April 11th, 1699, the year's accounts were "seen and allowed." The following summary is given:—

	£	s.	d.
Leekfrith...	54	16	09
Tittesworth	16	11	10
Heaton	15	16	05
Rushton Spencer	14	02	01
Rushton James...	26	10	09
Leek	38	08	05
Warrants and other things ...	08	14	04
In all ...	172	00	08

This amount appears to have been more than the overseer had received, for he thus summarises:

	£	s.	d.
Received	165	00	00
Disburs'd	172	00	03
Out of purse...	007	00	08

Then follow the signatures of 25 persons, of which we give a *fac-simile* and transcription :—

J. HAWKSWORTH, Delt.

JOSUAH POTTS,   ED. BUTLER,
WILLIAM ARMETT,   RICHARD GOODWIN,
JOHN GENT,   THO: FFISHITT,
THOMAS PLANT,   THOMAS PYOTT,
RALPH MOUNTFOORT,   WM. NICKSON,
JOS: WHITSALL,   WILLIAM ALLEN,
WILL: HULME,   SAM: GOODFELLOWE,
RICHARD CLOULOW,   JAMES BRADDOCK,
JOHN DRESSER,   JOHN COOKE,
RICHARD WOOD,   CLULOW GRINDEY,
JOHN BURTINGHAW,   JOHN ALLEN,
WILL: BORSHONOUGH,   JOHN POTTS.
WILL: BROUGH,

Amongst the curious items of expenditure (the details of receipts are not given) we find the following:

	£	s.	d.
John Nichson	02	19	10
For 2 yds. and an half of linen cloth to make him a shirt	00	01	11
James Davenport, blind	08	18	00
His house-rent	00	12	00
John Dording, before and in his sickness	00	14	06
Laid out att his funeral	00	02	06
To Vicar, tolling, and grave	00	02	01
For coffin and carriage	00	04	08
Affidavit, bier, and carrying him on horse back to Leek	00	01	10
Ye Vicar, for coming from Leeke to Meerbrooke, with his fees...	00	03	01
Paid John Hulme for Ruth Barber's table (board) when she lay in of a bastard child and for midwife...	00	10	00

My charges for going into Hartington parish about tabling Ruth Barber's child and seeking after its father 00 13 06

For 3 peck and an half of meal for John Alloby, sick 00 04 00

For a coat for Tho. Goodwin and in his sickness 00 05 09

Spent att making my accounts 00 05 00

Joyce Plant, Blind 03 00 00

For a wastcoat and shift for her 00 05 00

Meat and drink at Will Sherratt's funerall 00 02 06

Cloths for Aron Hunt and pair of clogs... 00 06 04

Margeret Clows in her weekness 00 04 06

Cloths for Tho: Shipplebothom's girl and making up 00 05 06

The funeral of Thomas Lowns, of Pool, for a sheet,* tolling, grave, and Vicar ... 00 04 08

For a warrant for Charles Brindley for bringing me his child 00 00 06

For warrant of good behaviour against Ellis Moss 00 02 06

First time meeting of overseers at Leek, spent 00 00 06

Spent at monthly meeting at Cheddleton on Samuel Goodfellow, Edward Butler and myself... ... ... 00 03 06

Charges of two men for pursuing and apprehending Ann Shaw for over-running her child, and for lodging, meat, drink, and attendance 00 07 06

*This was at a time when only the upper crust of the poor were treated to a coffin with a false bottom.

For keeping Matthew Stubbs his wife one
night ... ... oo oo o6
Paid to surgeon for curing Emanuel Wood's
child's thigh and Tho: Cope's hand ... oɪ oo oo
Towards burying Alice Ffisher's child ... oo o5 oo
To Barbarah Spilsbury and her son both of
'em being sick ... ... oo 12 oo
Paid for house room for Matthew Stubbs's
wife, and to John Shipple Bottom ... ... oo o5 o5
Paul Aderton, for 3 weeks' boarding for a
bastard child of Tho. Knight's ... ... oo o3 o6

Altogether there an airiness about the accounts that
would astonish Mr. John Dolby or any other district
auditor. The overseer of those days was evidently a
man to be trusted, and the vestries had to take a
good deal for granted. The charming innocence of
lumping together the relief granted before and during
a man's sickness would not pass current for innocence
in these days; and it is just possible that something
might be said about the entries for personal expenses,
which appear to have an odour of strong ale about
them. One thing, however, is quite clear, and that
is that it was possible to be buried at a cheap rate.
The uniform charge in 1698 was 2s. 1d., and this
sum included "vicar, tolling and grave." Now the
charge is 9s. 6d.

The accounts for 1710, however, shew that the
vicar, clerk, and sexton had raised their charges to 2s. 8d.,
and that the items for "meat and drink" at funerals
varied from 10s. to 4s. 6d. In that year relief to the
poor was "stipended and paid." The summary runs as
follows :—

	£	s.	d.
Leekfryth	76	19	07
Tittesworth	06	18	03
Rudyard	11	01	06
Heaton	12	11	10
Rushton James...	42	02	09
Rushton Spencer	19	18	00
Leek poor	14	02	04
By chances	32	03	09½
Other payments	00	13	00
	208	08	04½

" Chances " appear to have been payment by a
note," " by consent," or " upon a certificate," and
among others are the following :—

Paid to Doctor Charles Hulme my proportion
for business to several poor persons ... 00 08 03

Charges for taking John Trafford before a
justice and boarding him for 20 weeks... 00 15 10

My charge for taking John Chappel to
Caverswall, his work, and hiring a mower
in his stead 00 05 09

Charges about Matthew Beech and Sarah
Gardner, which he ought to pay if he be
catch't, but I have paid 01 15 06

Ffor 12 weeks' table for Sarah Gardner at
at 1s. 8d. per week 01 00 00

A shift for her 00 01 08

To ye Doctor for her 00 02 00

Charges another time for takeing Sarah
Gardner before a justice and hiring a man
and woman to attend her all night and
to go the next day to Knipersly ... 00 07 00

Ffor tabling Sarah Gardner a month before
  she was delivered and a month after and
  for burying her child 00 18 08
Spent at Leek at dividing the poor ... 00 02 10
Spent at makeing my accounts 00 13 04

    The autographs attached to the year's accounts are
those of—

JOSUAH POTTS,	JAMES NICKSON,
JHO. GOODFELLOW,	RICHARD WOOD,
WILLIAM SUTTON,	JOHN ALLEN,
WILL: GENT,	WILLIAM HIGSON,
THO: PYOTT,	DANIEL DALE,
WM. POTTS,	JOHN BURTINSHAW,
JOHN DRESSER,	THOMAS WOOD,
RICHARD CLULOW,	CLEWLOW GRUNDY,
THO: MOUNTFORD,	JOHN BRADLEY,
WILL: HULME,	RALPH BRADLEY,
JOHN COOKE,	JEREMY BUXTON,
THOMAS PLANT,	GEORGE WOODWARD,
THOMAS TUNORK,	JAMES HULME.

The Leek Poor Law Union.

THE Leek Union comprises all the extensive parish of Leek, most of the parish of Alstonefield, namely, Warslow, Upper and Lower Elkstone, Longnor, Heathy-lee, Hollinsclough, Quarnford, and Fawfieldhead; and the parishes of Horton, Norton-in-the-Moors, and Sheen.

    The town of Leek is comprised within the townships of Leek and Lowe, Leekfrith, and Tittesworth—chiefly in the first-named township.

May Fair and Pie Powder Court.

ROM copies of some Chancery writs in the possession of Mr. W. S. Brough, we find that after an inquisition at Stafford on June 10th, 1629, Charles I granted, on July 14th of the same year, to "Thomas Jodderile, gentleman, his heirs and assigns, full and absolute license, liberty, power, advantage and authority to have, hold and keep within the said Manor and Village of Leek and the precincts thereof, one Fair or Market yearly for ever, on the 7th, 8th, and 9th days of May yearly, to be held and kept and for all those days to continue, together with a Court of Pie Powder there at the time of the said Fair or Market aforesaid, and with all liberty and free Customes, Tolls, Stallage, Pickage, Fines, Amerceiaments, and all other profits, commodities, and emoluments whatsoever to a Fair or Market of that sort and to a Court of Pie Powder belonging, happening, contingent, or in any manner appertaining."

We may state that a Court of Pie Powder was a court held during fairs to do justice to buyers and sellers, and to redress disorders committed in them. The court was also known as "Dusty-foot Court." "Pickage" is an old law term, signifying money paid in a fair for breaking up the ground in order to set up booths, stands, or stalls.

The Old Almshouses.

ONE of the most ancient blocks of building in Leek is that formed by the old almshouses at the foot of Compton, and which was dedicated to the poor of Leek in the time of Charles II. The quaint, simple architecture contrasts favourably with the palatial residences near the Cemetery, designed by Norman Shaw, which are also almshouses.

The former were bequeathed by Dame Elizabeth Ash, eldest daughter of William Jollif, of Leek. She was twice married: (1) to Sir John Bowyer, of Knypersley; and (2) to Sir — Ash, of Halstead, Kent. She granted in trust to Sir John Bowyer, Benjamin Jolley, and William Ash, Mixon Hay and other lands near the Spout-yate—the house on the same intended for an almshouse—an annuity or rent-charge of £40 per annum, tax-free, out of Thomas Jollif's grant to her at Mixon, called Keywall Green, Jack Flatt, Long Croft, and two Round Crofts, by four quarterly payments to the Vicar, for eight poor people of the said almshouse, on every Sunday 1/8 each, and to have yearly on Christmas Eve a new violet gown.

The qualifications for candidates are, "(1) to be poor widows or maidens of sixty years or upward, or else disabled to work; (2) constant comers to church;

(3) no men or married women; (4) their settlement residence to be in the parish; (5) not to take and no inmate, except as a nurse; (6) not to frequent ale-houses; (7) no scold or disturber of neighbours; (8) not of an ill life, or guilty of any other misdemeanor, in such case liable to be turned out again by the trustees.

Mr. John Sleigh says the elections before Loxdale's day appear to have been carried on "with no little heat, intrigue, expense, and trouble."

Leek and Bach's "Passion" Music.

BACH's "Passion according to St. Matthew" was performed (the first half) in Leek, on March 26th, 27th and 28th, 1877, in West Street School. It is believed that it had at that time never been produced in the provinces except at Manchester, and there only once and never under the same circumstances : local amateurs taking the entire *role*. The narrative was sung by Mr. W. Dishley, the other soloists being Misses Rider, Smith, Sugden and Walwyn, and Messrs. Beckett and J. Gwynne. Mr. W. W. Vorne-Palmer was at the piano-forte, and Mr. S. Howard at the organ. The choir numbered about 200, including a chorale choir of about 53 girls, and there was a small band led by Messrs. Lockett and B. Tomlinson : the conductor being Mr. Samuel Gee, A.R.A.M. It was produced after six weeks' rehearsing. Several gentlemen acted as stewards.

The First Leek Improvement Commissioners.

N Act of Parliament of the sixth year of the reign of George IV, and which came into force on the 20th of May, 1825, is entitled "An Act for lighting, watching, cleaning and improving the town of Leek in the County of Stafford." The Act consisted of ninety clauses. The prolix preamble, of which we give a photo *fac-simile* of the first page, states after giving as reasons for the action, that the management of the internal affairs of the town was not proper or effectual, that Joseph Badnall, Richard Badnall the younger, William Birch, Thomas Carr, William Challinor, Toft Chorley, Charles Coupland, William Critchlow, John Cruso the elder, Henry Cruso, Richard Cutting, Charles Flint, Hugh Ford, John Fowler, John Fynney, Thomas Fenton Grosvenor, John Gaunt, Richard Gaunt, Josiah Gaunt, Josiah Gaunt the younger, Thomas Griffin, George Ridgway Kilminster, Samuel Lucas, Samuel Phillips, William Phillips, John Sleigh, Hugh Sleigh, Thomas Sutton, George Thompson, Anthony Ward, James Wardle, Hugh Wardle, Benjamin Woolfe, and Samuel Young and their successors should be appointed Commissioners of the town of Leek, their authority to extend twelve hundred yards from the old Market Hall.

GEORGII IV. REGIS.

●●

Cap. lxxi.

An Act for lighting, watching, cleansing, and improving the Town of *Leek* in the County of *Stafford*. [20th *May* 1825.]

WHEREAS the Town of *Leek* in the County of *Stafford* is large and populous, and a Place of extensive Trade and Manufacture, and greatly increasing, and is also a great Thoroughfare for Travellers, and where many Fairs are held: And whereas the Streets, Highways, and other public Places within the said Town, are not lighted or watched, nor are the same properly cleansed; and it would tend greatly to prevent Thefts, Robberies, Disturbances, Breaches of the Peace, and other unlawful Proceedings, which in the Night-time are frequently committed and happen in the said Town, and would add to the personal Safety, Comfort, Convenience, and Advantage, not only of the Inhabitants of the said Town, but also of all other Persons resorting to and travelling through the same, if the Streets, Highways, Market Place, and other public Places in the said Town were properly and effectually lighted, watched, and cleansed, and the present Nuisances abated, and all future Nuisances, Annoyances, Encroachments, and Obstructions prevented: May it therefore please Your Majesty that it may be enacted; and be it enacted by the King's most Excellent Majesty, by and with the Advice and Consent of the Lords Spiritual and Temporal, and Commons, in this present Parliament assembled, and by the Authority of the same, That *Joseph Badnall, Richard Badnall* the younger, *William Birch, Thomas Carr, William Challinor, Toft Chorley, Charles Coupland, William Critchlow, John Cruso* the elder, *Henry Cruso, Richard Cutting, Charles Flint, Hugh*

Commissioners.

The qualification for a Commissioner was a yearly income of £50 from land or the possession of personal property to the amount of £1,000. This qualification might be also in the right of the Commissioner's wife.

The form of oath required a statement as to the last paragraph, and the Commissioner had also to swear (or being a Quaker to affirm) that he would truly and impartially, according to the best of his skill and judgment, execute and perform the several powers and authorities reposed in him as a Commissioner. It is interesting to note that hotel and innkeepers and wine and beer sellers, or those having any interest, directly or indirectly, in any bargain or contract with the Commissioners, were debarred from becoming members of the Board, with exceptions of justices of the peace or creditors on the rates or assessments.

The first meeting of the Board was appointed to be held on the third Tuesday after the passing of the Act, in the Town Hall, at eleven o'clock in the forenoon, and the Commissioners after appointing a chairman and taking the oath should adjourn for a period not exceeding two months. The first annual meeting of the Commissioners was appointed to be held on the first Monday in July, 1826, and the annual meetings were ordered to be on the first Monday in July in each year.

The Board were given power to engage paid officers, with the proviso that the clerk should not act as treasurer and *vice versa*, and that if any officer should receive a bribe or reward on account of his employment, he should be disqualified from his office and should forfeit and pay the sum of £20 for every such offence.

The powers given to the Commissioners gave them
the right of sueing and being sued, or being proceeded
against at law or otherwise, and of entering into
contracts with respect to the lighting and improving
of the streets and public places of the town, no contract
(with the exception of the lighting of the town with
gas) to be for a longer period than three years from
the making thereof. Things engaged to be done should
be fulfilled, with the exception that the Commissioners
might compound or agree with anybody for penalties
that might have been named at the time of the
contract.

The Commissioners were specially empowered as
to the lighting of the town with gas, and a number
of provisions were made for this purpose, among which
is to be noted that they should not allow any refuse
from the gas works to enter any place where it might
possibly cause contamination, under a penalty of £1,000
for any such offence. The copious clauses in this
part of the Act might now appear to be vexatious;
such matters as the method of laying gas and water
pipes (such pipes not to be joined before laying;
water pipes to be from four feet from gas pipes, etc.)
being described in great detail. The offence of breaking
a gas lamp was to be punishable with a fine of £5,
or imprisonment for a space of time not exceeding
three months. Lamps accidently broken were to be
paid for, the justices assessing the damage.

The Commissioners were empowered to employ
watchmen and to erect watchhouses and watchboxes
in such situations as they should think proper and
expedient for the security and good order of the town,

and they might appoint a committee or committees for the purpose of managing, regulating, and appointing watchmen or night patrols. The duties of the watchmen were wide and extensive, and they were required not only to use their utmost endeavours to prevent fires, but also to prevent murders, burglaries, felonies and other outrages, disorders and breaches of peace, and to that end they were empowered to arrest and apprehend all night-walkers, felons, malefactors, vagrants, beggars, disturbers of the peace, and all disorderly and suspected persons who should be found misbehaving or wandering in the said town and to lodge them in the watchhouse, to be safely kept until they might be conveniently brought before a justice of the peace to be dealt with as their case demanded. The watchmen were accountable for their regular attendance and the due performance of their duty to the Commissioners, for any neglect of which they were to be fined 20s. and immediately dismissed from service. The penalty for harbouring a watchman in a public-house or premises during the time he should be on duty was a sum not exceeding £5. The Commissioners were empowered to grant rewards in money to watchmen who might be disabled or wounded in the performance of their duty. Any person who assaulted or obstructed a watchman in the perform-ance of his duty was liable to a fine of £10 or imprisonment for three months at the discretion of the magistrates.

An enactment for the purpose of preventing "future projections" into the roadways, highways, or footpaths, ordered that if in the opinion of the Commissioners they were an encroachment or obstruction, they might

give notice to have them removed, and that in default
of such removal the person or persons responsible for
their erection should be liable to a penalty of 10s.
per day. Any doors that opened outwards on public
places or highway were ordered to be made to open
inwards.

The penalty for the defacement, by sticking bills,
writing in chalk, or in any other way, of churches and
chapels, was £5.

Among the numerous definitions of street nuisances,
for which a fine of 20s. was to be paid, is to be seen
"the baiting of any bull, bear, or other animal," and
"the throwing at any cock or fowl in the manner
called cock-throwing."

Unwholesome meat might be destroyed by an
inspector of provisions, appointed by the Commissioners.

The exemption from rates included those persons
who should occupy a house of less than the yearly
value of £3, and those persons who by reason of their
poverty only, might be excused, the rates in such a case
to be paid by the landlord. If any collector should
wilfully over-rate any person, or should otherwise mis-
behave himself, he should forfeit a sum not exceeding
£5, and should be discharged or retained in service at
the option of the Commissioners. The penalty for
refusing to be an assessor was £20. The Commissioners
might amend, raise or reduce any assessment, and persons
aggrieved by any rate or assessment had the right of
a further appeal to the Quarter Sessions.

To raise any penalties, the Commissioners were
empowered to distrain on goods and chattels under
warrant from a justice, but all penalties imposed by

this Act on the Commissioners, and which were not specially directed to be otherwise applied or disposed of, should be paid to the overseers of the poor of the parish in which the penalty was incurred, and by them applied to the poor rates of such parish.

No order, verdict, rate, assessment, judgment, conviction, or other proceeding touching or concerning any offence against the Act, could be quashed or vacated for want of form only, or be removed or removable by *certiorari*, or any other writ or process, into any of His Majesty's Courts of Record at Westminster, any law or statute to the contrary notwithstanding.

An Extraordinary Bill.

THE following is a copy of a bill sent some fifty years ago by the landlord of an inn between Buxton and Leek :—

	s.	d.
Aos afada	1	6
A	0	3
Atakinonimomagen	0	6
	2	3

TRANSLATION.

	s.	d.
A horse half-a-day (stabling)	1	6
Hay	0	3
A taking of him home again	0	6
	2	3

The Source of the Churnet.

PWARDS of forty members of the North Staffordshire Naturalists' Field Club undertook, some years ago, the task of finding the source of the river Churnet, as it did not appear to have had any name beyond Upperhulme, and considerable doubt existed on the point. There are several confluents at and above Upperhulme, one the Dane brook, the springs of which supply the town of Leek with water, and flow into the Churnet below Upperhulme mill. This brook is no part of the River Dane, which flows on the other side of the watershed in a westerly direction, but is so named from a corn mill called Dane Mill, situated on its banks at the foot of Hen Cloud. Dane brook has been thought by some to be the real Churnet, but that is not so, the main stream crosses the Buxton road close to the joining of Dane brook with it. The valley is bounded in this part by Bramcott and the Knowl on the west, and by the Morridge slopes at Hurdlow on the east, above which is seen the Mermaid Inn at Blakemeer. There were several good sections of the Yoredale sandstones and shales in the river course dipping under the Roaches at an angle of 20° to 30°. A tributary of considerable size, but not quite so large as the main stream, was met with nearly a mile from the starting point of the expedition. This is a stream which is said to find its origin in Blakemeer or Blackmeer, on the highest point of Morridge, not unknown to legendary lore, a small pool of dark water and said to be of unknown depth. This brook is by some called the true Churnet, but we think not upon sufficient authority. It flows down a deep and wild ravine from the top of Morridge, and its future exploration would prove interesting botanically, as in the short distance from its source to its junction with the Churnet there is probably a difference of about 1,000 feet in level. The party then proceeded up the valley, passing a small fault which runs into a greater one traversing the distance between Thorncliffe and Flash, and, leaving the upper Yoredale measures, came into the rocks and shales of the Millstone Grit, which comprise in this district the first, third, fourth and fifth grits, with intervening shales, the second grit, or Haslingden flags, being absent, having thinned out near Stoneway Head, near the river Dane. This is a flaggy grit of not more than 100 to 120 feet thick, in the Lancashire part of the Pennine range. The first bed of grit the party came across was the fifth or lowest of the series, and may be considered as the junction between the Yoredale series and the true Millstone Grit. It is not of great thickness, and is succeeded by a thick blackish shale containing an abundance of *goniatites lingula*, and the beautiful shell *aviculopecten papyraceus*. These fossils are not uncommon in the Yoredale shales, and are the characteristic forms of this geological horizon. No fossils were observed in the sandstones or grits, although in some parts of the neighbourhood, as at the Kniveden and Waste quarries, there is an abundance of *lepidodendra*, *calamites*, *stigmaræ*, and other plants common to the carboniferous formation.   After traversing some barren and wild moorland valleys, which lie low down at the foot of Ramshaw Rocks, the party arrived at a bifurcation near Stake Gutter, and both streams being nearly of equal size, it was decided to divide the party and trace each to its source.   The stream (the most eastward) being a little the larger seemed to claim the name Churnet, and up that the majority of the party proceeded, passing several pretty but short waterfalls.   The stream drawing much of its water from the natural drainage of the moors, and which entered at every bog and gulley, soon became dwarfed into very small proportions, until at last it was run to earth in a well which supplies a very small farm-house, called "White Middle Hills," with water, and also a small artificial drain from a field not 100 yards from the well.   Sampson Erdeswick (1603) says : "Churnet at Rowcester entering into Dove upon the west side, hath its first spring within less than two miles of Dove's Head, and passing through one of the barrenest countries that I know hath not any place worth the naming till it comes Dieu-le-Cresse, an abbey founded by the last Ranulfe, Earl of Chester." The distance between Middle Hills and Dove Head is more than three miles.   The land here is a peat moss, and has been converted from heathery mossland to good grazing-land by drainage and cultivation. There are now no trees growing in that part of the barren and bleak moor, which is the abode of numerous colonies of grouse.   The well and the farm are situated

between the roads to Warslow and Longnor, and within
about 300 yards from the inn called "Royal Cottage," said
to be so named from Prince Charles having called there.
At this point the reading of the aneroid gave a height
of 800 feet above Leek, and taking the datum station,
which is at the bottom of Stockwell street, and is 603
feet above the Mersey at Runcorn, the altitude would
be upwards of 1410 feet above the sea. At the Royal
Cottage the party found welcome rest and refreshment,
and also the contingent which had gone up the other
branch at the bifurcation. They reported tracing that
stream until it lost itself amongst various boggy sedges
of the moor, a little south of the Royal Cottage, and
not far distant to the well alluded to above which was
unanimously considered to be the fountain head of the
Churnet, and was christened "Churnet well."

Reference to the river is made in the first Latin
edition of Camden's *Britannia*, published in 1586, as
follows: "The northern part of Staffordshire swells
gradually into slight mountains, which rise something
like the Appenines of Italy, elevated into a continuous
mountainous ridge like a back-bone as far as Scotland,
though often changed in its name—here it is called
the Moorlands—there the Peak, afterwards Craven, then
Steanmore, and at length the parts divide, as it were,
in the shape of a horn, and are called Cheviots;
from these hills many rivers emerge into the plain,
the principal of which are the Dove, the Hanse, the
Churnet, and, that which ultimately takes both into
the Black Sea, the Trent. The Dovus, or Dove, whose
banks have been ploughed out of the solid stone, and
the stones of which being burnt are used for manuring

fields, closely bounds the eastern parts of the land, and separates it from Derbyshire. First of all there is the Hanse river, which, after being absorbed and lost, breaks out again about the third mile, and thence increased by the Churnet, flows by Utcester, in the Saxon language called Uttockester, a place celebrated for its flocks and herds, and flourishing meadows."

As to the origin of the word Churnet, Mr. Sleigh is of opinion that it is derived from the Gaelic *Car*, "turn or bend," and certainly the Churnet is a river of many twistings, turnings, and bendings.

"Serena" Sneyd.

HONORA, daughter of Edward Sneyd (Major of Oxford Blues), of Lichfield, was at one time the fiancée of the unfortunate Major André who was hanged as a spy near New York, 2nd October, 1780, æt. 29. She married 17th July, 1773, Richard Lovel Edgworth, of Edgworth's-town, Ireland; who, on her death, 30th April, 1780, married on 'Xmas day in the same year, her sister, Elizabeth, who ob. Nov. 1797—

> Sweet Evelina's fascinating power
> Had fast beguiled of sleep her midnight hour;
> Possessed by sympathy's enchanting sway,
> She read unconscious of the dawning day.
>   —*Hayley.*

The "Double Sunset" from Leek Churchyard.

HE accompanying account of the "double sunset" behind the Cloud appeared in the *Gentleman's Magazine*, with an exceedingly quaint woodcut, here reproduced and re-arranged, in July, 1738 :—

The four following schemes represent the four successive Phases of the Sun in his Approach to, or Recess from, the Summer Tropic, as he gradually emerges from, or absconds behind, a Hill in *Staffordshire* called the *Cloud*, six miles distant from a Spectator in *Leek* Churchyard; as it has been observed from thence many years, for two or three days before and after the 10th June [old style] (see p. 264).

The reference is to an article in the May number of the same year, being a letter from Mr. R. Brookes to the editor, touching a dispute as to the variation of the Obliquity of the Eliptick, and from this we quote :—"What I mean, is a Solar Occultation behind a Hill called the *Cloud* on the Borders of Staffordshire; which Dr. Plot has given the World an account of sixty years ago. This Hill is so situated with respect to the Churchyard of *Leek* a Market Town in the

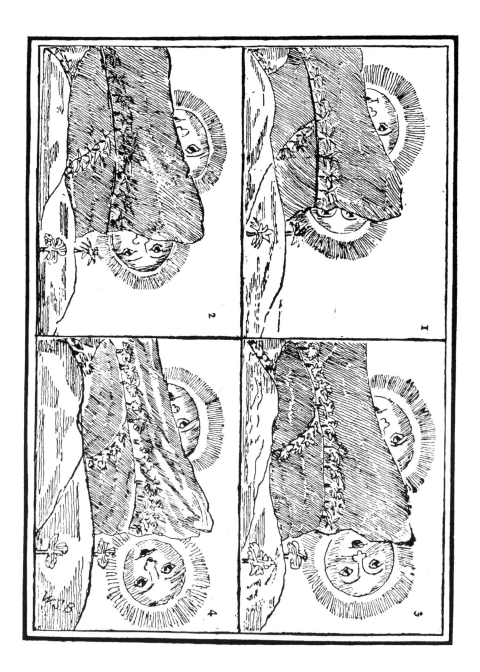

same County, and six miles distant from the Hill,
that a spectator standing there of an Evening three
or four days before the 10th of June, when the sun
enters the Beginning of *Cancer*, beholds the Disk of
the Sun gradually Emerging from beyond the Northward
Side of the Hill, which is nearly perpendicular; and
this in such a manner, that a very sensible Difference
is perceived in the Sun's motion every Evening, and
at length the whole Disk Emerges for three days
together, but the second very evidently more distant
than the first and last."

Plot in his "Natural History of Staffordshire"
(1786) says:—"The first thing I met with relating to
the Heavens, and one of the first too that I heard
of after I set to work in earnest, was a pretty rural
observation, of late years made by some of the
inhabitants of the town of Leek in the Moorlands,
of the setting of the Sun in the Summer Solstice,
near a Hill called the Cloud, about six miles distant,
in the confines of Staffordshire and Cheshire; which
appearing almost perpendicular on the Northern side,
to such persons as are standing in the Leek Churchyard, the Sun seems so nicely at that time of year
to cut the Edge of it at setting. That notwithstanding
what is taught by Astronomers, that the Sun whilst it
occupies the Cardinal point, appears Stationary for
some time without giving any sensible increase or
decrease to the length of the days; they can plainly
perceive by the help of this Hill that no two days
are equal, but that there is a sensible difference every
day; just as at the Temple of Teutiris in Egypt
where there are as many Windows as days in the

year, so placed, that the Sun rising in a different
degree in the Zodiac every day, it also sends its
beams every day into a distinct window from the day
before. For when the Sun comes near the Solstice,
the which disk of it first sets behind the Hill, after
a while the Northern Limb first appears, and so every
night gradually more, till at length the whole Diameter
comes to set Northward of it, for about three nights;
but the middle night of the three, very sensibly more
remote, than the former or the following, when
beginning its recess from the Tropic, it still continues
more and more to be hidden away every night, till
at length it descends quite behind it again. Which
Phænomenon though worth notice for its own sake
alone yet might be render'd of much more use to
the Publick, would the Curious that for the most
part reside thereabout, make annual and more strict
observations for the future by suitable instruments,
noteing every year the day precisely, that the Limb
of the Sun first cuts the edge of the Hill, and how
many digits or parts of digits, of its own Diameter,
it daily advances; also carefully noteing the nearest
distance b'twixt the edge of the Hill, and the Rim
of the Sun, on the very day of the Solstice, and
lastly the mean between both: For by this means in
time the Sun's greatest Northern Declination (which
Astronomers say is less now than heretofore) may be
gradually adjusted, and at length perhaps limited;
Which I take to be an Experiment of so valuable
consideration, that I cannot but recommend it to my
worthy friends the Worshipful Thomas Rudyerd of
Rudyerd Esquire, Mr. Parker, and Mr. Thomas Gent;

at least that they would take care in some one year
or other, when there is least of Refraction upon
account of the Atmosphere, from some fixt point, so
as to adjust the distance betwixt the Hill and the Sun
on the day of the Solstice by an Azimuthal Quadrant,
the new Micrometer, or some other agreeable Instrument, that future Ages however (if it cannot be in
this) may see the difference."

W. S. B.

A Natural Prodigy.

THE *Dublin University Magazine* published in 1868
an interesting account of a Longnor prodigy of the
last century. The name of this natural wonder was
Charles Charlesworth, son of Richard Charlesworth, a
carrier, of Longnor. He was born under the common
size, but he grew so amazingly fast that by the time
he was four years old he was four feet high, and in
strength, agility and bulk was equal to a boy of ten.
At five he measured four feet ten inches, weighed
eighty-seven pounds; could, with ease, carry a man
fourteen stone weight; had every sign of puberty, and
worked as an adult at his father's business. This was
the time of his full vigour, from whence gradually he
began to fall in strength and bulk like a man in the
decline of life. At the age of seven his strength was
gone, his body totally emaciated, his eyes sunk, and his
head palsied. He died with all the signs of extreme old
age, and as if the months he had lived had been years.

The Moorland City Plague.

IN the year 1857, an Order in Council was issued to close the surcharged graveyard at the Parish Church on a certain day, except in the then existing walled graves, whereupon a number of persons, having more gold than brains, set upwards of eighty workmen at work to construct wall graves, being horrified at the idea of being buried in the new Cemetery. At the same time the street gullies of the old sewers of deposit were being trapped, and no attention paid to the trapping of the house drains. The stench emitted from the churchyard was so great that the men could only be induced to continue the disgraceful work by constant supplies of brandy and other spirits. The work proceeded day and night for about a fortnight, when an epidemic of diphtheria broke out and caused great alarm. The appearance of the following lines and a representation to the Home Office had the effect of putting a stop to the disgraceful proceedings :—

Still night o'ershadowed the fair Moorland town,
Its natives, ten thousand, ne'er happier known,
In calm sleep reposed undisturbed by a sound—
Breathing the purest of air to be found.

No voice came in dreams to the happy abode
To tell the fond mother of danger abroad,
That threatened herself, her babes, and their sire,
With pestilence worse than war, famine, or fire.
Thus nestled all snug till the morning they lay
When in vain they hark'd for the birds of the sky;
No songster's sweet note of the morn to awake
The Moorlands, nor heard from the banks of the lake;
The groves on its picturesque slopes were as mute
As the still lake that echoes their choir's sweet note.
The joyous throng of the Westwood retreat
Were dumb, and the squire had forsaken his seat.
No strain floated o'er from the old Abbey wood—
Once the seat of devotions, true brotherhood;
Who taught the first-born of the Moorlands to raise
To heaven the holiest anthems of praise.
The sacred trees round the church were forsaken,
No chat'ring daws on the steeple were talkin';
St. Edward's clock's tick was heard in the calm,
As faint as a lisp that heralds a storm.
The rising sun peeps o'er the eastern hill,
Looked amased, looked again, on Leek so still;
He gazed an instant, then with modest grace
Behind a cloud concealed his crimson face,
Created nature here, in her calmness, wore
A look of sadness ne'er observed before.
Calm Contemplation, with her list'ning ear,
Could one articulated whisper hear
Fall from keen-eyed Science who, beyond the gloom,
Saw Folly's mischief in the distance loom—
Half what grave Science in her whispers told,
Would make a British parent's blood run cold.
All else seemed dumb, except the healthy stream
Gushing from the mountain Roaches sandstone seam,
Ever rebuking as it murmured down
To waste, within sight of our thirsty town.

Time's faithful voice within the sacred tower
Hoarsely at length spoke forth the morn's sixth hour;
When croaking Folly's well-known tramp was heard,
With "donkey cart" and sewering men prepared
With traps to seal street gullies o'er the sewers,

And force rank poison to men's very doors
When untrapped drains, want of water and thought,
Forms with the sewer a perfect retort,
Which naught but chemical science and skill
Plotting destruction, could ever excel.
But knowledge and skill were never yet found
Parts of incompetent follies compound;
Therefore, let reason in drawing the line,
Never suspect a mischievous design.
A second rude band! Oh shame, deeper shame!
Well stocked with liquor to the churchyard came;
With pickaxe and spade they madly prepare
The sacred ground to mar and to tear;
Remains of the dead were torn from their rest
And wickedly thrown north, south, east and west,
By men without sense whom Folly had fee'd,
And made drunk to commit the horrible deed.
The stranger cried "Shame!" and retired in pain,
Whilst mothers wept o'er their child's corpse again;
The stout-hearted native sighed and then said,—
"Wretches! Why sport with the skulls of our dead?"
Shroud, coffins, and corpse lie in fragments around—
Not even a watch o'er the dogs was found;
The stench so increased, so noxious became,
That tar was burning to drive away shame.
Grave Science cried "Cease, a plague will appear,"
But Ignorance cursed and demanded more beer;
Churchwardens and magistrates gathered around,
Tried means to stop further breaking of ground,
But Folly's rude agents, drunkenly bold,
Said "All was improvement, and bricks must be sold."
The voice of the Vicar was heard in the wail,
But Folly was deaf to Reason's appeal.

Plague's potent king took the town as by siege,
And Ignorance fought for its sovereign leige;
Proud, self-seeking man much power had obtained,
And might o'er right had a victory gained.
Conceit mocked at science, water, and sewers,
At chemists' preventions and doctor's cures;
The Press bore insult, while Folly and Wealth
Crushed the best efforts of law upon health;

The dead were torn up, God's laws set at naught,
And the air with the deadliest poisons fraught.
Death's subtle harbinger then found a seat
In the happiest moorland homes retreat,
Where he lurked unseen, unfelt as it seemed,
Infecting the blood through the lungs as it streemed,
Diffusing poisonous atoms well known
To taint food, water, and air of the town.
So forc'd came that foe from the sewers underground,
And grasped by the throat the victims around;
Held fast in his toils the healthy and strong,
Condensing his venomous breath on the tongue;
His slime of contagion soon found its way
To the uvula, stomach, and blood of his prey.
This folly-hatched fiend with serpent-like smile
Then laughed at the anguish, the fruit of his guile,
And with his cold hand struck a death-like note,
Sealed up the lip, left his blast in the throat.
Bereav'd were then told, 'mid anguish and care,
How Christians the will of the Lord should bear;
Whilst synanche, maligna, diptheria, the same
Fill'd registrar's columns with public shame.

Thou cruel Fanaticism! curse of the land,
Back with thy ignorant, blaspheming hand!
For Reason, Science, and Nature declare
That God never caused such misery there;
The hand was not that which fades autumn flower—
The blight was man's own the touch was his power;
Let justice, stern justice, remember the deed,
And smite the bold folly that made the heart bleed.
Means to save life were suggested and known,
But contempt was on ages of wisdom thrown:
Laws—ancient and modern—their framers wise
Were mocked like fiction, and foes in disguise.
For days, weeks, months has the plague cry being heard,
And yet is the demon of death still abroad;
His wings still o'erspread our mournful retreat,
And Folly spurns Reason laid at his feet.
Death is triumphant! he smites and we're slain,
And nothing wise done to stay his proud reign.
We hear not his voice, yet he speaks in wrath,

We see not his form but only his path—
The ghostly bill of his deaths the year past
Is greater by far than his cholera's last.
Our youths' sweet voices that greeted the sun,
Are hush'd mid the grief of a town undone;
The once happy pair, in all but love poor,
Gaze o'er their desolate homes in despair;
Young mothers weep o'er their babe's form with pain,
Who'll breathe no more on her bosom again.
The spouse, left alone like a death-stricken dove,
Sighs o'er the ice-frozen lock of her love;
Those the destroyer hath spared in the past
May fall a prey to his poison at last—
Meantime they seem as if left on a steep,
Like willows to bend o'er the ruin and weep.

Tell not ye, angel throng who on us gaze,
Such shame to the tribes of the southern seas,
Or the healthy savage, free from such pest,
Would scorn intelligence in proud disgust.
Shall Plague longer reign or longer disgrace,
Pollute, and infect the whole moorland race?
Shall a valley by Nature's hand so blest
By foul maligna for ever be curs'd?
Shall oppression, disease, death, and the grave,
Devour a race once so happy and brave?
Shall a civilized people's noblest pride
By plague and dishonour be thus belied?
Shall proud-fronted Folly's fest'ring breath
Besmear the sceptics' sacred gold with death?
Shall the immortal annals of our fame
Contain an immortality of shame?

A.

Acreage of Leek Parish.

EEK parish comprises no less than 34,300 acres of land, extending about six miles north and west of the town and four miles eastward, and rising from the picturesque valleys of the Churnet and other rivulets to some of the boldest heights of the moorlands. On the north side it is separated from Cheshire by the river Dane; on the east it is bounded by the parishes of Alstonefield, Butterton and Waterfall; and on the west by Horton, Norton-in-the-Moors, and Stoke-upon-Trent. It is divided into ten townships, viz :—

	Acres.
Bradnop	3,000
Endon, Longsdon, and Stanley	5,500
Heaton	2,300
Leekfrith	7,500
Leek and Lowe	6,000
Onecote...	5,000
Rudyard	1,500
Rushton James	1,000
Rushton Spencer	1,500
Tittesworth	1,000

Total, 34,300; all in the northern division of the hundred of Totmonslow.

Ashenhurst.

NESTLING in a verdant valley to the south-east of Leek, is Ashenhurst, the seat of the ancient family of that name. Their connection with Leek dates as far back as the time of Edward I, when one Ralphe de Ashenhurst is believed to have owned the town. In 1597, John Ashenhurst died and was buried at Leek, and from that date the family may be traced for a century, when the estate appears to have passed into other hands. On June 3rd, 1828, William Phillips, of the Field House, Leek, and his brother Samuel, bought the estate from the assignees of the late Richard Badnall, and it is now in the possession of his nephew, Colonel Phillips, J.P.

Tradition ascribes considerable medicinal properties to Ashenhurst Well, or "Egg Well" (from its elliptical form), which is of Roman origin and bears the following inscription :—

> Renibus, et splein, cordi, jecorique medetur :
> Mille malis prodest ista salubris aqua.

Various translations of these lines have appeared from time to time, of which we quote the following :—

> Whate'er of inward ailings may be yours,
> A thousand such this healing water cures.
>
> —*C. Flint.*

Ashenburst
C.W.R. Knan

The racking stone, its tortured victim leaves;
Spleen, heart, or liver ailments cease;
A thousand evils own this water's power.
                    —*S. Whittaker*, R.C. priest, 1830.

The reins, the spleen, the liver, and the heart,
This wholesome water cureth every part.
                                    —*Mrs. Chorley*.

Whate'er the liver, reins, spleen, heart endure—
A thousand ills this wholesome spring can cure.
                                    —*W. Challinor*.

A stone in the pavement of the house commemorated a great fodder famine in April, 1741, in the following quaint terms:—" Fodder was the dearest and scarcest that had been known in any body's time living, hay being sold at 6/-, 7/-, and 8/- a cwt. and none to be had for money. Mr. Hollinshead, [the owner] sold at least 200 tons at £4, in about ten days, which was of great service to the country, they coming from all places ten miles round. The last day of the sale was supposed to be 40 carts and waggons, and no less than 200 horses, but could not near all be fitted. All eatables were very dear, the best wheat at near 8/- a strike; oatmeal, 1/3 a peck; cheese (which had been as low as 16/-), 35/8 a cwt.; bacon 6d. a lb; butter, 7d.; oats, 3/- a strike; oat straw, 12d. a thrave; beef and mutton, 4d. a lb."

The Sneyd Family and the War of Independence.

ON the 10th of June, 1776, the Americans captured in Long Island Sound a British ship, the *Bombrig*. Among the prisoners were Edward Sneyd, the commander; John Coggin, boatswain; John Russell, carpenter; and William Cook, seaman; and these were sent to Windham Gaol. They remained there about six months, when they made their escape, but subsequently were, with one exception, drowned. While the prisoners were at old Windham Gaol, they carved an image of Bacchus, the god of wine, and presented it to the Widow Cary, the hostess of the tavern. Probably the kind-hearted landlady had favoured the home-sick prisoners with dainties from her well-kept larder, and perhaps now and then a thimbleful of old Jamaica. At any rate she placed them under obligations, and they reciprocated by carving this image as a tavern sign. It was carved out of pine log, was 26½ inches high, and 21 inches long, and represented Bacchus, crowned with grapes, astride of a cask of wine, and holding a basket of fruit; a work which, though rude, still was cleverly executed. In 1856 it was blown in a hard

gale from its place and somewhat disfigured. Then
for some years it was stored away in a wood-house,
and finally sold for 25 cents. to a Mr. Brooks, whose
pet idea had been to discover some of the descendants
of the Windham prisoners, and who had a history of
the Bacchus image published. One of the books was
addressed to Henry F. Sneyd, captain in the Royal
army. It appears that he found that he forwarded it
to his cousin, Dryden Sneyd, of Ashcombe Park, near
Leek, Staffordshire, who in January last wrote acknowledging the receipt of copies of the history of Bacchus
and enclosing a genealogical table of the Sneyd family,
which was dated back to 1310. He says:—" I am
very distantly related to Edward of whom you write.
A Capt. Edward Sneyd, who I suppose to be the
same, was uncle to the Rev. Walter Sneyd, now of
Keele Hall, near Newcastle, in this county, and was
drowned in America in 1776. I should have rather
supposed Edward Sneyd had been born at Keele, but
it may be otherwise. He, undoubtedly, was brought
up there. Keele was a grant from Henry VIII. to
Sir William Sneyd, Knight, but my family have resided
in the county of Stafford for over 600 years, and now
own large tracts of land. Keele Hall is one of the
finest gentlemen's seats in England, and was built by
Ralph Sneyd in 1580, and was restored at the enormous
cost of £140,000 about 20 years since by Ralph, the
brother of Walter, the present owner. The family of
Sneyd is numerous, but Walter and his son Ralph
are the only male descendants of the name, of Ralph
and Barbara, the parents of Edward Sneyd, who was
drowned in America." Our contemporary adds that

Capt. H. F. Sneyd came at the request of the writer of this letter to make a personal inspection of this figure, and spent a day with Mr. Brooks. In company with Mr. Brooks he visited Windham Green, dined at the old Widow Cary tavern, the identical building, and under the espionage of the venerable Judge Swift, an authority in historical affairs, and Mr. J. Griffin Martin, saw the foundation of the old gaol and other points of interest. Capt. Sneyd was enthusiastic over his visit. So it will be seen that around this bit of rude carving cluster many romantic historical incidents. The apparently hopeless task of ferreting out descendants of the most conspicuous of the prisoners was by persistent efforts accomplished, and although no value attaches to the discovery, except a sentimental one, yet there is a good deal of satisfaction felt on both sides—by the owner of Bacchus and by the wealthy and aristocratic descendants of Commander Sneyd.—*Hartford* (Connecticut) *Courant*, and reprinted in the *Leek Times* of August 27th, 1881.

William the Conqueror in Staffordshire.

FREEMAN, in referring to the final subduing of Staffordshire, says:—"To the north, Staffordshire was in arms, and though this is the only movement of which we have got no details, and must have been one specially to be dreaded, as it was the only one which needed William's presence to quell."

A Strange and Wonderful Prophecy.

LILLY'S

Strange and Wonderful

PROPHECY

Being a Revelation of many Universal Accidents that will come to pass in the YEAR

1681,

According to the Prognostications of the Celestial Bodies, as well in this our English Nation, as in all parts beyond the seas: With a Sober Caution to all by speedy Repentance to avert the judgements that are Impendent.

As likewise a Strange and Wonderful Discovery at a place called LEEK in Staffordshire:

By Men Digging in the Earth for stones to pave two Streets, where they found a Pavement of smooth Stone, several Pots full of Ashes and Men's Bones: and under a Grave-Stone a pot of Oyl sweeter than Perfume, in which was a Parchment containing a Wonderful Prophecy, directing them to dig 40 Arms deep, and they should find inestimable Treasure, in having been preserved about 500 Y. and subscribed *Anselem*, with many strange things contain'd in it.

As also an Account of the
GREAT STREAM OF LIGHT,
By some termed a BLAZING-STAR;

Which was seen in the *South-West* on *Saturday* and *Sunday* the *11th* and *12th* of this instant *December*, between Six and Seven in the Evening: with several *Judicial Opinions and Conjectures upon the same.*

Printed for *P. Brooksby* in *West Smithfield*, 1680.

"Now we shall proceed to give the Reader an account of a strange Prophesie which was found in the Earth at a place called *Leek* in *Staffordshire*, the manner thus:

Several Labourers being set on work to Dig for Stone to pave Two Streets, having dug a 100 Load, about six yards in the Ground, found a broad Pavement, under which was an Iron Pot full of Bones and Ashes; as likewise several other Earthen Pots that contained the like; but with a touch fell all into the Dust: Under them was a grave-stone, which being taken up had under it a Pot of Oyl close covered, in which was a Scroule of Parchment preserved by the same, in which was Written these words in old English.

The Words found Written on the Parchment.

When the Year Sixteen hundred Fourtys tows is well nigh gone, Folk shall gang here together stane; when Gold is most esteem'd Monk Men, then let 'um Digg here Arms deep four times Ten, and they shall ha' that which is their sole desire, but then let them beware, for amongst hearts there shall be as Naked din, because many shall have their Lamps to trim, yet shall share the Debonire of me gurk hay la

tim: But first let um digg Forty arms deep, and
then into a Cave they shall peep, then let 'um take
out what's in that hole, and give some to every
poor soul; and whilst they digg give hungry Bread
free, and they shall great Treasure see.

ANSELEM, &c.

The meaning of these words are,—That in the
year 1680, near the end of the said year, men shall
gather to that place to get stone and digging in the
Earth 40 Arms deep, shall find a Cave in which is
great Treasure, yet if they use it not according to the
intent of the owner, which is to bestow it amongst
the poor, it will become a snare to them.

This *Anselem* as neer as can be computed, about
500 years since was an Arch-Bishop of *Canterbury*, and
a very great *Stickler* for the Pope, against the King,
viz., *Stephen;* and did not only Excommunicate him,
but caused his subjects to Rebell, and caused a long
War to ensue between him and *Henry* the second,
son to *Maud*, the Empress Daughter to *William* the
Conquerour, nor would he Absolve him till he had
bought his Peace, and made a Golden Composition
with the Bishop. Likewise, this *Anselem* did much
contradict the opinions of many Learned Chimicks of
that Age concerning their opinions as to the Trans-
mutation of Mettle; till himself at last by Study, found
it to be true; and with a certain powder did change
abundance of Silver and other fine Mettals into Gold,
some of which he has hoarded in this place, where
according to Antient Chronologies, a Monestry had
formerly stood but we will leave it till we hear further.

—*From a rare tract in the library of Mr. Brough.*

A Singular Agreement.

HEREAS Benjamin Endon the elder of Dunwood, in the parish of Leeke and Countie
of Stafford yeoman did (about the begininge
of Maie last past) loase a horse coveringe cloath from
under his hackney saddle, as he came downe Moore-
lane to Gillow-heath. And before such time as he
could returne to the place where he left it, a certaine
man with a weane and two horses that weare loaden
had taken up the said cloath, and the said Benjamin
demandinge the said cloath from him, hee the said
carrier refused to restore it, sayinge that it was his,
in regard he had found it and had it in possession—
where upon a controversie and dispute arose betweene
them, and som hott words passed. And whereas the
said Benjamin Endon the elder is fallen into a desease
which is call'd the Mellancholley, and is much troubled
in his mind about this controversie that happened
suspectinge some trouble to ensue there upon. Now
know all men by theise p'sents that I Benjamin Endon
the younger of Dunwood aforesaid & countie of Stafford
aforesaid for the consideration of ffive Shillings in hand
received from him the said Benjamin Endon the elder
Doe Covenant promiss and agree with him the said

Benjamin the elder that I will fully and cleerely stand
betweene him and any shuite, trouble or incumbrance
that shall or may at any time happen to be or arise
betweene the carrier and him concerninge that controversie about the horse coveringe-cloath then in debate.
And will take the shuite to myselfe and free him
from any trouble about it. And unto this agreement
I doe here unto subscribe my name.

Dated the 24 of october anno 1693.

BEN. ENDON, Junior.

In witness of Tho. Endon.

(indorso:—" Benjamin's engagemen't to mee.")

[" Our first chyld Tho. Endon departed this life the
23d of Octob'r, 1696, at Mr. Nichols' house (his
then maister,) in Spannish-Town, in Jaimaica, in
the 23d yeare of his age: and was Buried withall
Decency in Spannish-Town church, at the Charge
of our most loving Cossin Mr. Gervas Sleigh—
the charge whereof was 26*li* 13*s* oo*d*, according
to bill sent over. His maister was the principle
Secretary of the Hand and hee his principle
Clerke."]

A Wealthy Bride.

ON April 15, 1771, *Aris's Birmingham Gazette,*
published the following notice of marriage :—" On
Monday last, at Leek, Simon Debank, Esq., to Miss
Birtles, an accomplished young lady, with a fortune
of £50,000.

The Roe Buck Hotel.

THIS ancient hostelry has been an architectural feature of Leek since 1626, when, according to Mr. John Sleigh, its framework was brought in detached pieces from Shropshire. Writing in 1862, Mr. Sleigh regretfully refers to the building, which was formerly the Sun, as "about the last of the white-and-black houses left in the town, now that the picturesque old Black's Head has disappeared. *Esto perpetua.*" To the present writing the wish has been observed, and the engraving we give below, which appeared for the first time in the first edition of the *History of Leek*, is an exact presentment of its present appearance, albeit Mr. George Chell's draper's shop on the western side has been swept away in favour of the Congregational Church. Two years ago, during some alterations by the present tenant, Mr. Wm. Knowles, the builder, found an interesting Leek Token bearing the inscription: "Iohn Gent, in Leek, his half-peny, 1666."

On September 28th, 1876, the ancient building was offered for sale by the Lownds family, in whose possession it had been for many years. Mr. Robert Mellor Fergyson was the auctioneer, and the event

drew together the leading gentlemen, lawyers, **and**
tradesmen of the town. In submitting the lot to
competition, Mr. Fergyson, said the hostelry was built
in the time of Charles I, and was of great historical
interest. It was, consequently, a beautiful and interesting
souvenir of days long gone by, and he should regret to

see so-called "modern improvements" efface its antique
beauty by destroying the grand old front. He contended
that under proper development and judicious management the house would in a very short period regain
its ancient prestige and be as in the days of yore the
first family and commercial hotel in Leek. Estimating
the license to be worth £1,000, and the commercial
value of the land at £3 per yard, the buyer should

pay for it about £5,000. "The first bid," says the
Leek Times of the period, "was £2,000, speedily
augmented to £3,000 by several apparently eager bidders.
By hundreds, the offer was increased to £3,600, when
Mr. Hy. Cartledge, of Rudyard Hotel, quietly intervened
with '£3,700.' A pause here took place, and after
a consultation with the solicitors, 'an open sale' was
declared by the auctioneer. £3,720 was the next bid,
and after some demur was accepted by Mr. Fergyson,
who expressed a predilection for fifties. By twenties
the fight was then carried on until the large sum
of £4,000 was reached, Mr. Cartledge and Mr. Radley
(of Congleton) being the leading combatants. One of
those sweet intervals, so welcome to the thirsty souls
who 'never miss a property sale,' then occurred, and
£4,100 was soon afterwards reached. A few minutes
later, amid much excitement, the property was knocked
down to Mr. Cartledge, for the large sum of £4,120."
The late Mr. Cartledge afterwards explained that he
had purchased the property for Mrs. Byrom, who he
said had no intention of altering the ancient front.
The property remained in the possession of the Byrom
family until 1888, when it was purchased by private
treaty by Messrs. Bell & Co., the well-known Burton
brewers.

An Ecclesiastical Census.

WE give the following extract from " An Account of the Province of Canterbury, Anno 1676," deposited originally in the library of the Duke of Sussex, and now in the Salt Library at Stafford.

This "account" is the answer by the clergy of the respective parishes to queries addressed to them by the Crown respecting the number of " Conformists, Papists, and Nonconformists'" in their parishes.

From a note under the return for Bristol and Bath and Wells, the age of sixteen is mentioned as the correct limit for the return, so that we arrive at the conclusion, if we may rely on the accuracy of the information, that in or about the year 1676 the population of the parish of Leek above the age of sixteen years was 2,480, of which seventeen only were Dissenters, and none were Roman Catholics.

It is quite uncertain, however, whether the limit of sixteen years of age applied to the diocese of Bath and Wells only, or to the whole of the return. It would appear that not all the clergy were equally desirous of accuracy, Cheddleton's level 300, Cheadle's level 1,000, and Checkley's 500 were probably guesses! It will be remembered that the parish of Leek included Endon, Stanley, Longsdon, Leek and Lowe, Tittesworth, Bradnop, Onecote, Rudyard, Leekfrith, Heaton, Rushton James, and Rushton Spencer. The total population of the whole parish in 1881 was 16,165.

This return throws some light on the state of Nonconformity in the reign of Charles II. Its date is just that period when the most stringent laws were in force against Dissenters. Three years earlier the Test Act had become law. For ten years the Nonconformists of England had endured the persecution involved in carrying out the Conventicle and and Five Mile Acts, under which it was a crime punishable by fine, imprisonment, and transportation for more than five persons to meet together for religious worship, unless the Book of Common Prayer were used.

This "account" will be found instructive, not merely for the sake of its local information, but as showing how the Dissenters were, in numbers, but a small and feeble folk. Yet what may not be inferred of brave, stalwart independence, and perhaps obstinate "contumacy" on the part of the one Papist at Grindon! What heroism must not he of Cheadle have exhibited in that year of grace to stand alone the one Nonconformist in the midst of 1,000 neighbours who regarded him as a recusant and an outcast—in his somewhat smaller way a veritable Athanasius against the world. Yet was the fewness of their numbers not always disadvantageous, for where there were less than five they could all meet together, and yet defy the Conventicle Act. The following extract gives so much of the census as relates to the Archdeaconry of Uttoxeter :—

Name of Parish.	Confor-mists.	Papists.	Noncon-formists.
Uttoxeter	1963	5	32
Grindon	156	1	43
Draycott in ye Moores...	88	—	12
Chedleton	300	6	20
Gratwich	52	—	2
Kingstone	121	—	—
Abbotts Bromley ...	506	10	31
Ruston Chapel ...	116	—	10
Leek	2463	—	17
Dylhorne	351	2	11
Butterton	106	—	—
Wetton	138	—	10
Rocester	223	5	—
Croydon (Croxden)...	129	—	—
Bradley	45	—	—
Waterfall	39	—	—
Ellaston...	273	24	3
Bueslem (Burslem)...	427	17	—
Horton	322	8	7
Cauldon	28	—	—
Alurton (Alton)... ...	400	14	2
Biddulph	333	15	12
Carswell (Caverswall) ...	205	15	7
Ipstones	403	12	73
Bromshall	97	—	4
Sheen	55	—	—
Chedle	1000	4	1
Coulton (Calton) ...	140	30	30
Leigh	500	35	—
Checkley	473	39	6
Blore	152	—	—
Mathfield (Mayfield).	268	2	13
Kingsleigh	399	1	3
Itam (Ilam)... ...	167	1	6
Alstonfield	454	1	2

Dialect of the District.

BIDE. Bear or endure.

AFFEARED or AFFEART. Frightened.

> Each trembling leaf, and whistling wind they hear,
> As ghastly bug does greatly them affear.—*Spenser.*

AND THEN. A very common phrase, used at the end of an order or request, generally as a threat.

ANENST. Against.

> And many a sink poured out their rage *anenst* 'em.—*B. Jonson.*

APIECES. In pieces.

> Tombs were hacked and hewn *apieces.*—*Weever.*

ASK WIND. East wind.

AVEROUS. Avaricious or covetous.

AYE! BY GONNY. A very common affirmative expression.

BARE AS A GOOSE GREEN. Scanty herbage.

BAWT. Without.

BEASTINGS. The first milk of a cow after calving.

BECK. Peak of a cap.

BE-MOILED. Daubed with dirt.

> How she was *be-moiled.*—*Shakespeare.*

BILLY-WIFFLING. Dodging, gammoning.

BLENCH. To catch a glimpse or sight.

BLENCH. To flinch.

> Though sometimes you do *blench.*—*Shakespeare.*

BOASTIVE. Presumptuous.

> How must his fellow streams
> Deride the tinklings of the *boastive* rill!—*Shenstone.*

BODGE. To bungle.

> With this we charged again ; but, out, alas !
> We *bodged* again.—*Shakespeare.*

BOWK. To point.

BRAST. Burst or broken.

> The craggy rock, when Moses cleft and *brast.*—*Fairfax.*
> That e'en the temple, wherein she was plac'd,
> Did quake to hear, and near asunder *brast.*—*Spenser.*

BREXFUST. Breakfast.

BRID-NASE. Bird's nest.

BRUE. Brow.

BRUNT. Burnt.

BUN. Bound or costive.

BUR. The sweetbread.

BUSSING. Kissing.

> Thy knee *bussing* the stones.—*Shakespeare.*

CANTLE. Canfull.

CAP. Better than or superior to.

CARPETMANTEL. Carpet bag or portmanteau.

CAUTION.—A superlatively clever man or rogue.

CAVY. Submission. (A corruption of "peccavi.")

CHUFFY. Friendly. Shakespeare uses the substantive to nominate a coarse blunt clown.

> Hang ye, gorbellied knaves, are ye undone ? No,
> Ye fat *chuffs.*

CHUMMER. Grumble.

CLAP-HATCHES. Double swing gate.

CLUSSOMED. Very cold, frozen.

COB. Superior; as "That beats (or caps) all."

COLLYFUGLE. Deceive or swindle.

COLLYWOBBLES. —Diarrhœa.

COLLY WESSON. Reversed.

COMBE. A valley between two hills.

> Till round the world, in sounding *combe* or plain,
> The last of them tell it the first again.—*W. Browne.*

CONNA.   Cannot.

COTE.—A cottage.

> Come every day to my *cote* and woe me.—*Shakespeare.*

CRACK.   To boast.

CRAP.   Crop.

CRUDS.   Curds.

CUMBER.   Cucumber.

DAMPORT.   Davenport.

DANDY COCK.   Game cock; spruce young man.

DARKSOM.   Dark, gloomy.

DARSEY.   An expression of doubt.

DECK.   A pack of cards.

> The king was slily fingered from the *deck.—Shakespeare.*

DEEP.   Cunning, or knowing.

> *Deep* versed in books, and shallow in himself.—*Milton.*

DENAY.   Denial.

> To her in haste; give her this jewel; say
> My love can give no place, bide no *denay.—Shakespeare.*

DESPUT.   *i.e.* "desperate," used instead of "very," as "desput bad weather."

DEY.   Day or die.

DIMBLE.   A dingle.

> Deep in a gloomy *dimble* she doth dwell.—*B. Jonson.*

DO NOWT.   Idle, worthless.

DOOMENT.   Jollification.

DOOLE.   Sorrow.

> And much argument against her *doole.—Spenser.*

DROWNT.   Drenched or drowned.

EARNE.   A great longing.

> Als Una *earn'd* her sorrow to renew.—*Spenser.*

EGG.   Provoke, stir up, set on.

> They *egged* him forward still not to spare the nobility.—*North.*

EKE.   Eternity; as "Will he eke?"—"Will he ever."

ESS. Coal ashes.

EYNE. Eyes.

> Our watery *eyne.* —*Shakespeare.*

FAUSE. Cunning, subtle, or false.

FINE AND WET. Very wet.

FIRK. Inquisitive or curious.

FIT. Ready to recommence.

> Come to the bride ; another *fit*
> Yet show, sirs, of your country wit.—*B. Jonson.*

FOREBY. By.

> He took her up *foreby* her lily hand,
> And her re-comforted the best he might. —*Spenser.*

FORENENST. Opposite to.

> The lands *forenenst* the Greekish shore he held,
> From Sauger's mouth to crook'd Meander's fall.—*Fairfax.*

FOWSPOKEN. Scurrilous.

> *Foul-spoken* coward. —*Shakespeare.*

FUNK. To be afraid; cowardly.

> The best part of veal, and the Greek for *hunc,*
> Is the name of a man that makes us *funk.*
> —*Proctor's Epigram on J. Burton.*

FUST. First; mouldy.

GERN. Yawn.

> And gaped like a wolf when he did *gerne.*—*Spenser.*

GET A GATE. Begin.

GIESORP'NY. A mean or miserly person (derived from "Gi' us a half-penny?")

GIRN. Grin.

> This is at least a *girn* of fortune, if
> Not a fair smile.—*Davenant.*

GLIDE. Squint.

GOT QUIT. Acquitted or discharged.

GREWND. Greyhound.

GROYNE. Groan, grunt.

> Some were of cats, that wealing still did cry,
> And some of beasts, that *groyn'd* continually.—*Spenser.*

GUMPTION. Sense.

HARD FACED. Impudent or bold.

HATCH. Gossip.

HEFT. Throw.

> Out of his headpiece Cambell fiercely reft,
> And with such furie backe at him it *heft.—Spenser.*

HILL UP. Earth up or cover up.

HIT. Agree.

> Pray you, let's *hit* together.—*Shakespeare.*

HOG. A mound of potatoes.

HOLLED For hurled.

HOLT. Woodland.

> About the rivers, vallies, *holts*, and crags,
> Among the ozyers and the waving flags,
> They neerly pry.—*W. Browne.*

HOUSLING. One fond of the house or fireside.

HUSKER. Superlative adjective, good or bad.

INSENSE. To make to understand.

INVENTIOUS. Ingenious, clever.

> Thou art a fine, *inventious* rogue.—*B. Jonson.*

JIRT. Jerk or throw.

> She's gien me mony a *jirt* an' fleg.—*Burns.*

JOBATION. Jolly time, a scolding.

JONNOCK. Fair, honourable.

JUBOUS. Dubious, doubtful.

KAWF. Calf.

KEPEN. To keep or take care of.

KICKED UP A DUST. Caused a quarrel or wrangle.

KILT. Killed.

> But what art thou, that tells of nephews *kilt.—Spenser.*

KNOISENED. Known or noised abroad.

KNURL. A knot in timber.

LEASH. Lease.

LET. Met, as "I *let* upon him yesterday."

LIF. Rather, or as soon.

LIKIN. Likely.

LOVE CHILD. An illegitimate.

LOZEL. Idle, wasteful.
> And, *lozel*, thou art worthy to be hanged.—*Shakespeare.*

LUNJOUS. To strike heavily.

LUNY. Silly or mad.

MANKS. Lark, practical joking.

MEAZELLY. An expression of contempt.

MISH-MASH. Mixture, hotch-potch.
> With the whole *mish-mash* of their composition.—*Lee.*

MOITHER. Bother or plague.

MUN. Must.
> And aye ! but I winne that ladyes love,
> For dole now I *mun* die.—*Percy's Reliques.*

MUNNA. Must not.

NAZZY. Short or ill-tempered.

NEELE. A needle.

NESH. Tender, weak, or cowardly.

NODDY. A stupid fellow.

NON ALL THEER. Not right in his head. "Only about ten to the dozen."

NOT A SMITE. Not a bit.

NOWT. Nothing.

NOWT ELSE. A common expression, meaning "Nothing so sure."

NUMPS. A silly person.

NUZZLE. To hold a child to the breast.

O'ERDONE. Exhausted, beaten.

OLD ANCIENT. Old friend.

OPINIATED. Opinionated.

OSS. Offer or attempt.

OUTIN. Holiday.

PASH. To strike violently.

PUT. Compelled.

RABBLE-YEADED. Full of nonsense.

RACK OF THE EYE. To dig without a line.

RAPATAG. An idle, worthless person.

RATCHILLY. Stony.

REECHY. Smoky, dirty.

RID. Get on with, as "I conno' *rid* my work."

ROMMOCK. Romp.

SAM IT UP. Arrange or set straight.

SAWT. Salt.

SCROIKE. Cry or shout in pain.

SHAPE. Able to do a certain thing, as "He *shaped* right enough."

SHIVE. A slice of bread, cheese, or meat.

> And easy it is
> Of a cut loaf to steal a *shive.*—*Shakespeare.*

SHOMMOCKS. Feet.

SHONNA. Shall not.

SHOON. Shoes.

> Gramercye, my liege, the tanner replyde,
>   For the favour thou hast me showne;
> If ever thou comes to merry Tamworth
>   Neale's leather shall clout thy *shoon.*—*Percy's Reliques.*
>
> It were mair meet that those fine feet
> Were well laced up in silken *shoon.*—*Burns.*

SHUFFS. Feet.

SHUTE. Suit (of clothes).

SKENS. Squints.

SKEW-WIFFED. Lop-sided; on one side.

SKINNY. Mean, miserly.

SKRIKE. To cry. "The chilt's been skrikin' all mornin'."

SLAT. To dash or throw down.

> *Slatted* his brains out, and then soused him in the briny sea.
> *Marston.*

SLATTED.   Spilled.

SLUTHER.   To slide or drag the feet along.

SNEAP.   To rebuke or check.

> I will not undergo this *sneap* without reply.—*Shakespeare.*

SOJERS.   Soldiers.

SPERR.   To bolt or fasten up.

> With massive staples
> And corresponsive and fulfilling bolts,
> *Sperr* up the sons of Troy.—*Shakespeare.*

STRENE.   Strain, descent.

> Sate goodly Temperance in garments clene
> And sacred Reverence, yborne of heavenly *strene.*—*Spenser.*

STONE COLD.   Cold as a stone.

SURRY.   A common word by which anyone is accosted.

SUSTENE.   To sustain.

> That with her soveraine power and scepter shene
> All faery land does peaceably *sustene.*—*Spenser.*

SWEAL or SWALE.   To waste or melt away.

SWOP.   Exchange.

> We'se gie ae night's discharge to care,
>   If we forgather,
> And hae a *swop* o' rhymin' ware
>   W' ane anither.—*Burns.*

SYKE.   A person fond of drinking at another's expense.

TELD.   Told.

> Sir Calidore up-chear'd, and to her *teld*
> All this accord to which he brudar had compeld.—*Spenser.*

THIN AGEN.   Until.

TIDY MON.   A good man.

TON O' TOTHER.   One or the other.

TWINK.   An instant.

UNDOUBTFUL.   Beyond a doubt.

> This fact, till now in the government of Lord Angelo,
> came not to an *undoubtful proof.*—*Shakespeare.*

UNVULGAR.   Above what is common.

> Heat my brain with Delphick fire,
> That I may sing my thoughts in some *unvulgar* strain.—*B. Jonson.*

UPBRAST. Burst open.

> But Calidore with huge resistless might
> The dores assayled, and the lockes *upbrast.*—*Spenser.*

UNBETHOUGHT. Reminded.

WAKKEN. To awaken.

WERRIT. Worritt.

WICK'UN. A knowing one.

WOSSER. Worse.

> Our *worser* genius.—*Shakespeare.*

YATE. Gate. (Nearly obsolete).

> And when they came to King Adland's hall,
> Until the fayre hall *yate,*
> There they found a proud porter
> Rearing himselfe thereatt.—*Percy's Reliques.*

YELL. Ale. (Old Leek phrase, " A glass o' gude lousy old *yell.*")

YEN. Endon.

Ibenry Mewcome.

HENRY NEWCOME, Vicar of Leek, 1654. (A learned and pious Puritan; founder of the old Dissent, in Manchester; author of a " Plain Discourse about Rash and Sinful Anger," as a help for such as are willing to be relieved against so sad and too-generally prevailing a distemper, even amongst professors of religion. Being the substance of some sermons preached at Manchester, in Lancashire, by Henry Newcome, M.A., and a minister of the Gospel there.—London, printed for Tho. Parkhurst, at the " Bible and Three Crowns," in Cheapside, near Mercers' Chapel, 1693).

Leek and the Lincoln Militia.

N Saturday last a division of the South
Lincoln Militia, commanded by Colonel
Sibthorp, arrived at this town on their route
to Ireland. Several of the principal inhabitants being
apprised of their coming, raised a very handsome
subscription to furnish them with refreshments. On
their arrival the whole town was illuminated, the bells
rang, and every mark of attention was paid to the
accommodation of the brave fellows. Colonel Sibthorp
expressed his thanks to the inhabitants in the following
note :—" Colonel Sibthorp in passing thro' Leek to
Congleton, made acquainted of the great kindness
presented to the division of his regiment on their
route, by many inhabitants of the town, begs that they
will believe that he feels most gratefully and obliged,
and accept his sincere thanks for the honour conferred
on himself in the favours bestowed on his soldiers."—
Staffordshire Advertiser, September 15th, 1798.

Ireland at this time was in a state of insurrection,
and the Lincoln Militia formed part of the reinforce-
ments which were sent to Lord Lake. The troops
passed through Leek three or four months after the
battle of Vinegar Hill and the evacuation of Wexford.

The Roches.

DR. Plot says:—"The vast Rocks or Roches, as they call them, that bear no grass, but here and there a turf in some cleft or hollow, stand as bare as a stone wall, some of them kissing the clouds with their tops and running along in mountainous ridges for some miles together. The first of these I met with on Wetley Moore, which at a distance I took for some prodigious ruins, these representing them as much bigger than truth, as the Florentine stones doe less; but when I came to Leek and saw the Hen Cloud and Leek Roches I was quickly undeceived, though my mind was still heightened to see such vast rocks and such really stupendous prospects which I had never seen before, or could have believed to be anywhere but in picture, and that which yet further increased my wonder was, how they should become thus bare, having no turf upon them or earth to produce one, which, whether so from the Creation, or uncovered by the Flood or the perpetual deterrations which have happened since upon the rain to all mountainous parts, is hard to account for."

Mr. John Sleigh says:—" Here are those high stony grounds, called the Roches, composed of coarse

Roaches.

sandy grit rock, whose bold and still varied outline, backed by the heathery moors, adds so much to the general picturesqueness of the country; though the Cheese Press or Loaf and Cheese on the Hen Cloud; the Rocking Stone or Loggan Rock, the Sun Dial, and the Tip Cat, four of their more fantastic and remarkable features, were a few years ago wantonly destroyed."

King James used to say of Staffordshire :—" 'Twas fit only to be cut out into throngs to make highways for the rest of the Kingdom." His Majesty thus innocently prognosticated the use of Staffordshire stone for road metalling.

Leek Pottery.

MARRYATT's "History of Pottery and Porcelain" says with "the more modern manufacture must be mentioned a fabric marked Mason's Ironstone China, made near Leek, Staffordshire, which, however, is not an ironstone but fine porcelain; at least such are the specimens in collection of the author, consisting of a pair of ewers large size, finely moulded, rich in gilding and painting, and most creditable to this manufacture, which from the expensive nature of its ware failed of success. For good and cheap articles these manufactures are unrivalled. The French hard paste production show more taste in colour and ornamentation, but cannot compete with the English soft china in other respects."

"Lumpy=Tums."

The following lines were written by Joseph Allen, of Onecote, shoemaker, about 1855 :—

Taters they are windy meat,
Un frumity it is a treat;
Puddin's good when stuffed wi' plums
Bu' gie mi plenty lumpy-tums.

Its put yer kettle on th' fire,
Un bring th' meal a little nigher;
When th' milk it boils un foams,
Then's yer toime fur lumpy-tums.

A poultice made o' milk un meal
A hungry stomach soon will 'eal;
When hunger throo yer bowels roams
The very best cure is lumpy-tums.

Bafe, mutton, veal, poke, ducks or gase,
Fresh fish or fowl or bread un chase;
O gie mi thase when dinner comes,
Bu' at supper gie mi lumpy-tums.

Would yo ya tender offspring rear,
Wi bodies fit fatigues t' bear;
Paumper 'um not wi' deenty crums,
Bu' bring 'um up on lumpy-tums.

Just view our labourers' robust race—
Theer rosy chakes, theer ruddy face;
They'n nerves loike stale, they'n hearts like drums
Because they were reer'd on lumpy-tums.

Just view those healthy country girls—
Theer rosy chakes, theer glossy curls;
Th' rosiest chakes un reddest combs
Han girls ut are reer'd on lumpy-tums.

Th' plow lad when his work war done
Returned wom wi' th' settin' sun;
Some fag eend of a sung he hums,
When hae thinks o' his wom un lumpy-tums.

Wae well remember Robert Peel,
Who kindly lowered th' proice o' meal;
Its a poor look out at folks' woms
If they han noo meal for lumpy-tums.

Jim Shaw,* that vallient mon who slew
Ten of the French at Waterloo,
His powerful arms dealt them theer dooms
For hae wur reer'd on lumpy-tums.

Let pale-faced wimmin sip aw dey
On slape-destroying strung grane tea,—
Th' acrid juice th' nerves benums—
They's none such juice i' lumpy-tums.

Koind heavens, listen too mi prayer,
Un grant mi whoile oi tarry here;
Oi eks no' wealth's uncounted sums,
Bu' health un peace un lumpy-tums.

* Born at Cossall, near Nottingham.

The Nine Hours' Movement.

THIS popular movement, which has now spread to almost every industry in the kingdom, owes its local introduction to Messrs. Brough, Nicholson & Co., who on January 26th, 1872, posted up a notice to the effect that in future the nine hours' system would be adopted. The innovation, aided by agitation on the part of the operatives, became rapidly adopted throughout the silk trade, and subsequently spread to other departments of local labour.

John Jones, Schoolmaster.

N 1787 there came to Leek a young gentleman named John Jones, who set up a school probably in Backsides (now Pickwood Road), but who met with scant success. Strangers were not received in those days with open arms, but were rather looked upon as trespassers upon preserved land. Nothing was then known of the young gentleman's antecedents, but it gradually became known that he was the son of a Welsh clergyman, was intended for the Church, and had been educated at Chester, but who, when his father died, deserted his home and went to sea. His father was William Jones, B.A., Jesus College, Oxford, and Rector of Penmorva and Dolbenmaen; who married Margaret Owens, one of the daughters and coheiresses at law of Humphrey Owens, of Lasynys, near Harleigh, Merionethshire. The marriage proved a direct contradiction of the old proverb, "Marry in haste and repent at leisure," for although the couple eloped, and while on horseback, were followed by the irate squire, and fired at with a duelling pistol, the union was a singularly happy one. When the Rector died in 1769 he was buried under the altar steps in Ruthin Church of which he

was for some time Curate; and after mourning her
husband for fifty years, his widow joined him in 1819,
her body being placed in the coffin containing his
bones and dust.   This is a remarkable statement to
make, but we give it on the authority of Mary Walker,
of Ruthin (sister of John Jones, the subject of this
sketch), who died in 1854.   Writing from Coed Garven,
on September 25th, 1819, she said to her brother,
" I am sorry to tell you that our dear old mother is
no more. We laid her in her husband's grave ; indeed,
in his very coffin, which wonderful to say was not at
all decayed, after lying in the ground fifty years.
They took the lid off, and put her close upon the
poor bones, laying her coffin into his.   Such a thing
they say was never known, that they should lay in
the same coffin after so long a separation"; and in a
subsequent letter she says, " I have been at Conway
for three weeks since my ever to be lamented mother's
death."   Her brother, Mr. William Jones, resided at
Conway, and was a surgeon.

Returning to John Jones, we find that he was
married at Astbury Church to Sarah, the daughter of
William and Sarah Bullock, and that the first of a
family of 14 was born at Kiln Lane, Leek, in 1787.   In
the following year he opened a School, having previously (October 7th, 1787,) been appointed Master of
the Leek Church Sunday School.   At a vestry meeting
on May 23rd, 1791, he was appointed Master of
Endon Free School, but whether Endon did not suit
him, or he did not suit Endon, or whether his roving
propensities proved too strong for his own interests, is
not known ; but certain it is that he left Endon for

Chester in 1793, where he identified himself with the
Methodist New Connexion body. A few months appear
to have convinced him that Chester was not an El
Dorado, for during the same year he entered the
services of Messrs. Tate and Brown, cotton spinners,
Deansgate, Manchester, presumably as a Clerk, seeing
that he wrote a good hand and was an expert
arithmetician. His salary, however, could not have been
a high one, for we find that in order to add to his
income and provide for his fast increasing family, he
opened a night school in Fleet Street, Manchester.
1806 found him at Stanningley, near Bradford, and
the same year he flitted to Stockport, back again to
Stanningley, and then returned to Stockport. There he
tried the experiment of a night school, but discontinued
it after three or four months, on the birth of his
twelfth child. It is not known whether his school was
adequately patronised or not. Proceeding on the even
tenour of his way, his fourteenth and last child,
Thomas (whose only surviving son is Mr. Thomas
Jones, of Westwood Terrace, in this town, clerk to
Messrs. Challinors and Shaw, solicitors, Derby Street,)
was born to bless the family, although his welcome was
not as warm as it would have been if the fold had
not been so full. He remained at Stockport until
about 1819, when he returned to Leek after an
absence of twenty-eight years. During his ramblings
he had become imbued with the notions of Swedenborg, and on May 9th, 1824, a meeting was called
by him at Leek. The event is thus recorded in a
neatly written but loosely kept diary :—" May 9th, 1824,
being the first time the readers and lovers of the

Hon. Baron Swedenborg's works met in the Blackamoor
Yard, in Leek, at my School, in order to instruct
ourselves in the divine truth and good of the Word
of God." The meeting was probably held in the same
room as John Wesley had preached in in 1772-88,
and which had also been used by the persecuted
Methodists. In 1827, at which time Mr. Jones was
73 years of age, he took a house in the Blakamoor
Yard, for which he paid six pounds ten shillings per
annum. He afterwards lived in Mill Street, where he
taught school and kept a small grocer's shop. Amongst
those who passed through his hands were Mr. William
Goostrey, gentleman, Mr. Uriah Davenport Hudson,
surveyor, Mr. Thomas Davenport, confectioner, Mr.
Joseph Broster, sen., silk manufacturer, a son of the
late Dr. Fynney, of Compton House, the late Mr.
Edward Pickford, chemist, the late Mr. Thomas
Rowley, relieving officer, Messrs. John and William
Barlow, of the Red Lion Hotel, and others; and he
is remembered as a man of good education and
ability, and as a strict disciplinarian. He died on
April 9th, 1833, aged 79 years, and was buried three
days later in the Leek Churchyard. His widow lived
until February 7th, 1843, and she was buried with her
husband on the 9th of the same month.

The late Mr. Thomas Jones, who died at Leek
in 1882 (son of the schoolmaster), had a windfall in
1857 under the will of the Mrs. Walker above
referred to, in the shape of a legacy of something
over £100 in money, and a silver tankard and two
silver nipperkins, each bearing the arms of Humphrey
Owens, esquire, his maternal grandmother's father.

On the 24th February, 1889, the said Mr. Thomas Jones, of Westwood Terrace, received the following letter from his cousin, Mrs. Davies, in reply to one from him. Mrs. Davies is a sister of Mrs. Thomas, wife of the Rev. David Morgan Thomas, M.A., Jesus College, Oxford, of Llanelian Rectory, Abergele, North Wales :-

"Eryl Mar, Penmaenmawr, February 23rd, 1889.

"Dear Mr. Jones,—I always understood that the arms on the plate left by aunt Walker belonged to the Humphrey Owen branch of our family. (I mean those with little birds on.) My grandfather (Dr. Jones) had a seal with a lion on, which he used to shew me when I was a little girl, and he told me many times that it belonged to the Jones's, but I have not seen it on any of the plate.

"I remain, yours very sincerely,

"MARGARET DAVIES."

Value of Land in 1587.

ON April 18, John Bullock, husbandman, of Leek, for a consideration of £50, conveyed to Thomas Jollye, mercer, of Leek, Bullock's meadow, near to the water of the "Chornette," with ten days' work in Leek fields, near "Catteslowe and the Bromy-fflatt.

George Smith of Coalville.

FEW have not heard of the above-named large-hearted brickmaker, who has devoted the best years of his life to the task of rescuing from ignorance and immorality the children who once made our brickyards and canal boats a dreadful disgrace to Christian England; and fewer still are aware that in the neighbourhood of Leek he probably obtained some of the experiences that caused him to devote his health, strength, and money, to the blessed work that has linked his name with the illustrious roll of nineteenth century saviours of society. It would be far from our present purpose to give the details of his interesting life, but they may be gleaned from the many biographies of him that have been written, and also of the numerous books of which he is the author. It is rather our business to connect him with old Leek, and in this pleasant relation we have been assisted by a few notes which he has kindly placed at our service.

Born at Clayhills, Tunstall, Staffordshire, on February 16th, 1831, George Smith (whose portrait we are able to publish by the courtesy of the Editor of the *Christian Globe*), when only seven years of age, commenced working for his father, a brick and tile maker. At nine years of age he was working harder than labouring men do now, and was, moreover, brutally treated, the marks of which he will carry some day to an honoured grave. He says:—"On one occasion I had to perform a very heavy task. After my customary day's work I had to carry 1,200 nine-inch bricks from the maker to the floors on which they were placed to harden. The total distance walked by me that night was not less than fourteen miles, seven of which I traversed with eleven pounds weight of clay in my arms, besides lifting the unmade clay and carrying it to the maker. The total quantity of clay thus carried by me was five-and-a-half tons." Even amidst these terrible circumstances he found time for mental improvement, and thus unconsciously began qualifying himself for the crusade that has been so gloriously successful.

Marrying early in life he left Tunstall to make a home and fortune for himself, and came Leekwards. He first worked for Mr. West, at the Ladderedge brickyard, and lodged in the further of the two cottages near the Leek wharf, opposite to Woodcroft. He made the first blue bricks and sanitary ware ever produced in the neighbourhood, his first work being to make pipes to carry a spring of excellent water to Mr. West's house, a mile away. From Leek, he journeyed, as he says, "with my wife and bag and baggage,

through Leek by the Mermaid Inn to Reapsmoor."
Arrived there he started a small brick and tile yard
on his own account, and introduced to the district
blue bricks, glazed ware, and roof tiles, there being
nothing of the kind to be obtained within twenty miles.
These he carted chiefly to Buxton, numbering amongst
his customers the Duke of Devonshire, the Duke of
Rutland, and Sir John Harpur Crewe, Bart. In those
years, however, he found that the dearness of coal
and the long distances from canal and rail, were
insuperable bars to success, and he left Morridge for
Leicestershire. Whilst at Reapsmoor he began to prac-
tise that which he subsequently preached so eloquently,
and declined to employ children under thirteen, or
girls or women; and refused to permit his young boys
to work overtime or on Sundays. Whilst at Reapsmoor, living in an old ivy-clad cottage, his wife bore
him two sons; and about 1856 he started the first
Wesleyan Sunday school in the neighbourhood, and
was superintendent nearly the whole of the time he
lived in the locality.

On one occasion he had a very narrow escape of
losing his life. One dark winter's night, whilst riding
rapidly downhill, between the Mermaid and Reapsmoor,
from the Potteries, his horse, an old one, fell and
pitched him headforemost. Mr. Smith struck the ground
violently, within six inches of a huge rough stone,
receiving a tremendous shock, from which he did not
speedily recover, whilst the accident proved fatal to the
horse. The tens of thousands of poor children, whose eman-
cipation Mr. Smith has since brought about, may " thank
the goodness and the grace " that he escaped with his life.

On another occasion he risked his life in preventing what might have been a serious, perhaps fatal, accident to Lady Crewe. Whilst on his way to Warslow, he met a pair of runaway ponies, attached to a carriage in which were seated Lady Crewe and her maid. The unmanageable animals were dashing along at a tremendous pace, and at great risk Mr. Smith succeeded in stopping them. Lady Crewe thanked the poor brickmaker, and the ponies were led to Warslow Hall.

We conclude this sketch of Mr. Smith's connection with Leek in his own words:—" Since then many changes have taken place, but in the midst of them all my mind has often been at the old spots near Leek."

We may add that having revolutionised the condition, educational and moral, of 20,000 brickyard children, and vastly improved the surroundings of about 40,000 boys and girls on our canals and rivers, Mr. Smith is now hard at work for 50,000 gipsy and van children, on whose behalf he hopes during the present Parliament to add to the statute book his Movable Dwellings Bill—which under one name or other he has been promoting since 1877—a measure that will bring them under educational and sanitary influences. All his old Moorland and Morridge friends, we may safely say, wish him God speed in his good and great work.

"The Queen of the Moorlands."

THIS "town on a hill in a valley," called by its people "the Metropolis," or, better still, "the Queen of the Moorlands," is certainly, in its way, one of the most interesting places in the Midland Counties. Its charm is a little difficult to put into words: plenty of other towns are surrounded by beautiful country, have hilly old streets, a picturesque market place, a fine old church with chiming bells. This town has these and something more; something which one feels in approaching it, which grows clearer and deeper every day, till at last one is possessed with a sort of sense of individuality in the place, and studies and knows it like a human being.

Perhaps something of the charm of this town lies in its remoteness; no main line of railway passes it, or goes very near it, and this means that it is a long and tiresome journey from everywhere. But once visited, one does not think of the journey when one visits it again; and as to getting away, the regret at leaving it is such, that the small annoyance of waiting

at stations hardly seems worth considering. Let us
travel to it from the south-west. We leave a great
region of smoke and dimness—the Potteries—and pass
through red ironworks flashing and gleaming, where
black figures move very like demons on a background
of flame. Uncanny little trucks run up and down a
narrow line near a black canal, without engine or
visible means of guidance; then come great bare banks
and fields; then, by degrees, a lonely country, first
flat and ugly, then becoming rocky and bold, with
fir-woods, hills, and streams. This is the plainest side
of our town. It is not exactly smiling; wild, and
rather sad. But in this short half-hour the Potteries
are quite forgotten, and we feel that the moorland is
not far away. We are among the hills with all their
mystery, their half-melancholy beauty, so strongly felt
in autumn and winter time; we breathe their air, and
feel ourselves in another world, even as we climb up
from the station, with its puzzling archways and
tunnels—"a bad place to get to after dark," says a
kind old porter at a station on the way—into the
paved streets of the old moorland town.

The main street, St. Edward Street, leads up-hill;
broad and paved, large old houses mingled with shops
looking down upon it, shady gardens and open country
behind them. This town, with 13,000 people, seems
to have hills and trees—or, at least, a view of them—
at the end of every street. Among the old red houses,
mostly square, and of a last-century aspect, tower the
romantic gables of two or three half-timbered ones,
already looking old. These have been built by one
of those inhabitants who love their town so truly,

that they ask for nothing better than to spend their
lives and fortunes there. There are several of these
families, whose names have been known in the town
for generations; and perhaps, in these changing days,
here again is one of the secrets of its charm,—a sort
of feudality not yet extinct; a history of its own, in
which, as century follows century, the same names
appear. Famous beauties have lived in the old country
town; very great people have danced at its balls;
and the stopping of the coach at the beautiful old inn
has been an affair of great excitement in its day.
By-the-bye, we hope it is not true that the "Roebuck"
is to be pulled down. Surely the people who are so
loyal to their town, homesick wherever they go, and
coming back to die there from the ends of the earth,
have more feeling than this for their *monuments
historiques.*

From the "Roebuck" we may wander up into
the Market Place, a broad paved square, sloping up
to the great red house that fills all its north side,
and looks down upon it kindly. The square is
generally empty and silent enough, with its great lamps
and its drinking-fountain; but on one day of the week
it is crowded and very picturesque, with a great store
of pots, chiefly "seconds" from the Potteries. There
one may spend a few pence with wonderful result,
shape and colour being exactly suited to the aspirations
of the present day. The north east wind whistles very
bitterly down the square, however, and the pottery-
woman tells us that she has sometimes stood there
knee-deep in snow. We have, indeed, heard it said
that these moorlands are the coldest part of England;

but then, the air is dry, and the real old inhabitants
do not mind. As we stand in the market, the church
clock falls suddenly to chiming, almost over our heads.
It chimes all the quarters, and four times a day plays
a tune. The paved streets of the town have almost a
foreign effect, narrow and twisting as some of them
are, with little dark shops looking out of corners; one
fancies *sabots* clattering over the stones, but then the
bells break in with "The Bailiff's Daughter of Isling-
ton," or "Believe me, if all those endearing young
charms," or some other familiar air, to remind us that
we need not go abroad for that undefinable thing
"romance," or poetic suggestion, or quaint picturesqueness; all are to be found in a Staffordshire moorland
town, a dozen miles from the Potteries.

A certain old stone house by the churchyard has
a tradition of its own. Prince Charles Edward asked
for shelter there, when he was hopelessly marching
about England in the winter of 1745, and the mistress
of the house—too loyal, shall we say?—pushed him
away by the shoulders and shut the door upon him.
There are plenty of other stories of different kinds in
the history of the town, which has been written, and
fills a large book.

The most striking thing in the town is the old
Church of St. Edward the Confessor—"Owd Church,"
as the poor people call it—standing on the north
edge of the hill, the churchyard raised high, with its
centuries of graves and two old curious crosses, above
the paved street that runs under the wall. To the
south is the town with all its busy life; to the north
the ground slopes sharply away from the ridge on

which the church stands; first, a hillside covered with
graves, then the deep green valley of meadows and
trees through which the Churnet flows. On the farther
bank of the little river are some old farm buildings,
and here are to be found, scarcely traceable now, the
last relics of the abbey which was once master of the
town. But our eyes wander on, over meadows and
river, to the wild, varied view beyond; hills and
valleys breaking away, clothed with woods, still beautiful
in their wintry brownness; solemn clumps of dark fir;
hills wilder still, of strange craggy shapes, suggesting
the lonely waste of moorland that one knows to lie
beyond them; and then all the changing mystery of
clouds in a country like this—flying mists through
which the hills show like a vision, or fierce dark
masses threatening storm, perhaps a ray of sunlight
shooting through on some rocky point or group of
pines that flashes out like gold.

There is a foreign element in the town, too, and
the *sabots* may not always have been quite imaginary.
Down to the north-west of the church there is a small
crowded colony of poor houses, called " Petty France,"
where a tribe of French prisoners lived once upon a
time. *Petite France!* poor things—what a cheerful
courage there is in the name, and how they must
have shivered in this dark, cold, rugged North, the
great churchyard, with its piled-up tombstones, between
them and the sun! Several of the common surnames
of the town seem to be of French origin; and one
of its chief officials has as much the air of a soldier
of the Empire, that one expects to see a bit of red
ribbon in his button-hole. . . . Her silk mills are

celebrated; one of them is on its way to a world-wide reputation. We find here stuffs "to dream of, not to feel;" a beauty of colour and design which impresses the most ignorant with the unmistakable sense of being in the presence of *true art*—and how much of the show and glitter and artistic upholstery of the time fails to give this impression!—a school of embroidery which is gaining fresh fame day by day; the whole thing carried on with a kind of unconscious naturalness which surely must be the atmosphere Art really loves. It all takes one back to an older England; and coming out from the square red house with its world of beauty into the hilly street where twilight is falling, and St. Edward's bells are chiming down, sending their music over town and hills and away to moorland, one feels one's self, in some indescribable way, several hundred years nearer to the days when Art was born.

The attraction of the place is perhaps all these things, and yet it is none of them: it is something more hidden still. The task which seemed a little difficult has proved almost impossible. One may go on writing for hours, and yet fail to convey to those who do not know it the subtle, nameless charm of this "town on a hill in a valley," this chief city of the Moorlands.—*The Spectator*, Dec. 31, 1887.

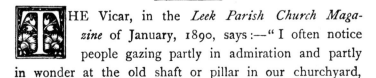
The Old Parish Church.

THE PILLAR IN THE CHURCHYARD.

HE Vicar, in the *Leek Parish Church Maga-zine* of January, 1890, says :—" I often notice people gazing partly in admiration and partly in wonder at the old shaft or pillar in our churchyard,

and trying to make out what the mystic letters
H.Q.C.C. on the basement can possibly mean. Well,
the pillar and its base are certainly an ill-assorted pair,
and the matter for wonder should be how even the
church folk of Leek allowed such stones to be mated.
We rather rebel against a very old man marrying a
very young wife, but that is nothing compared to this
ancient cross—for cross it would be, were it perfect—
standing on a stone which bears the date MCLXXX,
i.e. 1180. Mr. Sleigh, in his *History of Leek*, says:
'The monogram H.Q.C.C., Hugo Quintus Comes
Cestriæ, *i.e.* Hugh the fifth Count of Chester, was
transcribed from an ancient stone found near the base
of the cross, which would lead to the supposition that
the cross itself was erected as a memorial to this
curious old earl.' But the cross is certainly of much
greater antiquity than the year 1180, and it is very
confusing to the antiquarian mind to see that date
on its pedestal. In a pamphlet on the Ilam crosses
by the Rev. G. F. Brown, B.D., F.S.A., I come across
a reference to our cross, which may interest some of
my readers. He says: 'It is curious that Staffordshire
and the neighbouring county of Chester have more of
these early sculptured shafts than any other counties
have. Derbyshire has two or three examples, one at
Spendon and one at Bakewell. Beyond these counties
they are exceedingly rare. In the complete monument
the shaft was roughly cylindrical for some six feet
from the ground; above this the cylinder was cut into
four plain faces, each with decoration: at the top the
stone spread out again and formed a cross, either of
the kind known as the cross pattée, or a 'wheel'

cross. There is no complete monument of the kind known. The nearest to completeness is in the great pillar at the east end of the Church of Leek, in this same county; it has all the parts except the cross head, of which only a little bit of the lowest part is

left at the top of the pillar. Some idea of the antiquity which may be claimed for this kind of stone may be gathered from the fact the pillar near Valle Crucis Abbey has on it a long inscription, which no one can date later than A.D. 850, while many date it much earlier than that.'"

PUBLISHING THE BANNS OF MARRIAGE AT THE MARKET CROSS.

In olden times it was the custom to publish the banns of marriage at the Market Cross, in proof of which we give the following extract from the Leek Parish Register:—"The bands of marriage between Robert Fernihough, carpenter, of the parish of Ipstones, and Ellen Smith, of ye same place, were duly published at ye Market Cross, at Leek, in ye county of Stafford thre several times on July 15th, 22nd, and 29th, 1657, and were marryed Sept. 15th, 1657." There are other entries of a similar character, including that of John Godwin, of the Low, and Annie Booth of the same, were published the 20th of May at the Market Cross, and were married the 27th of May, 1657;" and also of the marriage of a couple who had been published at the Market Cross of Stone, and were married at Leek on August 17th, 1657.

The above mode of publishing the banns of marriage was discontinued in December, 1658; and in January, 1659, the banns of marriage between Richard Myatt and Mary Heath were published three several times in the Parish Church.

THE ORGAN AND ORGANISTS.

The old organ, which was removed in 1878, was probably erected in 1772. Upon its front was a record of the early organists, and we are indebted for

a copy to the Rev. A. W. W. Vorne-Palmer, at one
time organist at the Old Church, and now curate of
South Ashford, Kent. The first organist was John
Francis Stanton, who was appointed on April 18th, 1772.
Of the second there is no mention, but in the vestry
accounts for 1777 there is an entry—"Gave to the
organist Hambleton, when he left Leeke, 2/9." On
April 10th, 1777, John Clark was appointed; and on
January 20th, 1782, Thomas Jackson succeeded Clark.
Jackson also appears to have undertaken to tune the
instrument for two guineas per annum, the work having
previously been done by one Wych for twice that
amount. The fifth organist was named Alcock, who
succeeded Jackson on March 15th, 1804; and he in
turn gave way in 1807 to Edmund Larkin, who was
appointed on June 24th. John St. Valentine followed
the last-named on October, 1813, and was succeeded
in 1815 by Jonathan Barnes, who was elected on
March 25th. Then came Johnson, Benjamin Barlow,
Alfred Barlow, A. W. W. Vorne-Palmer, Alfred Barlow,
and Herbert Barlow, the last-named still holding the
appointment.

The vestry book contains no entry of the total
cost of the instrument, which was built by Glyn and
Parker, of Manchester; but on May 23rd, 1773, an
item was paid—"Richard Parker's balance on account
of organ £32 11s.," and on the same date J. Daintry
was paid £2 18s., "interest on the above for two
years." One of the pipes in the swell organ bore the
following inscription—"This organ was repaired and
revoiced, and a dulciana added to the swell by J.
Schultz, December, 1807." Upon the new front, the

old one having been covered up by the extension of
the manuals, was a plate—" This organ was enlarged
and rebuilt by public subscription A.D. 1814. Rev. T.
H. Heathcote, vicar; Rev. J. Barnes, curate; John
Russell, churchwarden. Ren————, (query, Renshaw,
builder, Manchester."

THE PARISH CLERK'S SALARY.

The Old Church vestry minute book, under date
November 29th, 1774, contains an entry to the effect
that whereas in the past it had been customary to
pay the parish clerk a portion of his salary in " seed
oats and other contributions," it was resolved that in
future he be paid the sum of ten pounds in money,
in addition to the usual fees for weddings, burials,
and the churching of women.

A CHURCHYARD LEGEND.

The following lines upon Robert Emerson, churchwarden of Leek, who died on March 2nd, 1820, are
believed to have been written about 1815 by Eli
Cope or Alfred Fynney, of Leek, surgeons :—

Not many weeks since, if report does not lie,
A theft was committed—pray, whom was it by?
The public declares it to be the Churchwarden,
Who from the churchyard took soil to his garden.
His wife, in a longing condition, 'tis said,
Begged of her dear husband to make a hot-bed;
That she might have radishes early in spring
When other great folk had no such a thing.

"My Anne," he replied, "'t shall be done in a trice,
There's soil i' th' churchyard which will do very nice;
I'll fetch it at midnight, for fear lest the clowns
Should tease me and vex me with menacing frowns."
The soil it was brought and the seed it was sown,
And in process of time the radishes grown.
Some scores to the table were very soon brought,
And madame selected the best as she thought;
Her mouth was half-open, her taste to regale,
When the Radish screamed out, "Don't bite off my
tail!
The top of my head, legs and arms I bewail,
But pray, my dear madam, don't bite off my tail!
Near the sexton's old house my mangled limbs lie,
And I beg that my tail may be buried hard-by."
The radish ceased speaking, and vanished from sight,
Leaving Sponsy and Anne half dead with affright,
The soil was "took back;" and, the spirit at rest,
The churchwarden owned "to be honest was best."

THE CHIMES AND CLOCK.

In April, 1668, the following entry appears in the
Leek Parish Register:—"Ch. Wans.* account for making
ye chymes and repairing ye Clock £11 11s. 06d., of
which sum

Leek and Lowe churchwardens paid ...	01	15	00
Leekfrith	... 04	00	10
Endon Longsden & Stanley ...	... 02	17	10
Bradnop & Onecote ...	... 02	17	10
	£11	11	06

The amount paid per annum for mending the clock
and bells was £00 06 00."

* Churchwardens.

INSCRIPTIONS ON THE BELLS.

1st.—The Lord to praise my voice I'll raise. V.R.

2nd.—Our voices shall with joyful sound,
Make hill and valley echo round. V.R.

3rd.—God be our speed. A.R. 1721.

4th.—Reverence my Sanctuary.

5th.—Glory be to God on high.

6th.—Prosperity to all our Benefactors.

7th.—Prosperity to this Town. 1721.

8th.—On Earth Peace, Good Will towards Men.
A.R. 1721.

AN ANCIENT RECORD.

When the Old Church tower was opened out in 1867, some plaster was removed and underneath was discovered three oaken boards, about three feet six by eight, and one inch thick, bearing the following :—

CHVRCHWARDENS.

DANIEL FENTON   RICHARD MOBBERLEY

WILLIAM WOOLLEY   TIMOTHY FALLOWES

Iohn Ball Carpenter, 1647.

The two first lines are upon one board, and perhaps served to indicate that the pew above which it was fixed was reserved for the persons named. The other lines have each a board, and probably were for a similar purpose, especially when it is remembered that the boards had evidently been fitted end to end so as to form one long line of letters.

A MODEL WIFE.

The Rev. John Daintry, vicar of Leek, writes in the death register of St. Edward's Church, Leek, under date November 19th, 1738, of Elizabeth Sutton, the wife of Mr. John Sutton, of Endon, as follows:—"She was an obsequious wife—a tender mother—a rare economist—her temper was even—her passions calm—her understanding clear—her conversation was pleasant, instructive, and pious, without any savour of pride, raillery, or affectation—the whole course of her behaviour, the constant series of her actions were the result of rational and religious principles—she died with the same character she lived—she was known to me several years—I never heard or knew she had an enemy, and am sure she never deserved one. All this and more I know to be true."

Badnall's Charity.

WILLIAM Badnall, of Leek, silk dyer, left by will dated the 11th January, 1806, one thousand pounds in the public funds, the interest of which is to be annually laid out in bedding, clothing, or other necessaries, to be distributed amongst twenty poor widows resident in Leek, who are not less than 60 years of age.—Pitt's *Staffordshire.*

The Cricket Club.

RICKET in Leek had been played with little or no organization until 1844, when a meeting was called on May 20th to start a club on a proper basis. The gathering took place in the Town Hall (which was demolished in 1872), and Mr. William Challinor presided. Mr. Sawkins, solicitor, was appointed treasurer, and Mr. J. G. Whittles, grocer, was elected secretary. The rules were settled and ordered to be printed.

A general meeting was held two days later, under the presidency of Mr. William Milner, when the uniform was decided to consist of a white serge jacket, edged with blue woollen binding, and fastened by hooks and eyes, with the Staffordshire Knot in blue on the collar ; white trousers ; and a plain blue cap, with a beck, without braiding. It was also decided to rent a meadow at Barn Fields from Mr. Leech, at a yearly rental of five pounds ; and on May 30th it was resolved " on the playground," to meet every Thursday at six p.m. until further notice.

The first roll of members included the following :— Messrs. W. B. Badnall, G. Sawkins, W. P. Morley, management seems to have been practised about this time, for in the following year a resolution was proposed by Mr. James Bloore, seconded by Dr. Walters, and unanimously carried, "That a vote of thanks be passed to Mr. W. Allen for his kindness and attention to the Leek Cricket Club during the time he has willingly spent his leisure for their amusement and recreation." In the same year the blue cap was discarded and a grey one adopted. A friendly match was arranged with Ashbourne, Stockport was arranged with in 1854, and in 1855 Longsight was again taken on. It was in the last mentioned year that we find Leek's first professional, and an exceedingly modest beginning it was. The thin end of the wedge was inserted at the annual meeting on April 5th, when Mr. W. Allen proposed and Mr. G. Bloore seconded—"That Mr. J. Copson be elected an honorary member of the club," and the accounts for the year show that he was paid at the rate of one shilling per match for nine matches! In addition to this he had free dinners and one pound per annum for carrying the club bag. The accounts for 1858, show that he was also paid £2 as bowler, £1 as ground keeper, and other smaller sums for rolling and mowing.

The all-important office of secretary often changed hands after Mr. Allen's three years' spell, for we find that between 1852, when he resigned, and 1857, Messrs. Bacon, Squire, Shufflebotham, and G. Wardle successively held the office. In 1856, a special vote of thanks was passed to Mr. John Davenport "fully acknowledging the kindness and generosity which he has for several years past particularly displayed in granting to us gratuitously the use of a splendid cricket ground." This and other annual votes of thanks were printed upon white satin, and Mr. Davenport used to say that he was very much pleased to receive them.

The accounts of the first year—1844—show that the turn-over was £11 12s. 4d., and that the year ended in a balance due to Mr. Sawkins of 7s. 7d. The members were 22 in number, 17 of whom paid 10s. 3d., and the remainder 10s. Their names were :—W. Badnall, W. P. Morley, G. Sawkins, W. Milner, E. J. Walters, J. Ward, T. Redfern, junr., H. Sleigh, L. Hunt, W. Challinor, J. G. Whittles, G. A. Smith, J. Nall, J. Robins, junr., A. Wedgwood, Joshua Smith, A. J. Worthington, T. Carr, junr., E. Heaton, Joseph Challinor, and the Rev. J. Barnes. In 1845, H. Sleigh was fined threepence, G. A. Smith ninepence, A. Wedgwood one shilling, and E. Heaton eighteenpence, but the nature of their delinquencies are not stated. Then, as now, it was the rule of the club to pay expenses for out matches, for in 1847, the accounts included an item of £3 4s. 6d. " expenses of members to Hanley "; in 1848 one of £4 15s. for " carriages "; and in 1851 one of 15s. for " tollgates and expenses of driver and horses to the match at Congleton, also dinners for scorer and umpire." The amount of subscription changed from 10s. 3d. in 1844 to 10s. 6d. in 1847, and still remains the same.

From this time until 1860, when the record ceases, the club appears to have been carried on successfully, though the scoring-books, with the exception of one from 1857-69, are missing. The minute book's secrets, too, end with 1860, and it will be sufficient to record a few of the players' names who figured prominently prior to the last-named year, in addition to those already enumerated. Amongst them we find Messrs. T. Maskery, T. Wardle, W. Smith, G. Walker, J. Eaton, E. Jackson, T. Stretch, W. Shufflebotham, R. Dean, R. Lockett, W. Howard, C. H. Badnall, G. Wardle, John Russell, W. D. Sneyd, T. Hammersley, J. Plant, H. Brunt, J. Gould, and J. Dean.

We cannot close this sketch without acknowledging our indebtedness to Mr. William Allen for the very kind help he has given us; and to Mr. William Shufflebotham, also an old-time secretary, both of whom have placed at our service invaluable documentary evidence.

The Grammar School and Free Scholars.

HERE is and long has been a good deal of misapprehension as to the Leek Grammar School, built by the first Lord Macclesfield, and supposed to have been endowed by him. The fact is that the school has not been endowed by Lord Macclesfield or anyone else. The misunderstanding has probably arisen from the fact that by his will, dated October 21st, 1712, the Rev. George Roades, vicar of Leek 1692-98, left a sum of money "to the Vicar of Leek for ever" to be applied by him in "teaching poor children to read." Until thirty years ago, when the then vicar, the Rev. Thomas Henry Heathcote, died, the money, £8 17s. 8d., was regularly paid to the master of the Grammar School, and the payment was continued up to the appointment of Mr. Joseph Sykes, but not afterwards. It was then diverted by the new vicar, the Rev. George Edward Deacon, to Mill Street School, and the payment has been continued by the present vicar, the Rev. C. B. Maude. The statement in the *History of Leek* that the sum was left for "teaching poor children to read English at the Grammar School of Leek," was taken by Mr. Sleigh

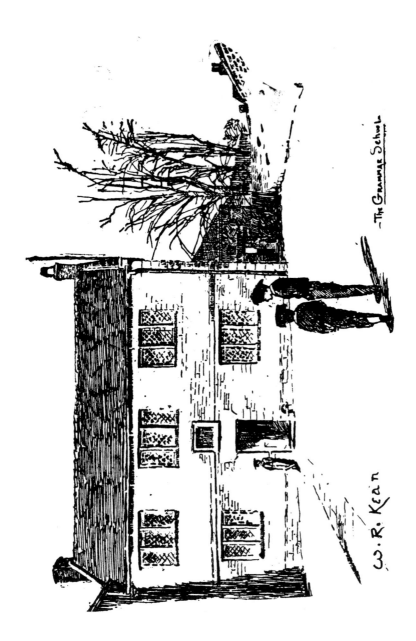

The Grammar School

W. R. Kean

from Loxdale's MSS. at the Leek Vicarage, and appears to be unwarranted. The will itself, dated 1712, could have contained no mention of the Grammar School, which was not founded until 1723, eleven years afterwards.

Benefaction tablet No. 5, now in the belfry of St. Edward's Church, disposes of the matter in these words—"to be laid out in Lands, the rents thereof to be applied by the Vicar of Leek in Teaching Poor Children to read;" and in the *Parish Magazine* for June, 1889, the present Vicar says:—"The charity is now in the hands of Charity Commissioners, and the late Vicar in his discretion gave the income (£8 17s. 8d.) to the Mill Street School, and I follow his example, as that school seems to best further the intention of the founder of the charity."

It seems clear, then, that Loxdale made a mistake in saying that Roades left the money for "teaching poor children to read English at the Grammar School of Leek;" and that other historians copied the error. It is, therefore, equally clear that the Grammar School is unendowed, and that free scholars were only taken at the Grammar School during the time when the then Vicar, in his absolute discretion, saw fit to hand over to the master for the time being the small sum which has occasioned so much misapprehension.

The following lines appeared in the *London Magazine* of November, 1733, addressed "to Mr. Thomas Bourne, master of Leek School." Mr. Bourne was

the first master of the school, which was "erected by
the Earl of Macclesfield, Lord High Chancellor, Anno
Domini, 1723."

Aid me ye powers in this, convey me hence
To some bless'd unknown heavenly state; from whence
Poets divinely great are ever taught
To glow, with extasy seraphic fraught.
Where the harmonious sisters sacred dwell :
Where Homer learn'd Ilion's just doom to tell :
Where Tully lay entranced ; that font of wit :
Where Milton labour'd and where Virgil writ :
There would I go.   There would I be inspir'd,
And listen to those powers that Waller fir'd ;
There amongst choirs of crowding heroes mix'd,
By Dryden's awful shade attentive fix'd,
Made pure, my muse for you should sound her lays,
Though words ethereial echoe forth your praise :
Thousands should view me mount, and in my way, ⎫
All your refulgent merit should display,   ⎬
Through realms imperial, and eternal day.   ⎭

Friendship nor urges me these rights to pay
Nor flattery, that base plebeian way,
From no such venal, unpure fountains flow
These tributary trophies to your brow ;
By gratitude alone am I inspir'd,
By justice prompted, and by merit fir'd.

Lo !—Where I see amongst the gods a throng
Of bards exalted by the Roman tongue.
But who taught me such distant bliss to view,
Or bear such heav'nly harmony, but you?
Your hand first till'd the rudiments of wit
Taught me how Ovid charm'd and Horace writ :
Homer's bewitching beauties have I heard
And in each Iliad hug'd the Grecian bard.
You every classic lustre did display,
And arm'd my youth against the op'ning day ;
Watch'd my endeavours with paternal joy,
And ever viewed me with a father's eye.
And shall I now forget how much I owe?
Shall springs forget the fountains whence they flow?

Or shall the wretch in record grateful stand,
Restor'd to sight, nor own the healing hand?
Take these then, take an earnest I am grate
The utmost present of my present state.
Receive this pledge till heav'ns shall prove more kind,
And raise my power equal to my mind.

" H.C."

"Tom Oakleigh."

MR. Abraham Kershaw Killminster died at Moorland House, Leek, on Christmas Day, 1858. A contribution to the *History of Leek* states that he was a gentleman of retired habits and of manners indicative of nervousness. The world at large little suspected that in him was to be found an author of no very mean repute—namely, the well-known "Tom Oakleigh," of literary sporting celebrity,—author of the article on "Shooting" in the *Encyclopædia Britannica*,—and a large contributor to magazines, principally between the years 1830 and 1845. After his death a large unfinished work on "Angling" was found among his papers, and several MSS. on astronomical subjects, astronomy having in his late years occupied much of his attention. He had at considerable expense erected an observatory and furnished it with a powerful refracting telescope, having an object glass, by Dolland, of nearly eight inches diameter.

Some Old Soldiers.

HIDDEN away in an obscure part of the Leek Cemetery, without a stone to prate of their whereabouts, lie the remains of a brave old soldier, whose record is one of which the town of his birth has reason to be proud. Leek heroes are not so plentiful that one should be left unsung, and in the present case the

Disastrous chances
Of moving accidents by flood and field
Of hair-breadth 'scapes i' the deadly breach,

were of a character that deserved chronicling whilst the memory of the hero was green.

SAMUEL BOWCOCK was born at Leek on Barnaby day, in 1774, when George the Third was King, and in the year preceding the American War of Independence. When eighteen years of age, and whilst engaged in hand-piece weaving, he enlisted in the 92nd regiment of Highlanders, and for the first time saw active service in Holland in 1799. From that time until the battle of Waterloo he was engaged in fighting for his country, and the following copy of the official record of the twenty-three engagements in which he took part shows that he had more active service than falls to the lot of soldiers nowadays :—

THIS IS TO CERTIFY that Corporal Samuel Beaucock, of the 92nd regiment of Highlanders, has served with his regiment in the following engagements viz. :—

Holland...	10th September, 1799.
do.	2nd October, 1799.
Egypt	13th March, 1801.
do.	21st do. do.
Rioge	7th August, 1807.
Corunna	16th January, 1809.
Fuente d'onor	5th May, 1811.
Ri de Molyna ...	28th October, 1811.
Almorass	19th May, 1812.
Alva de Jormes ...	10th November, 1812.
Vittoria	21st June, 1813.
Heights of Mayo ...	25th July, 1813.
do. do. ...	30th do. do.
do. do. ...	31st do. do.
Entering France ...	10th November, 1813.
Crossing the Neave...	9th December, do.
Bayonne	13th do. do.
Gallice	15th February, 1814.
A Riveveta	17th do. do.
Orthees	17th do. do.
Aire	2nd March, 1814.
Quatre Bras ...	16th June, 1815.
Waterloo	18th June, do.

AND. HILL, Lieut., 92nd Regiment.

Throughout this busy period our hero was only wounded twice. He was slashed in the face with a sabre in Egypt in 1801, and in the Peninsular War was prodded in the leg with a bayonet. The hardships, however, of such an arduous career at last told upon his fine constitution, and for some affection of the lungs he was invalided and sent to the Royal Hospital, Kilmainham, about three years after the fall of Napoleon Buonaparte. The lung trouble having become chronic he was discharged on November 25th, 1818, at the age of 44, and after nearly twenty-seven years' service. The following is an exact copy of the terms of discharge :—

"Royal Hospital, Kilmainham.—This is to certify that Corporal SAMUEL BEAUCOCK, the bearer hereof, was examined on the 25th day of November, 1818, before the Governor of the Royal Hospital, and that he is an out-Pensioner of the said Hospital, from the 92nd Foot, at 1s. 3d. per day, served in the army 26 years 191 days. He is about 44 years of age, about 5 feet 8 inches high, brown hair, fair complexion, and was discharged unfit for further service, being pulmonic, and that he is to reside at Leek.—Given under my hand, free of erasures, WILLIAM PLUNKETT, Audtr. and Registr."

Upon his return to Leek he resumed the occupation of a weaver, but at the time of his death, which took place on December 23rd, 1858, in his 84th year, he was a wet doubler at Wreford's silk mill, and resided in London street. He was interred in the Cemetery, which had been opened during the previous year, on December 26th, the ceremony being performed by the Rev. C. Knowles. His grave, the 187th opened, is situated about the middle of the outer line nearest the Junction road, and is numbered 2194. His wife, Janet, who lived in Russell street, died on June 3rd, 1863, at the age of 82, and was buried with her husband on June 5th, by the Rev. G. E. Deacon.

Corporal Bowcock's medals, with the original documents which we have copied, are in the possession of his nephew by marriage, Mr. William Gould, of 81, Grove street, whose kindness has enabled us to supply an important gap in our local annals. The oldest medal is for services in the Peninsular War, and has four bars— Vittoria, Fuentas d'onor, Corunna, and Egypt. The other is commemorative of the battle of Waterloo, but appears not to have been issued until 1848, and bears on one side the words "Wellington, Waterloo, June 18, 1815," and on the other the head of George P. Regent.

———

JOHN HOWARD, a Waterloo veteran, who for many years resided on Clerk's Bank, died on March 29th, 1879. He entered the army about the year 1808, enlisting in the 51st Foot, in which he became a bugler. He was present with his regiment at Waterloo, and received three wounds. Although he was discharged in 1816, it was not until 1822 that his services were recognized. In that year, owing to the urgent representations of the late Colonel Carruthers, an order was issued from the War Office that all the men of Howard's regiment should have a pension for life of 1/3 per day. This he received until he died, as stated, in his 86th year.

———

His Royal Highness the Duke of York as Commander-in-chief was very popular in the army, and very good-hearted, as the following incident will show. THOMAS GARNER, a native of Leek, had enlisted, and being a very fine fellow had risen to the highest rank as a non-commissioned officer. One unlucky day he fell into gay company, when followed a plentiful "sowing of wild oats," and his absenting himself from his regiment. When he returned to his senses he was overwhelmed with shame and remorse, and fearing arrest, he became a wanderer. He came home, but could not rest in Leek, and like the moth that flutters round and is fascinated by the glare that destroys it, he went back to London. Being by trade a silk weaver, he found employment amongst the silk workers of Spitalfields. One day he met one of his late officers in the street. The recognition seems to have been mutual, for on glancing back after he had passed the officer he saw the latter had turned round and was looking after him. Afraid of being arrested he hurried away. He appears to have enlisted again soon after into another regiment, and upon it becoming known to him that His Royal Highness the Commander-in-Chief was going to review it, he took the very bold course of writing to the Duke, making known his case, and begging to be forgiven. It seems His Royal Highness took good note of the letter, for on the day of the review, when passing down the ranks he stopped opposite our townsman, who was ordered to fall out, on doing which he fell upon his knees before the Duke and begged to be forgiven. His Royal Highness spoke kindly to him, bade him rise, telling him he freely pardoned him, and saying he was a fine fellow.

Garner saw some fighting in the great French war but escaped unhurt, and returned home and settled down again to his weaving. He died some sixty odd years ago, and was laid to rest in the old churchyard, and a townsman, an old acquaintance who was a stone carver, kindly placed a stone over his grave.

JOSEPH BRADLEY, who died on November 10th, 1879, was born at Leek on the 17th April, 1782. His father was what was known as an "outrider" for a silk manu-

for him a high degree of respect, and his death is deeply deplored."

A few paces to the west, and within the railings of the Van Tuyl-Bullock tombs, is an inscription to the memory of "JOSEPH BRINDLEY, who died April 11th, 1841, aged 39." He was associated in business, before he obtained his diploma, with Mr. Chadwick, and was of much the same gay and festive temperament. On the day of his death he was hastening round the turn from Abbey Green to Mill Street, when a stirrup leather broke, and he was thrown violently to the ground and suffered a fatal fracture of the skull. He was very fond of boxing, and old inhabitants tell funny tales of his exploits in this direction.

In the new ground, but under the shadow of the elm tree, on a flat tombstone, is the following:— "Here lie the remains of JAMES DAVENPORT HULME, M.D., formerly of Ball Haye, near Leek; he died in Manchester, March 7th, 1848, aged 75."

To the north-west of the above is the grave of the seventh surgeon, as testified by the stone:—"Also of CHARLES FLINT, who died November 10th, 1864, aged 74." He at one time resided in Stockwell Street, in the house until recently occupied by the late Miss Smith, and died at Compton House. For some years, however, he had given up the active work of his profession, but was frequently called into consultation with other practitioners. He was greatly respected.

The last of the octave lies in the new ground, and under the wall of the garden attached to the house wherein was born on July 23rd, 1666, the first

Lord Macclesfield, Lord Chancellor of England in 1721. The tomb bears the inscription:—"In affectionate remembrance of RICHARD COOPER, M.R.C.S., L.S.A., born October 2nd, 1802, and died on January 23rd, 1872. 'And I heard a voice saying unto me, Write, Blessed are the dead which die in the Lord from henceforth; yea, saith the spirit, that they may rest from their labours; and their works do follow them.—Rev. xiv, 13 v.'" Mr. Cooper, by indefatigable attention to his patients, and by his affectionate regard for their temporal wants and spiritual welfare, endeared himself to all who sought his professional assistance, and died generally and deeply respected. He was a staunch Wesleyan, and in the *Circuit Year Book* for 1887 it is stated that "he was a class leader of long standing, of deep but unobtrusive piety, and a generous supporter of the cause of God."

Two other noted doctors have been buried at St. Edward's, but not in the "Corner." JAMES ROBINS, who died on July 15th, 1856, aged 56 years, lies buried far away under the north wall in the new portion; and THOMAS FENTON GROSVENOR was interred inside the church, a memorial stone, erected by George Nathaniel Best and situated near to the font, recording that he died on December 3rd, 1831, in his 73rd year, and that "the poor will lament one whose ear was ever open to their cry." In the Milner vault next to the Robins-Gaunt tomb and close to the exit to Foxlow, is buried "PETER MILNER, surgeon, late of Mirfield, Yorkshire, who departed this life April 30th, 1846, aged 26 years," who died in Leek whilst on a visit to his elder brother, Mr. William Milner, who at that time was a banker and is now head of the firm of Milner and Son, silk manufacturers.

A Doctor's Charges in the 18th Century.

THE following is an exact copy of bill sent to a resident of Leek by the executors of James Fenton Grosvenor, M.D. :—

1735.		£	s.	d.
Aug. 10—Ointment of Poplin Hoj		0	9	0
Mellilot suet		0	2	0
Novr. 7—Pd Mr. Henry in cash		2	16	10
Astringent and sudorifick medicines		1	0	0
Decr. 8—Pd for burying fees at Cheadle ...		0	2	4
Tho. Stubbs for choiming		0	2	6
By a bill for fees at Draycott ...		0	8	4
To John Bill for Harnish and going to Foxholes twice		0	3	0
Pd for mending lamp and bridle...		0	0	4
Pd clerk's fees fer child		0	2	0
Expd at Winster for horses		0	8	6
Going and coming		0	4	0
Pd John Wolff for making 3 gowns		0	6	0
3 bushels of oats		0	4	6
1741. A pint of ale for Daniel Carr ...		0	0	2
Mar. 7—A febrefuge decoction		0	3	6
1748. A saline electary		0	2	0
Jany. 30—A pectoral linctus—Mr. Condlyffe		0	1	6
		£6	17	6

Bits from Dieu-la-cresse.

The Hermitage at the Abbey.

IT is a well-known fact that the founders of religious houses often placed their new monasteries on the spots which had already a reputation for sanctity, often as the abode of some celebrated hermit. We know from the history of Leek Abbey that such was the case here. The ghost which in Earl Randle's dream told him where to place the Abbey, told him to go to Cholpesdale "where was a chapel of the Virgin," and there to build. Now if this chapel had been a building it would have been incorporated into the Abbey church, as was the ancient chapel of St. Joseph at Glastonbury. But there is no trace of any such additional building at Dieu-la-cresse. We conclude, therefore, that the chapel was not a building, and especially since we have unmistakeable traces of a hermitage close by.

The early English hermit chose the sunny face of a rock in which to cut cells. And in the red sandstone rock as you go the Abbey from "Surey pavement" you notice a cave. Going to it you see further that it has been divided into three cells; two

occupying the now open front of the cave and one
behind them driven some feet into the rock. The
right-hand front cell was the hermit's living room; for
just inside his door—the right jamb (half buried in
earth) of which remains—he had his fireplace, and a
chimney groove creeps up the rock. The whole front
of the cave was protected from the weather by a wall

ω R Kean

or by wattling. A roof—the weather groove of which
still remains—was drawn over the open space from
the rock to that front wall, one large beam being
used to support it. The little cell to the left-hand
has a small awmbry in it for books, and the rocky
wall at the back of it is ornamented with rough
incised lines of a pattern which reminds one of the
seven branched candlestick at Jerusalem, as figured on
the arch of Titus at Rome. This was doubtless the

ancient chapel of Saint Mary. The whole cave is very interesting. It has been carefully and cleverly constructed both in the rock cutting and in the bit of frontal building (now entirely demolished) which has left its traces on the rock. And that it was a hermitage its nearness to the Abbey, and its otherwise remarkable seclusion, shew.

A line of hermits may have lived here, though for many hundred years the place has probably been a desolation. Who was the first hermit? Perhaps the first preacher of the Gospel in the wild woods which covered the district after the coming of the Saxons. This little cell may indeed be the mother, not only of the proud Abbey of foreigners whom the Norman earl seated near it, but of every Christian church in the neighbourhood. And it is just possible that the Old Church of Leek—so many centuries the parish church— was dedicated to St. Edward instead of St. Mary, because some perhaps royal preacher from the north of England had already given the name of St. Mary's to this hermit's oratory.—BLACK BEAR.

Value of Cottage Property in 1776.

IN 1776, Samuel Hyde, of Leek, sold eleven houses in Overton Row and Scolding Bank, to James Rowley, bricklayer, of Biddulph, for £40.

Overton Row has become Overton's Bank, and Scolding Row is the narrow passage leading from the Bank to the back entrance to the Fields.

Leek and Mary Howitt.

ROM *Good Words*, 1885, we learn that Mary
Howitt was born at Uttoxeter, of Quaker
parents, on "the 12th of third month, 1799,"
and not "early in the present century" as several
authorities have it. Her father, Samuel Botham, was
a native of Uttoxeter, and his ancestors were moorland farmers, who doubtless often brought their produce into Leek market. "He was descended from a
long line of farmers, who had lived for centuries in
primitive simplicity on their own property, Appsford,
situated in the bleak northern part of Staffordshire,
known as the Moorlands." And our author goes on to
describe the place in terms we can appreciate. "It
was a wild, solitary district, remote from towns, and
only half cultivated, with wide stretches of brown
moors, where the undisturbed peewits wailed through
the long summer. Solitary houses miles apart stood here
and there. Villages were far distant from each other.
There was little church going, and education was at
the lowest ebb. The town of Leek, in itself a primitive place, might be called the capital of this wild
district. It was the resort of rude farmers on the
occasion of fairs and markets." And here she gives a

sketch of things that are not at all creditable to the
people of that day, and which happily do not obtain
so much now. "Strange brutal crimes occurred from
time to time, the report of which came like a creep-
ing horror to the lower country. Sordid, penurious
habits prevailed; the hoarding of money was considered
a great virtue." The Bothams differed from their
neighbours in their habits and tastes, although it
cannot be said that they had much of either refine-
ment or learning. "They rode on good horses, saddled
and pillioned, to meeting at Leek on Firstday
mornings; and were a well-to-do, orderly set of
people." In the ancient record of the Staffordshire
monthly meeting, preserved by the Friends of Leek,
they appear to have been generally satisfactory members,
living up to the old standard of integrity of their
ancestress Mary; who, a widow at the head of the
house in the days of Quaker persecution, was
imprisoned in Stafford gaol for refusing to pay tithes."
From the next paragraph we gather something
relative to the Scottish invasion, and the doings of
the rebels in these parts. "Years glided uneventfully
on, generation followed generation, until 1745, when
the rumour that the 'Scottish rebels were approaching'
filled the scattered inhabitants of the Moorlands with
terror. Even the quiet Friend, John Botham, of
Appsford, might have prepared to fight; one thing is
certain, he hurried wife and children out of the way
and buried his plate and valuables. But there was
no need of fighting, and hardly of fear. The Scotch
and Highland soldiers that came to that secluded
spot only demanded food. They sliced the big round

cheeses and toasted them on their claymores at the kitchen fires." The superstition of the time is also touched upon. "In those days a popular belief in the occult power of so-called witches prevailed. The most noted witch of the period and locality was Witch Hatton, who lived in the high Moorlands."

The July instalment of these reminiscences deals chiefly with Mary Howitt's mother and maternal ancestry, and also contains a good engraving of "The House at Uttoxeter." It is in the current number of *Good Words* that we are first introduced to William Howitt, who, "having been to Lichfield Cathedral to see the monument by Chantrey, of the sleeping children, the daughters of the Rev. W. Robinson, came round by Uttoxeter ostensibly to visit his cousin, Susanna Frith." His evident culture and fine natural taste, made a very favourable impression upon the Bothams at their first meeting, and before the close of the year Mary became his affianced bride. In connection with this event she says: "Father, although he never allowed his emotions or even his affections to evince themselves, to our surprise almost laughed when the important matter was settled, hiding his pleasure by the remark, "It is all in the usual order! The young women of Uttoxeter Meeting were always sought in marriage; those of Leek but seldom." During their days of courtship they had, of course, many delightful walks, in "the Arcadian scenery" that surrounded them. She records: "We took him to our favourite Alton Towers, that wonderful region of beauty and romance, which was growing up year after year under the Earl of Shrewsbury's taste and reli-

gious ardour; to the secluded ruins of Croxden Abbey;
to the airy heights of the Weaver Hills; to the ancient
lordly oaks and birches of Bagot Woods; to the still
more hoary fragment of nature's antiquity, Chartley
Moss; to Tutbury and Sudbury." They were married
on "the 16th of fourth month, 1821."—W.S.B.

Height of Hills, &c., near Leek.

Feet above sea.

Axedge	1809
Shutlingslow	1661
Roaches	1600
Biddulph Moor	1210
Gun	1210
Cloud End	1190
Weaver Hills	1150
Mow Cop	1091
Butterton village	936
Rock above Thor's Cave	919
Throwley Hall	784
Bagnall village	728
Leek (Market Place)	599
Bed of the Manifold below Wetton	562
Cat and Fiddle	1750
Wrekin	1320
Clent Hills	900
Buxton	859
Beeston Castle	556
Macclesfield	500

James Brindley, "the Schemer."

AMES BRINDLEY, the great engineer who
founded the canal system, was born in a
modest cottage at Tunsted, a village about
three miles to the north-east of Buxton, in 1716. Early
in life his greatest delight was to examine water-wheels
and other machinery, and in this way he showed the
bent of mind that was destined to make him famous.
When seventeen years of age he was bound apprentice
to Abraham Bennett, a wheelwright and millwright, of
Sutton, near Macclesfield. In 1742, he came to Leek,
and started in business for himself, with, as Samuel
Smiles puts it, " no capital except his skill, and no
influence except that which his character as a steady
workman gave him. . . He gradually, however, acquired

a position, and became known for his skill in improving old machinery or inventing such new mechanical arrangements as might be required for any special purpose."

Whilst at Leek, he lodged the specification of a patent, dated December 26, 1758, No. 730, for a " Fire-engine for drawing water out of mines, or for draining of lands, or for supplying of cityes, townes, or gardens with water, or other useful purposes." He, moreover, made the acquaintance of the Duke of Bridge-water, and devoted his marvellous skill to the construction of the many waterways which were for a century connected with the fortunes of the ducal family.

Brindley is stated to have lived in Leek from 1742 to 1765, and to have had his smithy and workshop in Mill Street. He died on September 27, 1772, at the early age of fifty-five, of diabetes, contracted whilst surveying a branch canal between Leek and Froghall.

So with strong arm immortal Brindley leads
His long canals and parts the velvet meads ;
Winding in lucid lines, the watery mass
Minds the firm rock, or loads the deep morass ;
While rising locks a thousand hills alarm,
Flings o'er a thousand streams its silver arm ;
Feeds the long vales, the nodding woodland laves,
And plenty, arts and commerce freight the waves.

Nymphs, who erstwhile on Brindley's early bier,
On snow-white bosoms shed the incessant tear,
Adorn his tomb ! oh ! raise the marble bust,
Proclaim his honors and protect his dust !
With urns inverted round the sacred shrine,
Their ozier-wreaths let weeping Naiads twine :
While on the top mechanic Genius stands,
Counts the fleet waves and balances the sands.

ERASMUS DARWIN, M.D.

"The Old Wooden Plough."

HE following song, which has been and is popular in the Moorlands, and has been sung at many social gatherings in Leek, was composed by Mr. T. C. Sneyd Kynnersley, M.A., who for many years was stipendiary magistrate of Birmingham :—

Up by th' Blake mere o' Morridge, not long time ago,
There lived an old chap wi' an old wig o' tow :
His name wor Tom Morris, and I'll tell ye how
He made a discourse on an old wooden plough.
    Gee ho, Dobbin, gee ho, Dobbin,
    Gee ho, Dobbin, gee up and gee wo !

'Twor the tenth of October, and th' oats wor just ripe,
On the settle he sot, and he smoked his long pipe ;
And he thought a long time about this thing and that,
And said " Tommy, sit down, and I'll tell thee what's
  what.   Gee ho, Dobbin, etc.

These are terrible times, lad ; I prithee draw nigh,
And I'll give thee a wrinkle or two ere I die ;
I can't stand it much longer, it shortens my breath,
These new-fangled notions will soon be my death.
    Gee ho, Dobbin, etc.

They're going too fast, lad, I tell thee a deal!
There's Lord Talbot o' Ingestre, and Ralph Sneyd o' Keele.
And Sandon and Buller, and Mainwaring and Bill—
Lord! the stuff they've been talking—it mak's me quite ill.
       Gee ho, Dobbin, etc.

Wi' their bones and their acids, their drills and guhanner!
Thy grandfeyther, Tom, niver farmed i' that manner;
He'd ha' stared hard enough if he'd heard what they say
About boiling o' oil cakes and chopping o' hay.
       Gee ho, Dobbin, etc.

Then soughing a thing as, in course, they mun alter,
So they go a mon's depth for to get at th' top water,
And they scoop out the dirt wi' a thing like a spoon,
And for tiles—they'll be using o' baccy-pipes soon.
       Gee ho, Dobbin, etc.

Then they prate o' their carrots, and mangles, and sich;
(As if growin' o' carrots would make a mon rich)—
Of hoeing o' turmits and cleaning o' yallows—
Stuff and nonsense!—and growing o' wheat without
   fallows.   Gee ho, Dobbin, etc.

Why, it mak's me to laugh; without fallows indeed—
I think they mun ha' a soft place in their yed,
And what dun ye think they've been doing just now?
Why, they've got up a laugh at an old wooden plough.
       Gee ho, Dobbin, etc.

Aye, an old wooden plough; and they say, to be sure,
As the wide awake farmers mun use 'em no more;
They mun all be of iron, and wood there's no trade for,
Why, what do fools thinken as ash-trees was made for?
       Gee ho, Dobbin, etc.

Talk o' ploughs made o' iron! why th' next thing they'll do,
As sure as you live they'll be painting them blue,
Then they've two tits abreast, as they call a gee ho,
They may call long enough, but it never can go.
       Gee ho, Dobbin, etc.

No! gi'e me a good wooden plough as is strong,
And a good pair o' big wheels to help it along,
And four long-tail'd tits, a mon and a lad,
A good steady pace, and it shanna' be bad.
       Gee ho, Dobbin, etc.

Then Tommy, my lad, niver heed what they say,
But get thee on still i' thy feyther's old way;
They'll bring all their hogs to fine markets just now,
But stick while thee lives to the old wooden plough.
        Gee ho, Dobbin, etc."

Price of Leek Silk in 1800.

A RECEIPTED bill has been handed to us bearing date
August 27th, 1800. It has a faded, old-time appear-
ance, and is a good specimen of early commercial
printing. It is from a copperplate, the characters of
which are script or italic, and runs as follows:—"Leek,
Staffordshire, 27th August, 1800. Messrs. G. and D.——
Bot. of Sleigh, Alsop, and Sleigh, Manufacturers of
Ribbons, Buttons, Twist, Sewing Silks, Ferretts, &c.

	£	s.	d.
4oz. Blk. Scarf 24/-	0	6	0
1lb. Cloth Sewings 32/-	1	12	0
1lb. Legee Twist 32/-	1	12	0
2oz. „ „ Scarlet, 36/-	0	4	6
	£3	14	6
Discount ...	0	3	6
	£3	11	0

                Settled this Account   £3 11 0
                    for Sleigh & Co.,
                    Wm. Shufflebotham.

Some Bygone Elections.

FOR parliamentary purposes Leek, until 1885, was in the Northern Division of the county of Stafford. Since the passing of the Reform Act, 1832, the following elections have taken place, the Division being represented by two members.

General Election, 1832—

    Sir Oswald Mosley (C) 4,779
    Mr. E. Buller (L) 4,593
    Mr. Jesse Watts Russell (C) 3,387

At the General Election in 1835, Sir Oswald Mosley and Mr. Buller were chosen without opposition.

General Election, 1837—

    Mr. W. B. Baring (C) 4,233
    Mr. Buller (L) 3,181
    Sir Oswald Mosley (C) 1,839

In 1841 Mr. Jesse Watts Russell and Mr. C. B. Adderley (now Lord Norton), both Conservatives, were chosen without a contest.

General Election, 1847—

    Mr. Adderley (C) 4,076
    Lord Brackley (C) 4,072
    Mr. Buller (L) 3,353

Early in 1851 Lord Brackley resigned owing to declining health, and Mr. (now Sir) Smith Child (C) was elected without opposition. In 1852 Mr. Adderley and Mr. Smith Child were elected without opposition.

General Election, 1857—

Mr. Adderley (C) ...	...	...	...	4,116
Mr. Smith Child (C) ...	...	...		3,866
Mr. Buller (L)	...	...	...	... 3,029

In 1859 Mr. Adderley and Viscount Ingestre, both Conservatives, were elected without opposition.

General Election, 1865—

Mr. Buller (L)	...	...	...	... 4,628
Mr. Adderley (C)	...	...	...	4,416
Viscount Ingestre (C)	...	...	...	4,053

In 1868 Sir C. B. Adderley and Sir E. M. Buller were chosen without opposition.

In January, 1874, Sir C. B. Adderley and Mr. C. M. Campbell, both Conservatives, were elected without opposition.

In 1878, Sir C. B. Adderley was raised to the peerage as Lord Norton, and Mr. R. W. Hanbury, Conservative, was returned without opposition.

General Election, 1880—

The last election for North Staffordshire took place on April 14th, 1880, when Mr. William Young Craig (L) on the retirement through ill-health of Mr. C. M. Campbell, opposed the return of Messrs. Harry Tichborne Davenport and Robert William Hanbury (C), with the following result :—

William Young Craig (L)...	...	...	4,821
Harry Tichborne Davenport (C)	...		4,333
Robert William Hanbury (C)	...	...	3,764

General Election, 1885—

The first election of one member for the Leek Division of Staffordshire took place on December 8th, 1885, and the poll was declared as follows, Mr. W. Y. Craig having declined the contest :—

Charles Crompton, Q.C. (L) 4,225
Harry Tichborne Davenport (C) ... 4,063
General Election, 1886—

At the General Election in 1886, which followed Mr. Gladstone's Home Rule proposals, the contest in the Leek Division was decided on July 19th as follows :—

Harry Tichborne Davenport (C)... ... 4,324
Charles Crompton, Q.C. (L) 3,669

Improvement Commissioners, 1855.

THE first election of gentlemen to serve under the Leek Improvement Act, 1855, took place on September 25th, 1855. Sixty-four persons were nominated for the twenty-four seats, and the following proved successful :—

JAMES ALSOP,
JAMES BERMINGHAM,
JAMES BENTLEY,
THOMAS BIRCH,
JOHN BROUGH,
JOSHUA BROUGH,
JOSIAH BRUNT,
THOMAS CARR,
JOHN CRUSO,
NATHAN DAVENPORT,
MOUNTFORT FYNNEY,
MATTHEW GAUNT,
SIMON GETTLIFFE,
ROBERT HAMMERSLEY,
JOHN LOVATT,
GEORGE MASSEY,
JOHN RUSSELL,
JAMES RIDOUT,
SAMUEL TATTON,
JOHN WARD,
THOS. WEST,
JOHN WESTON, SENR.
JOHN G. WHITTLES,
GEORGE YOUNG.

608 persons were entitled to vote, but only 240 saw fit to do so.

The Market Place.

LONG known as one of the handsomest market places in the county, it has changed less than any other part of the town, and to recall a few of its better known features will be worth all the trouble. Granted that no martyr was ever burnt within its limits,—that the roof of the " Balcony " was never crowded with faces red with the glow of the Marian burnings,—still many of the houses have their own tales of interest.

THE BIRTHPLACE OF A LORD CHANCELLOR.

The house now occupied by Mr. J. W. Critchlow, at the north-west corner of the Market Place, was the birthplace of Thomas, first Earl of Macclesfield, on July 23rd, 1666. Called to the bar on May 24th, 1691, he became leader of the Midland Circuit in a few years, and was commonly known as " silver-tongued Parker," in the same way as the present Lord Chief Justice is called " silver-tongued Coleridge." On May 12th, 1718, he became Lord High Chancellor, and on November 5th, 1721, he was created Earl of Macclesfield. Two years

later he founded the Leek Grammar School. Impeached
by the House of Lords for corruption in the Court of
Chancery, he was tried on May 25th, 1725, found guilty,
and sentenced to pay a fine of £30,000. George I
promised to refund the money out of his privy purse, but,
dying in 1727, his successor exacted the full penalty.
Upon his removal to the Tower, the populace insulted
him with the oft-repeated saying that "Staffordshire had
produced the three greatest rogues ever known in England
— Jack Sheppard, Jonathan Wild, and Tom Parker !"
He died on April 28th, 1732, in Soho Square, London,
aged 66.

In the diary of Oliver Heywood, an ejected minister
and one of the founders of the Presbyterian congrega-
tions in the county of York, as quoted in his life by
Hunter (p. 179), is this curious notice : "July, 1666;
went to Leeke, in Staffordshire, and visited one Mrs.
Parker, Col. Robert Venables' daughter, who married
against her father's consent. The thing is sadly exag-
gerated, and he wonderfully exasperated against her.
She weeps bitterly. Hath buried two children." Lord
Campbell adds :—"This must have been immediately
before the birth of Thomas. Little did the Cheshire
squire think that he was to be grandsire to an earl,
and placed in the pedigree of an illustrious house."

A newspaper of the period, speaking of a visit to
Leek of Lord Macclesfield, on August 21st, 1723, says
—"Wedy. night ye rt. hon. Ld. Chancellor arrived at
Leek, the place of his nativity. He was met on the
road and conducted to the town by a great number of
gentry, clergy, and other considerable inhabitants of that
neighd."

THE BLACK'S HEAD.

The last to survive of the " magpie " buildings, as the old black and white houses used to be called, several of which once adorned the Market Place, was

THE BLACK'S HEAD.

The ancient building was photographed about fifty years ago by the Rev. F. Ribbands, then curate of Leek, and engraved by Llewellyn Jewitt for Mr. John Sleigh's *History of Leek*, and it is by Mr. Sleigh's kindness that we are able to use the original woodcut here. The old building was removed about the year 1850, and the present handsome structure took its place.

The yard of the inn, however, has more claims to historical distinction than the house itself, as it was the scene of some of the earliest struggles of the Leek dissenters. John Wesley is believed to have preached in the club-room down the yard on several occasions prior to 1782, and in that year, when he preached for the third time, it is recorded that he wrote :—" I never saw a more lovely congregation : they were like melting wax,

—just fit for divine impressions." The earlier Congrega-
tionalists, too, who had had a chapel in Derby street
since about 1690, worshipped in this room in 1830;
and about the same time the Swedenborgians also occasionally held services there.

In the old days the inn presented, as may be
inferred from the engraving, a vastly different appearance to that of to-day. It was then a low black and
white-washed house, the only entrance to which was
down a yard, a row of strong wooden railings guarding
the front windows. When the new building was erected,
it was expected that its palatial appearance would prove
so attractive that the " Angel " would spread her wings
and fly away, that the " Bird-in-Hand " would be no

better security than those in the bush, and that the
" Cocks " of Derby street and the Market Place would
have their combs cut and be left without a crow.

BULL-BAITING

was frequently practised in Leek until about fifty years
ago, and the centre of the Market Place was the spot
generally selected.   The unfortunate animal was tethered
to an iron ring let into a large block of stone, and the
master of the ceremonies, who was called the Bellot,
saw to it that only one dog at a time was slipped at
the bull.   Now and then, a more than usually strong
animal would break loose in his efforts to escape or
kill his brutal tormentors, and the assembled crowd
would fly for their lives in every direction.

BURNING CHAPEL SEATS.

The noble Market Place was disgraced about 1791
by a scene even worse than the baiting of a bull.   In-
flamed by the cry of "The Church in danger," a Church
and King mob invaded the Congregational (then called
" Calvinist ") Chapel, took out the seats and fittings, and
burned them in the Market Place.   This was at the
time of the religious commotion caused by Dr. Priestley.

RESIDENTS IN 1829

Peopling the Market Place in 1829, by means of
documentary and irrefutable oral evidence, we find that

the following tradespeople and others occupied the square
sixty years ago :—

Joseph Chell, Black's Head Inn.
Francis White, draper.
James Abbott, flour dealer.
Samuel Bower Whittles, grocer.
Benjamin White, Bird-in-Hand.
James Challinor, butcher.
William Allen, King's Head—" Meal Market."
Benjamin Woolfe, nail maker and ironmonger.
William Nunns, nurseryman.
Ann Maria Redfern, milliner.
Joseph Howard, tinman and brazier.
Thomas Pearson, draper and tailor.
Thomas Steers, salt dealer.
Private house, occupier unknown.
Jesse Challinor, druggist.
George Deaville, grocer.
William Critchlow, butcher.
John Cruso, solicitor.
Mrs. Fowler.
Robert Fergyson, draper.
William Travis, watchmaker.
Henry Beard, Cock Inn.
Samuel Braddock, Red Lion.
John Griffin, saddler.
William Birch and Son, drapers.
George Woolliscroft, grocer.
Samuel Smith, the Angel.
William Alcock, ironmonger.

MICHAEL JOHNSON.

The tradesman last mentioned occupied the shop
in which Michael Johnson, father of the great Dr.
Johnson, served his time with one Needham, a bookseller.
Respecting this Michael Johnson, we find the following
in Malone's Boswell's " Life of Samuel Johnson, LL.D."

(vol. 1, pp. 12-13) :—" A young woman of Leek, in Staffordshire, while he served his apprenticeship there, conceived a violent passion for him ; and though it met with no favourable return, followed him to Lichfield, where she took lodgings opposite to the house in which he lived, and indulged her hopeless flame. When he was informed that it so preyed upon her mind that her life was in danger, he with a generous humanity went to her and offered to marry her, but it was then too late : her vital power was exhausted ; and she actually exhibited one of the very rare instances of dying for love. She was buried in the cathedral of Lichfield ; and he, with a tender regard, placed a stone over her grave with this inscription :—Here lies the body of Mrs. Elizabeth Blaney, a stranger ; she departed this life 20th of September, 1694." In 1784, only two months before his death, Dr. Johnson visited Lichfield, his native city, for the last time, and Boswell says "he felt a revival of all the tenderness of filial affection, an instance of which appeared in his ordering the gravestone and inscription over Elizabeth Blaney to be substantially and carefully renewed." (Vol. 5, p. 257.)

THE MARKET CROSS.

Where Mr. W. Challinor's beautiful fountain is and where the ugly old Town Hall was, there stood at the beginning of the present century a market cross—an old and interesting relic of antiquity. " It was," says a writer in the *Leek Times* of September 23rd, 1871, " the last survivor of the Market Place of the middle

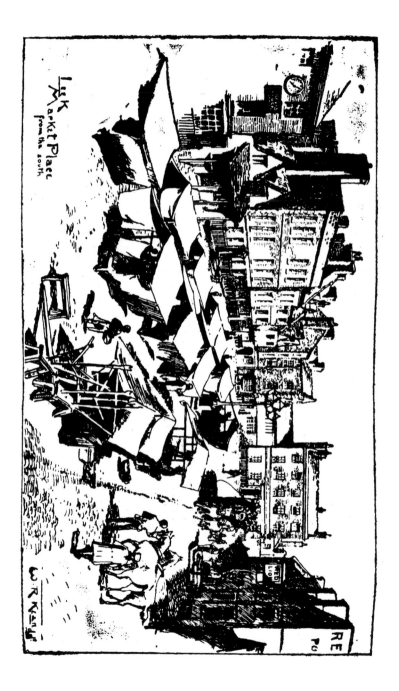

Leek Market Place from the south

Leek Market Place
from the north

W.R.Kean, delt.

ages—that quaint square of low and gable sign-decked
houses and shops, into which every week, gathered the
many coloured market throng of four hundred years since.
One of the Abbots of Dieu-la-cresse erected it as a
badge of the mutual dependence of the town on the
Abbey; and also, perhaps, of the Abbey on the market.
And at its foot, every week, one of the monks, or their
bailiff, attended to take the tolls. We can imagine the
dominus standing amidst the gay crowd (not the brown
and dusky throng of a modern market) in his beautiful
black robes. His face is plump and cleanly shaven,
and looks charmingly fresh, so snugly set in the ermine
lined cowl; whilst the splendid cloth of his long robes
and the extreme elegance of his lordship's fashionable
shoes are the pride and admiration of all the good
butter wives of the broad halidom. They cheerily crowd
around his 'lordship' with their baskets, or try to sell
him, if it be towards Eastertide, their myriad eggs.
And the good man is not a whit displeased with the
chatter of the buxom dames. The cross survived the
dissolution of the monastery. Even yet, after its shameful
removal, it lives in the hearts and parlance of the
market people. They still talk, as they heard their
mothers talk, about 'standing at the cross' with their
butter. Meanwhile, this ancient monument, this public
centre of busy life, has found a resting place in—the
Cemetery."

THE RED LION.

This prominent feature of the Market Place, originally known as "Leeke-hall," was built in 1627, by

Thomas Jolliffe, and for many years was the manor house of that family. In later days, the town's business was transacted there, and many persons living can remember the holding of the annual Court Leet and Court Baron, when the parish constables, head-borough, market inspector, town crier, beadle, bang-beggar, and pinner were elected. The justices, too, used to sit there, and County Court business was also transacted in the club-room. It was originally a large black and white half-timbered building.

On October 11th, 1836, Manuel Matthews Egidia da Silveria, of Rio Janeiro, Brazil, after alighting from the "Defiance" coach, entered the hotel, and immediately shot himself whilst in the water closet.

SELLING WIVES.

The story goes that sometime about 1830, a man who had found that marriage was a failure, put a halter round the neck of the woman he had vowed to treat very differently, and leading her to the Market Place, sold her for half-a-crown. Indeed, tradition gives several instances of local sales, and we have it on good authority that a gentleman now living in Leek was an eye-witness of such a transaction. Certain it is that a poet of the Moorlands once broke out with the following significant rhyme :—

> In Leek and Lowe the maids be so many,
> That you can get a wife for a penny.

In days more recent a woman, who lately died at Rudyard, was sold in the "Meal Market" for one shilling

and ninepence; and at the Talbot Inn, about 1854, a
man named Nadin sold his wife for a quart of ale, and
a right good wife she made her purchaser, an Irish
binding weaver.

STIRRING SCENES.

The Market Place was the scene of stirring events
in February, 1819, when the Blanketeers invaded the
town; and also when the Chartists marched through the
town to Burslem, on August 15th, 1842. On the latter
occasion, the late Simon Gettliffe closed his shutters
and chalked upon them " To let," thus saving his premises
from pillage.

"Waste Mot, Want Mot."

ABOUT 1786, a button merchant (Hugh Sleigh), living
at Ballhaye, having taken into his household as footman
one of his employés, was surprised whilst entertaining
a London friend at dinner one day, to find that
"Tummas" (Andrew Turnock), instead of attending to
his duties and quietly changing the plates, was noisily
discussing the remnants of the feast at a side-table.
On being remonstrated with, the only answer vouchsafed
was: "Lawks, mëaster, this mon hos'na hawf poiked
his boones."—*Reliquary, 1863.*

Leek Loyal Volunteers.

APOLEON BONAPARTE was the cause of the formation of the first company of Leek Volunteers, and below we give a copy of the original muster roll, which was called over on April 17th, 1810 :—

OFFICERS.

Davenport P W Captn
Sleigh Rd 1 Lt
Woolfe Benj 2 Lt

NON-COMMISSIONED OFFICERS.

Stonehewer Thos Sergt Majr
Ball Josh   Sergt
Cutting Richd „
Vigars James „
Walker Jas
Hambleton Geo—Corpl
Hulme Josh   „
Lee John   „
Pilsbury Ralph   „
Johnson William Drumr
Large John   „

PRIVATES.

Armit Iram   Boothe Wm
Abbott Saml   Bowcock Covns
Alsop Anthony   Bonsor Wm
Ball Saml   Booth Charles
Ball Wm   Bullock Wm

Cope Geo
Chappel Thos
Davenport Isaac
Eyre Thomas
Eyere John
Fallows Wm
Gratton Wm
Howard Samuel
Hambleton Josh
Hall Clemt
Holdride John
Holdride Josh
Hulme John
Hulme Wm
Hunt Saml
Jackson Geo
Kew Peter
Mellor Richd
Moss Geo
Morley Wm

Mollatt John
Mould John
Osborn Thos
Pickford James
Pickford Thos
Pilsbury Geo
Plant Eli
Plant Geo
Poynton Jas
Robinson Wm
Redfern Geo
Salt Isaac
Sterling Robt
Stonehewer Josh
Trafford Jas
Turner James
Wamsley Jas (twister)
Wamsley Jas (shoemaker)
Winterbottom Wm
Walker Charles

LEEK VOLUNTEER RIFLE CORPS.
APRIL 28TH, 1860.

Below we give the roll of members who revived the corps in 1860, when "wars and rumours of wars" brought into existence a great citizen army. It is worth while remembering that although the movement began late in 1859, the Queen reviewed 20,000 volunteers in Hyde Park on June 23rd, 1860.

WE, the undersigned, agree to become members of "The Leek Volunteer Rifle Corps," subject to the Rules and Regulations made by Government for the formation and maintenance of Rifle Corps.

No	Name of Volunteer.	Age.	Height		Occupation.
1	Thomas Hammersley...	25	5	10	silk manufacturer
2	George Allen Smith.....	47	5	9½	cashier
3	James Walker...........	20	5	7	articled clerk
4	Thomas D. Goodman...	20	5	7	ditto
5	William Russell.........	21	5	7¼	gentleman
6	William H. Squire	20	5	3½	warehouseman
7	Thomas Redfern, junr...	32	5	9	solicitor
8	Robert Nall..............	27	5	10	bookseller
9	William B. Badnall......	36	6	1	solicitor
10	Charles H. Halcombe...	28	5	10¼	silk manufacturer
11	John Russell, junr.......	25	5	10½	ditto
12	Charles K. Hyde........	20	5	9½	saddler
13	William Howard.........	25	5	10½	ironmonger
14	William Shufflebotham..	35	5	8	manager
15	Thomas Myatt...........	22	5	11¼	silk manufacturer
16	William Woodhead......	31	5	5½	iron founder
17	Henry Brunt............	23	5	7½	warehouseman
18	Robert Ridout...........	18	5	9	ditto
19	Ralph Hammond........	37	5	9½	silk agent
20	William Pilkington......	26	6	0½	warehouseman
21	William Walwyn.........	18	5	7½	joiner
22	William Heath...........	29	5	10¼	manager
23	Henry Hassall...........	29	5	10	stonemason
24	James Hall Tatton......	28	6	0	warehouseman
25	William S. Brough... ..	19	5	11¾	ditto
26	Arthur Nicholson........	18	5	10	ditto
27	Daniel Allen..............	21	5	5¾	cabinet maker
28	Henry Keates............	24	5	11½	shoemaker
29	James Lowe..............	24	5	7½	ditto
30	Charles Slagg...........	35	6	2	civil engineer
31	Edward Barton..........	21	5	5½	attorney's clerk
32	Job Tatton...............	36	5	10½	innkeeper
33	Wm. H. Hammersley...	27	6	0	silk dyer
34	John Malkin..............	33	5	7	silk manufacturer
35	Robert Gaunt...........	23	5	8	gentleman
36	Thomas Henry Booth..	24	5	8	shoemaker
37	Henry Albert Leigh.....	20	5	7	clerk
38	John Tatton..............	18	5	5½	warehouseman
39	John N. Faville..........	26	5	10	watchmaker
40	Samuel Heath...........	30	5	6½	saddler

No	Name of Volunteer.	Age.	Height.		Occupation.
41	John Weston............	29	5	10½	woollen draper
42	Frederick Gaunt........	15	5	7½	gentleman
43	Thomas Oakden.........	21	5	7	warehouseman
44	Samuel Shallcross*......	24	5	4½	ditto
45	William Needham.......	17	5	9	ditto
46	Henry Maskery..........	20	5	8¼	farmer
47	Robert Dalgleish*.......	32	5	10	cashier
48	Matthew Clee............	30	5	9½	painter
49	William Allen Eaton....	32	5	8	baker
50	Richard Clowes..........	31	5	6½	warehouseman
51	William Cater............	25	6	0	carter
52	William Hulme..........	29	5	8¼	twister
53	Robert M. Fergyson....	19	5	4½	furniture broker
54	Thomas Price*...........	40	—		attorney's clerk
55	William Ashton..........	23	5	7	painter
56	Thomas Rogers..........	28	5	8	rope maker
57	Charles John Smith.....	24	—		warehouseman
58	Samuel M. Fynney......	23	5	7½	farmer
59	Charles Eaton............	30	5	8	tailor
60	Joseph Wamsley.........	16	5	8	warehouseman
61	Edwin Mottershead.....	20	5	6½	ditto
62	Samuel Braddock.......	35	5	9	innkeeper
63	Joseph Doxey............	19	5	6	warehouseman
	The following joined at a later date or dates :				
64	Joseph Rushton.........	—	—		silk twister
65	Joseph Hall	—	—		ditto
66	John Snow...............	—	—		ironmonger's ap.
67	Silas Clowes.............	—	—		furniture broker
68	Henry Rider.............	—	—		silk weaver
69	William Tatton..........	—	—		silk dyer
70	William Lees.............	—	—		weaver
71	Henry Nichols..........	—	—		iron founder

* Names erased.

The original is written upon parchment, and, with
the exception of the last seven, the signatures are auto-
graphs. Framed and glazed, the document occupies the

place of honour in the orderly-room, and never fails to interest local visitors, who are sure to find the name of some past or present friend. Perhaps its most striking feature is that the corps was composed of vastly different material to that of which it is now constituted. A large majority of the recruits were engaged in trade as master-men, and freely devoted more than their leisure to the loyal labour they had undertaken. About one-third of the members have died, and only one—Quartermaster-sergeant Thomas Oakden—is still connected with the corps.

The officers were :— Captain, William Beaumont Badnall ; lieutenant, John Russell, jun. ; ensign, Charles Henry Halcombe ; drill instructor, William A. Eaton, late 3rd Light Dragoons.

The first drill took place in Alsop's Shade, the first battalion drill was at Trentham, and the first camp was at Newcastle-under-Lyme, May 24th, 1874.

The Leek Canal.

THE Trent and Mersey canal and reservoir at Leek was completed in the year 1800, and the Aqueduct House was first occupied by Samuel Heath in 1805. Heath was a labourer or overlooker in the employ of the Canal Company, and was afterwards in the employ of the railway shareholders for fifty-nine years.

Earthquakes and Storms.

EARTHQUAKES.

 STAFFORDSHIRE paper of December 9th, 1755, says :—"At the beginning of last month was observed near the town of Leek a large opening in the ground, in length full one hundred yards, in breadth one yard and two yards. This our northern *virtuosi* can no otherwise account for than by supposing the small shock of an earthquake."

Lisbon was destroyed and 60,000 lives were lost by an earthquake on November 1st, 1755, and as the above occurrence is reported to have taken place at the beginning of the same month, the suggested cause of the "large opening in the ground" at Leek may be the correct one. It should also be remembered that the county is no stranger to such volcanic disturbances. On January 4th, 1695, "a terrible earthquake was felt" at Alrewas, near Lichfield; in 1678 a shock was felt at Brewood, near Wolverhampton; and on April 20th, 1805, a similar shock threw down a number of chimneys at Alton.

Dr. Johnson appears to have been in Leek on September 14th, 1777, and whilst here was informed that there had been an earthquake during the morning.   He had been travelling during the whole of the previous night, and it was only when about to go to church in the afternoon that he heard of the occurrence.   The shock, however, was a severe one, and had the effect of dispersing the congregation at St. Edward's ; and at Rushton Church the congregation were thrown into the greatest confusion.

AN EXTRAORDINARY FLOOD IN 1717.

An extraordinary flood was the one recorded by Whillock as having taken place at Leek on August 12th, 1717.   He says :—"Sunday was an extraordinary wet day, and ye biggest flood upon our brooks and some others about us yt had been for 20 years.   A son of Richard Robton, of Horton, and 4 horses were drowned at ye Abbey yt evening, going for lime.   Ye weather continued wet, windy, and turbulent for some time."

Sunday not appearing to be a favourable day for carting lime, the practice has been discontinued.

GREAT SNOWSTORMS.

The oldest persons now in Leek would be in their childhood when the great snowstorm occurred which marked the beginning of the year 1814.   For three weeks, with but brief intermissions, snow fell heavily, and a keen frost nailed it to the ground.   Gradually the roads became well-nigh impassable, and the mail and other coaches kept very bad time. The crisis came on January 21st, when no coaches came at all, and serious alarm was felt for the safety of those who were endeavouring to come to the town during the terrible weather. Country people, too, could only get to Leek with very great difficulty, and not a little inconvenience was felt on Morridge. The doctors of the town were frozen as it were to Leek, and their country patients were for the most part left to their fate.

A similar occurrence took place in 1826, when one of the mail coaches was brought to this town by eight horses.

On the 18th of May, 1837, there was a great snowstorm in Leek, and on the 16th and 17th of May, 1891, there was a heavy and continuous fall.

HURRICANE.

An extremely violent tempest swept over Leek on Sunday night, January 6th, 1839. Great damage was done to buildings and farming produce in and near the town, and one of the pinnacles of the Parish Church was blown off. At Westwood Hall, the seat of Mr. John Davenport, M.P., a number of stacks were unroofed, and a considerable part of two oat stacks and one wheat stack were thrown into a neighbouring plantation. Many of the slates of a two-stall stable were also removed, and a number of young trees uprooted. Nearly one hundred lives were lost in England by the same hurricane, and property to the value of one million sterling was destroyed.

A MEMORABLE THUNDERSTORM.

Mr. John Nunns, son of the late William Nunns, nurseryman (after whom the gardens near West Street are still called), writes from Wimbledon as follows :— " On August 28th, 1838, a terrific thunderstorm broke over Leek at five p.m. The atmosphere was very close, dark clouds rolling over the town, and there was every sign of an impending storm. Between 10 and 11 o'clock it was at its height. The forked lightning was very vivid, flash after flash following in quick succession. The Market Place (where my father lived) to my young mind seemed to be all in a blaze. The thunder peals were terrific, and the storm did a great deal of damage in the neighbourhood. Many cows were killed, and trees knocked down by the lightning. Four pinnacles on the Old Church were knocked off, the glass in the church clock was smashed to pieces, and the lead on the roof was damaged in many places. Mr. Philip Wamsley, of Church Lane, who was standing at his door watching the lightning playing upon the weather vane on the top of the church steeple, was struck by the electric fluid, and died from the effects."

Dr. Johnson.

RADITION says that Michael Johnson, the father of the great dictionary maker, served his apprenticeship to Joseph Needham, a Leek bookseller, whose shop stood at the corner of the Market Place and Derby Street. When he left Leek, it is stated upon scarcely reliable authority, that a Leek girl followed the young man to Lichfield, and died there of a broken heart.

Samuel Johnson, LL.D., visited Leek on September 14th, 1777, and in a letter to Mrs. Thrale he gave his opinion of the place in the following characteristic sentence—"An old church, but a poor town."

Sir Walter Scott at Leek.

N Sir Walter Scott's Journal (David Douglas, Edinburgh, 1891) there is proof that the great Scotch novelist and poet was once in the Staffordshire moorlands.

Sir Walter appears to have left Abbotsford for London early in April, 1828. It was on the first of that month that he coined a phrase that has only recently been accepted as modern and original. He wrote:—" The vexation of having to do with ladies, who on such a point must be unreasonable, is very great. With a man it would soon be *ended or mended.*" The following day was " a cursed morning of putting to rights, which drives me well-nigh mad. At two or three I must go to a funeral—a happy and interesting relief from my employment." He set off at eight o'clock on the morning of the 3rd, and " fought forward to Carlisle," where he slept. He quotes the following stanza from David Hume written on a pane of glass at the inn :

> Here chicks in eggs for breakfast sprawl,
> Here godless boys God's glories call,
> Here Scotsmen's heads do guard the wall,
> But Sorby's walks atone for all.

On the 4th he travelled through Penrith to Garstang, where he slept and encountered disaster. " As a petty grievance, my ink-holder broke loose in the case, and spilt some of the ink on Anne's pelisse. Misfortunes seldom come single. ''Tis not alone the inky cloak, good daughter,' but I forgot at Garstang my two breast pins: one with Walter and Jane's hair, another a harp of pure Irish gold, the gift of the ladies of Llangollen."

"April 5.—Breakfasted at Chorley, and slept at Leek. We were in the neighbourhood of some fine rock-scenery, but the day was unfavourable; besides I did not come from Scotland to see rocks, I trow."

On the following day, Sir Walter breakfasted at Ashbourne and journeyed via Derby to Tamworth, where he slept.

The Stile House Cross.

THE opinion that the old cross on Stile House Farm was a parish meeting place, founded on the fact that Frith Quarter held its meetings at Gun Cross, has just been confirmed by an item found when searching for something else. The item is an extract from the registers at the Old Church. "Act. of Richard Meakin being a Churchwarden in Bradnop quarter for the parish of Leek, 1666. Item: Spent in Oncot upon showing my acct att yt side of Morridge 1/6.—On consideration of the poverty of R. Meakin and pricking him wrongfully doe allow him towards his loss of time the money that he is out £1/8/5½ "—*St. Luke's Magazine.*

Leek and the Civil War.

ERY few scraps of information have come down to our day with regard to the local battles of the civil war of Cromwell's time. But Glover's *History of Derbyshire* and Hobson's *History of Ashbourne* tell us of a smart skirmish that took place in the winter of 1643. Then the Royalists under Lord Newcastle fell upon the Moorland Dragoons at Hartington and were sending 250 of them prisoners to Leek, when Captain Mollanus was despatched by Sir John Gell, of Hopton, to intercept them. This he did; but where the fight took place the historian does not say. In the latter battle five officers were killed, and thirty-five prisoners were taken. The Leek people had been ready to flee from their houses, and were huddling together, probably in the Abbey ruins, out of fear of the Royal forces; but when the Round-head captain came he stayed with them fourteen days, though all that time he dared not leave the town. In the end, however, he marched off up the Ashbourne Road with his troop. In 1642 the Parliamentary leaders had "sent some forces to Leeke to trayne and exercise theyre men of which at that time they stoode in great neede." The "men" here spoken of were, we suppose, the Moorland Dragoons—a rough troop of soldiers raised in the hills, who fought for hire, and were good "stout fighting men, but the most ungovernable wretches that belonged to the Parliament."

The Young Pretender at Leek.

WHILST searching recently amongst some old family documents, Mr. Thomas Burnett, of Buckfurlong, Grindon, found a letter which deals with the invasion of '45, and he has very kindly placed it at our disposal. We submitted the faded half-sheet of foolscap, which bears a water-mark—consisting of a crown, an undecipherable device in the centre, and the motto *Pro patria ejusque libertate* (" For fatherland and its liberty ")—to Mr. John Sleigh, who says : " The letter is most interesting and valuable, and confirms the Whillock account of the invasion. One or two of the words have puzzled me, but the sense of the whole is very plain ; and it is an excellently-expressed and grammatical one for the time (such as Macaulay would have delighted in), and far better than the ' Proonce ' himself could have written." We regret, however, that we are unable to state by whom or to whom the letter was written, but on the back, in the same handwriting, are the words, " Thomas Rogers, his book," and " Sarah Burnet, her book," and there are undoubted signs that at some time the sheet was pasted in a book. Upon this point Mr. Sleigh says :—" Was it written by a Rogers or by whom ? I should not be surprised to hear that it was written by the Whillock whose other account is already in print." [See *History of Leek.*] One thing, however, is certain : the letter has never before been published, and it is not too much to say that it is more circumstantial and local than any letter that has hitherto been discovered. The following is a copy *verbatim et literatim* :—

Gr [Grindon] Dec ye 22 1745

Dear Sir

I make bould to write these lines to give you an account of ye progress of ye Rebells in our countery not that I doubt but you have had many for I chused not to be the first wihter [writer] as judging it not my place but yet there may be particulars in this which you have not had and I shall give you an account of there journal [journey] on this side (Maccls ffeild) [Macclesfield].

They entered that town on Sunday 1st of Decbr and on Monday ye 2nd they marched there advanced guard to Congleton to decoy the Duke, as apears sure by drawing his forces from the Ashburn road.

Tuesday ye 3rd there advanced guard marched through Leek to Ashburn and the main body whith the pretender marched from Macclsffeild to Leek and there staid until 2 o'clock ye next morning and then marched out by favour of ye moon in great hurry allmost frighted to death and marched to Derby that night

And on Thursday they marched on for Lestor but were frighted back by apearance of about 12 dragoons near Swarkstond brigd [Swarkstone Bridge] Marched to Derby that night, and the next day being friday ye 6th they Ran to Ashburn in great confusion sorely frighted though nobody had fired at them

Saturday ye 7th they march there main body to Leek but advanced g. [guard] went to maclesfeild and were followed by all the Rest on ye next day.

To give you a full account of all outrgges [outrages] Roberies and murderes they comited in the fore mentioned progress would fill a large voloum What may be frfaimed [affirmed] of them in general is this that they were about 7000 in number. I viewed them all at a small distance and am satisfied that I saw 7000 Robers and 100 stolen horses at onest a strange sight to be sene in England, speiping [stripping] everybody of ther cloths that came near them, poulling ther

Over the Moors wi' Charlie.

shoes of there feet plundring there houses to the value of old blankets nay even the pots from there fireside threatning present deth to every body that would not bring them horses or obey there comands in every thin tho never so unreasonable. In some places they puled the corn out of ye barns to make there fires on there being great swarmes of them that had no breeches at all and so I shall say haveing no Room to say any more but from such mercyles vilans good Lord deliver us.

Tradition says that when the Young Pretender visited Leek on December 3rd (o.s.), 1745, they left in the Market Place a small barrel, which for some time remained unnoticed, but being ultimately claimed by the Jolliffe's, it was found to be full of specie, intended for the pay of the army, but which served to greatly enrich the family.

In a manuscript note to the above, Mr. John Sleigh states that the barrel was found at the house of one Stringer, whose sons, John and Joshua, kept a draper's shop at the house next the Red Lion, now occupied by Miss Hassall, milliner.

We have received the following interesting note from Professor John Prince Sheldon, of the Brund, Sheen, whose maternal great-grandmother was an Edge of Acre Farm :—

On the retreat of the Pretender's army from Derby in 1745 two of the soldiers were fed and succoured—

for how long a time is not known—by the Edge family, at the Acre Farm. Out of gratitude for this shelter and hospitality, one of the soldiers left his sword, and the other his gun, with the family. The gun is now in the possession of Mr. Richard Henry Edge, of Southport, a direct descendant of the family, who, according to Sleigh's *History of Leek* (ed. 1862, p. 215, foot-note), had been tenants of the farm at the Acre upwards of 800 years, and have left it in our own time. The whereabouts of the sword might perhaps still be traced; it was once in the possession of the late John Edge Gould, of Butterton Clowes, and was obtained from him by the late W. B. Sides, of Winster, at whose sale it was sold some fifteen to twenty years ago. I speak with certainty about the gun, which I saw not long ago; and conjecturally about the sword, which I saw when I was a lad. The gun has a long barrel, a flint-lock, and brass mountings.

Mr. Francis B. Nunns writes as follows :—" At Christmas, 1860, I visited my maternal great-uncle, Richard Edge, who resided at Balcombe, in Sussex. He was 96 years of age, and was born at Acre Farm, near Onecote, his ancestors being mentioned in Sleigh's *History of Leek* as having lived at Acre Farm for 700 years. I asked Mr. Edge if he could give me any information of events that had occurred at Leek within his recollection, and, amongst others, he mentioned that he had conversed with a man at Leek who remembered Prince Charles Edward Stuart entering Leek with his Highland army, and saw the army leave on their march to Derby. Thus, in two lives, I have had communicated to me an historical event which occurred at Leek 144 years ago."

John Gould, who resided with his mother, Dorothy Gould (at Brownhills, now called Warslow Hall), taking it into his head to study for the bar, went to read with Mr. Osborne, of Beresford Hall; but happening to visit some relatives at Lowe Hill, when the rebels passed through Leek, he joined them, although his friends followed him as far as Macclesfield trying all they could to dissuade him from his madcap enterprise. Here he gave them a broad sword, now in possession of Mr. Briggs, of Ashbourne. Going on with the rebels, he escaped unhurt from the disastrous battle which overthrew them, settled in Scotland, and died at the age of 92.—*The Reliquary* for 1863.

From Thos. Anson, of Shugbro', Esq., to his brother Commodore, afterwards Lord, Anson :—"I made my way to the Duke's quarters at Stone, where I learned that the rebels were at Leeke. Having been long tired to death, I got home as fast as I could, and found the rascals left Leeke at 1 this morning. . . . The Pretender's son, who was generally in the rear before the army was so near them, has since marched at the head. He is something under 6 foot high; wears a plaid, walks well, a good person enough, but a melancholy aspect, speaks little, and was never seen to smile."—Wednesday and Saturday, December 4 and 7, 1745.

Extracts from a letter from a gentleman at Derby,
13th December, 1745 :—"About 6 o'clock on Wednesday
evening were quartered on me 6 officers, (one a major,
as they called him) and 40 private men, with 8 picked-up
shabby horses, &c. But these wretches being fatigued with
their long march from Leeke that day, soon after they
came into my house stuffed themselves with bread,
cheese, and ale ; and then about 20 of them, before
a great fire in my hall ordered by them, called for a
large quantity of straw, nestled into it for repose ; and
the remainder of them did the like in a large laundry-
room, etc. The officers took possession of my parlour
and chambers they liked best, commanded what supper
and liquor they would have, and expected me, my
wife and whole family to wait on them, as if they had
been so many petty princes."—*Gentleman's Magazine,
1746.*

One Statham kept the "Cock" in the Market
Place, and old Uriah Davenport used to tell a rambling
sort of story about Mr. Joshua Toft being at the
hostelrie and putting into his pocket a copy of the
Gazette, which had just been brought down from town,
offering a reward of £30,000 for the Young Pretender's
head ; of Charles Edward's sending to Statham for
it, under threat of drumhead court-martial if with-
held, and of his not being able to find it until he
suddenly "unbethought himself" of sending up to Haregate in quest of it.

Ellen Wardle, of Butterton (ob. 1836, æt. 105 ?)
was aged 13 when the Caterans came through the

country, and used to say that they encamped at Harperlee, between Grindon and Wetton.

The Burnetts of Grindon had their history that they came over with the Pretender, and turned back at Ashbourne; and seeing a tract of land with only *one cote*, thought there was room for them to settle there.

LIST OF THE CHEVALIER'S OFFICERS AND TROOPS WHO MARCHED THROUGH LEEK DECEMBER, 1745.

Regiment.	Colonel.	Men.
Lochiel	Cameron of Lochiel	740
Appin	Stuart of Ardshiel	360
Atholl	Lord George Murray (Jas. Stewart, of Tulloch, carried the standard)	1000
Clanronald	Clanronald of Clanronald, jr	200
Keppoch	Macdonald of Keppoch	400
Glenco	Macdonald of Glenco	200
Ogilvie	Lord Ogilvie	500
Glenbucket	Gordon of Glenbucket	427
Perth	Duke of Perth (and Lord Pitsligo's Foot). This regiment alone wore scarlet coats, with the Drummond tartan	750
Robertson	Robertson of Strowan	200
Maclachan	Maclachan of Maclachan	270
Glencarnick	Macgregor	300
Glengary	Macdonald of Glengary, jr	300
Nairn	Lord Nairn	200
Edinburgh	John Roy Stuart (and Lord Kelly's Foot)	450
Maclean	Charles Maclean, of Drimrin	500
	In several small corps	1000

Horse.

Life-guards......Lord Elcho's, in blue roquelaures } 160
    Lord Kilmarnock's..................... }
    Lord Pitsligo's............................ 140
                8087

The "Hundred Pipers" were led by "Swaggering John Macgregor, of Fortingall," the Prince's own favourite piper.

Mr. John Hawksworth, of Leek, has in his possession a pack of cards said to have been left by the Young Pretender's adherents during the invasion of Staffordshire in 1745. The present owner obtained the cards, 45 in number, from his father's maternal aunt, whose grandmother lived near Ashbourne at the time in question. The latter's version was that some officers and men came to her house and took possession, helping themselves to anything they fancied. They ate all there was in the larder, and afterwards killed and cooked several fowls. The officers of the party drank a very large quantity of elderberry wine and beer, and caroused and played cards all night, the men faring as well as they were able in the stables. Upon leaving next morning the cards were left behind, but a valuable grey stallion was taken, which, however, was afterwards turned loose and returned home.

The cards are very singular in appearance, being illuminated in crimson, yellow, black, blue, and green. One card is headed by an owl, and in a half circle is the following :—" *Hispania Rex Carolv dei gratia.*" Another bears the following :—" *Grossvs nonvs Imperator es Romanovm, 1691,"* with a king of hearts in the centre. A third, between two Roman swords, bears the maker's name, "Techasen, Bordeaux." The remainder are of various designs, denominating one to nine, and representing pin-cushions, daggers, stars, and clubs. They are 3½in. by 2⅜in. in size, and are made of two pieces of foreign hand-made paper pasted upon a third piece of cartridge, and are burnished back and front.

Funny Surnames.

SOME very interesting Subsidy Rolls, or Tax Papers of the reign of Edward III, have lately been published. They shew what funny surnames were given to men when surnames first became used. "William of the Heath" was the chief man in Leek. Other names were Richard of the Wall, Richard de Easing, Richard the Miller, Benedict of the Clough, Hugh of the Lowe, Adam the Harper, Henry the Smith, William son of Mag, John of the Gate, Adam the Brewster, William the Fisher, &c. There was a Smith and a Harper also at Rushton, a Smith at Cheddleton, and a Harper at Butterton. Richard the Demon was an Ipstones name, and John-by-the-Brook lived at Waterfall.—*St. Luke's Parish Magazine*, March, 1890.

Church Goers in 1736.

HE following copy of a faculty, dated January 18th, 1736, for the allotment of the pews in the Old Church, furnishes an interesting insight as to the principal inhabitants at that period and where they lived. The Commissioners acting under the deed were—" Jno. Wedgwood of Harracles, Wm. Trafford Swithamly—Saml. Langford of Leek Manufacturer—Saml. Tomkinson Park lane—Thos. Turner Bradnop and Jno. Grindey, Leekfrith—"

No.	Kneelings.	No.	Proprietor.	Tenement.
1	7	1	Revd. Richd. Jackson...	Great Longdon
		1	Hugh Sherratt	Bank End
		1	Ra. Williamson, Esq.....	Upper Foker
		1	William Rogers............	Oxhay
		1	Thos. Sutton, Esq........	Oncot Lower Grange
		1	Mrs. Eliza Andrews......	Lowndes's Tenement
		1	John Hollins, Gent......	Hillswood
2	7	2	Rev. Josh. Dale..........	Gun Side
		5	Saml. Langkford..........	Houses in Spout street
3	7	7	Edward Sikes..............	Leek
4	7	2	Thos. Turner..............	Lower Bradnop
		2	Thos. Jolliffe, Esq........	Palmer's Tenement
		1	Thos. Wardle	Mixon
		1	Henry Lomas.............	Roch Grange
		1	Henry Davenport.........	Ball Haye

No.	Kneel-ings.	No.	Proprietor.	Tenement.
5	7	2	Thos. Jolliffe	Lower Foker
		1	Josh Toft, Gent...........	Hare Gate
		1	John Wedgwood...... ...	Godwyn's Tenement
		1	John Lockett...............	Bradley's Tenement
		1	John Botham...............	Apesford
		1	Richard Wood............	Roch Side
6	7	7	Thomas Smith............	Cowhay
7	7	7	John Smith	Wildgoose House
8	7	6	John Debank, Gent......	Benthead
	1	1	John Sutton...............	Hallwater
9	6	1	Josiah Lancelott glazier..	Spout street
		1	Wm. Gashill...............	Barnyates
		1	John Sherratt.............	White Lee
		1	Tim Godwyn..............	Spout street
		1	—— Gent.........	Hollybush
10	5	1	John Watson..............	Pool End
		1	Mr. Cheshire	Low
		1	Wm. Brunt................	Bank Top
		1	——	Stockwell street
		1	Ellen Ratcliffe, Widow..	Dun Lee
11	5	1	John Needham............	Spoutyate
		1	Lord Macclesfield........	Wooleys
		1	Whittakers	Rowley
		2	Charles Nicholls, Gent...	Coltsmoor
12	7	1	The Hrs and Exectrs of Sarah Hall...............	Brundockhollins
		1	Thos. Sherratt............	Parklane
		1	Walter Chetwynd, Esq...	Bridgend
		1	Wm. Concliffe, Gent.	Derby street
		1	Thos. Hollinshead, Esq.	Bullshead
		1	— Rodes, Gent...........	Bradshaw
		1	——	Old Red Lion
13	7	2	Wm. Sneyd, Esq	The Acre
		1	John Grindy...............	Middle Hulme
		1	Wm. Rogers...............	Stony Cliffe
		2	Thomas Hollinshead.....	Upper Tettesworth
		1	Mrs. Bradburn............	Lower Tettesworth
14	5	*	Michael Henshaw........	Leekmoor side

* Half seat.

No.	Kneelings.	No.	Proprietor.	Tenement.
		*	Sarah Fenton, Widow...	Hollin House
15	5	2	Lord Macclesfield	Ashes' Tenement
		3	Wm. Mills, Gent	Allen's Tenement
16	7	1	Thos. Mountfort	New Grange
		1	Thos. Birtles..	Market Place
		1	Wm. Gent.................	Upper Hulme
		1	Wm. Condlyffe.............	Upper Hulme
		1	Richd. Godwyn	Thorncliffe
		1	Roger Fernihough........	Thorncliffe
		1	— Ash, Esq...............	Mixonhay
17	7	2	Lord Macclesfield........	Brook House
		5	Wm. Mills..................	Plant's Upper House†
18	5	2	Thos. Burgh, Esq..	Wynyates
		1	Thos. Sutton...............	Oncot Upper Grange
		1	Mr. Read or Condlyffe...	Lymhouse
		1	—Swan, Gent.............	Lesser Longsdon
19	—	–	The Earl of Macclesfield	Rudyard Hall
20	—	–	” ” ”	” ”
21	7	1	John Wedgewood.........	Endon Bank
		1	John Sutton...............	Endon
		1	Josiah Lancelott	Spout street
		1	John Lockett..............	Blackamoor's Head
		1	Wm. Sneyd................	Waterhouse nr Oncot
		1	Thos. Hollinshead........	Revidge
		1	The owners of the Green Dragon...................	Leek
22	6	1	Hugh Sherratt.............	Hollinshurst
		1	Saml. Tomkinson........	Lowerhouse
		1	— Turner..................	Harehouse
		1	Jas. Bulkeley, Gent......	Bradnop
		1	Arthur Goodwin..........	Dunswood
		1	Thos. Jolliffe..............	Washbrook Head
23	6	1	Widow Godwin...........	Dunswood
		1	Enoch Tomkinson, clerk	Upper House
		1	Mrs. Bradburn	Lower Tettesworth
		1	Dudley Hulme, Gent....	Hilly Lees
		1	Josh. Stonehewer, Gent..	Foul Church
		1	Henry Lankford..........	Spout street

* Half seat.   † Plant's Lower House, Lowndes Tenements, The Fold, formerly Auston's Tenements, &c.

No.	Kneel- ings.	No.	Proprietor.	Tenement.
24	6	1	Wm. Murhall, Esq........	The Knowles
		1	Thos. Wardle..............	White Lee
		1	Sir John Harpur, Bart...	Broncott
		1	— Jurks, Gent............	Steelhouse
		1	Saml. Tomkinson.........	Lane End
		1	Wm. Mills	Spout street
25	6	2	Thos. Jolliffe..............	Birchall
		2	Thos. Hollinshead........	Middlecliffe
		1	John Bentley..............	Stockwell street
26	6	1	Thos. Sutton..............	Oncot
		1	Wm. Wood, Gent..	Bottom of the Frith
		1	Thos. Burgh...............	Water House
		1	Thos. Birtles.............	Spout street
		1	Wm. Murhall..............	Standley Head
		1	John Mills.................	Derby street
27	6	2	Josh. Stonehewer........	Derby street
		2	John Hough	The Cock
		2	Lord Macclesfield.........	Willyyate
28	6	1	James Grindey............	Pet Hills
		1	Thos. Gent............	The Low
		1	Joseph Myott.............	Leek
		1	Lord Macclesfield........	Highgate
		2	Josh. Stonehewer........	
29	5	1	Ralph Bagnall.............	Low
		1	Wm. Hulme..............	Jaggerslane
		2	Mr. Cheshire..............	Market Place
		1	Lord Macclesfield.......	Shufflebothams
30	5	2	Wm. Hulme..............	Near Market Cross
		2	Widow Hinton............	Spout street
		1	Widow Brown......	Spout street
31	4	1	Mrs. Judith Shaw.........	The Barn
		2	Thos. Turner..............	Smith's Tenement
		1	Thos. Hollinshead........	Church street
32	4	4	Wm. Mills, John Hollins, — Brough...	Red Earth, New Grange, Middle Hulme
33	—	–	Ralph Wood, Gent.	Abbey
34	—	*	John Lockett, senr........	Leek

No.	Kneelings.	No.	Proprietor.	Tenement.
		*	Benj. Mould..............	
35		*	Wm. Badnall..............	Mill street
		*	Richard Lancelott........	
36	—	—	Thos. Rowley, Gent......	Fernihough
37	5	1	Revd. Mr. Daintry.......	Taylor's Green
		1	Wm. Smith..............	Leek
		1	Wm. Statham.............	Stockwell street
		1	Thos. Parr.................	Franklings
		1	— Colclough..............	Park lane

* Half seat each.

The above list will be read with interest by the
descendants of the persons named. It should, perhaps,
be remembered that since September 5th, 1862, the
township of Onecote, formerly a chapelry under the
Parish Church of Leek, has been constituted with the
township of Bradnop, a separate ecclesiastical parish,
the living being in the gift of the Vicar of Leek. St.
Luke's Church, Onecote, was built in 1753-5, but was
not consecrated until 1835. There are 200 sittings, 60
of which are free. Meerbrook became an ecclesiastical
parish on March 11th, 1859. The church of St. Matthew
was founded in 1565, by Sir Ralph Bagnall, Knight,
of Dieu-la-cress, the living being in the gift of the Vicar of
Leek. Endon and Longsdon now form a joint chapelry.
The church of St. Luke's was re-built in 1730, and the
living is in the gift of the Earl of Macclesfield.

The Record of the Hills by O. L. S.

HEY stand unmoved, unchanged by aught that
moved
To joy or sorrow the vast human world.
What scenes have been enacted at their feet
Since first those jagged rocks their heads uprear'd !
All silently they stood, and watched, and still
Remained the same, unaltering and mute.

They looked upon the Monast'ry below
Nestling in quiet calm beside the stream ;
They watched the brothers, clad in white, each day
Go forth upon their duties varied ; some
To mill, and stream, and sunny garden fair,
Others to toil and labour in the fields,
As sent, for none might idle be, but all
Had work to do. They saw them homeward turn
As sank the sun to rest, a globe of fire
In glorious skies behind the western ridge,
And silence reigned.

And so the stately hills
Looked down upon the busy hive, until
A change took place. Those rocks perchance could tell,
Had they the gift of speech, of one sad day
When by a cruel king's command (who long
Had fixed, with greedy gaze, his eager eyes
Upon the houses sacred to the name
Of God and charity throughout the land),
The brothers forth were driven, and their home
Was desolated. They themselves must seek
A refuge where they might, and so some fled

Unto those very hills, who kept their secret well.
Thus never more were seen the white-robed monks
Of Dieu-la-cresse—the Abbey, ruined, fell.

Full in their midst, for ages long, has stood
The building where our fathers worshipped God.
Unwearied watch the hills have ever kept
Around the sacred temple, and have heard,
When rose the sun upon the sleeping world,
And when the night her reign of peace began,
The matin and the vesper bell ring out,
Calling on men their Maker to adore,
Creator of the hills and them alike.

The Church still stands, surrounded by the hills,
Though long ago the Abbey was destroyed,
And still the bells ring out, resounding far,
And waking echoes in the distant rocks.

And once they heard the sound of martial strains.
As through the town with banners flying free,
Prince Charlie came, and with him all that host
Who loved him, and for him had gladly died,
If so he might escape —such loyalty
Was theirs; and minstrels many a tale unfold
Of "bonnie Charlie" and his faithful train.

So through long ages, though the storms have burst
In wild, relentless fury o'er their heads,
They still have stood, and kept their calm, still watch.
And though the years roll on, and many men
Shall come and go, the "everlasting hills"
Will still remain, till Time shall be no more.

A. L. GEE.

Coaches and Four.

ROM the middle of the 17th century up to
about 1770, coaches each drawn by four
horses were kept by Mr. Hollins, of Mossley;
Lord Vane, of Westwood; the Whitehalls of Sharpe-
cliffe; the Whitehoughs of Whitehough; the Wedgwoods
of Harracles; the Traffords of Swythamley; and the
Sneyds of Belmont. At Belmont were two postillions,
father and son, each Joe Carden. The horses had long
tails, festooned with ribbons in dirty weather. Old Birtles
was footman, and stood behind the carriage in silk
stockings, &c.

At Rudyard Hall the Rudyard's were still living,
another branch of that same ancient and dignified family
being seated at the Abbey. The Bulkeleys lived at
Stanlow, a second branch being seated somewhere in

Bradnop. The Armitts were at Thornylee; and the Stoddarts had hardly died out from Rushton. The Ashenhursts, too, were hardly gone from Ashenhurst, where the Hollingsheads, of Bosley, succeeded them. Just over the hills, too, a gentleman of the name of Wardle was living at Boosley Grange, with a town residence in Leek. William Parker, Esq., was a magistrate of good position in the town, and the Bowyers over-topped all the local magnates. Joddrell, of Moorhouse, was quite as great a man as some of those mentioned; whilst the Turners, of Padwick, ancestors of the Turners, vicars of Meerbrook, dated back further in local history than the Wedgewoods. Mr. Doxey Hulme and Mr. Randle Wood succeeded the Rudyerds as residents at the Abbey. All these must have travelled sometimes and when they did no one horse could have dragged them up the steep slopes and over the rocky roads of the district.

At the present time, coaches and four are rerely seen in Leek. Occasionally, however, Mr. P. L. Brocklehurst drives through, and now and then we see the turnouts of the Earl of Harrington and the Earl of Shrewsbury and Talbot.

Cost of a Stage Coach Journey.

 MEMORANDUM of the expenses of a stage-coach journey to London, from Blackburn through Manchester and Leek, in March 1824, was discovered in an old pocket-book belonging to a commercial traveller of the period:—

	£	s.	d.
From Blackburn to London, outside	1	16	0
Coachmen (5, 1/- each)	0	5	0
Guard	0	4	6
Refreshments in Manchester	0	1	6
Supper at Leek	0	2	6
Breakfast at Northampton	0	2	0
Spirits on the journey	0	2	0
	£2	13	6

The whole journey occupied twenty-seven hours, and great punctuality was observed.

Marriage of Jimmy Maddock.

ON July 26th, 1821, Mr. James Maddock, a little gentleman well known at Leek market, standing only 24 inches high and 45 years old, was married to Miss Smith, a blooming and blushing damsel of 20. This extraordinary wedding is said to have been witnessed by at least 2,000 people.

Riot at Leek in 1715.

HE following account of the riot at Leek in 1715 is extracted from the *Flying Post* for September 1-3, of that year:—

"Leek in Staffsh. Augt. 5.

SIR,—These are to acquaint you that on 28th July, being our Fair, the Mob of this Town, mingled with a few strangers in disguise, did about ten o'clock at night break into our Meeting-house, pulled down the pulpit and pews and made bonfires of them for several nights, uttered abominable blasphemies, and cried out they were doing God good service. After they had proceeded so far they uncovered a great part of the roof, so that the Dissenters were forced to meet out of the town. There are too many here who have openly declared for the Pretender, and no doubt encouraged the Mob to such impudence. We have some gentlemen in and about town of very good estates that are jealous for His Majesty King George; but the Mob has been so Rampant that these gentlemen could not do what they would otherwise have done. Some idle Fellows went about in the day time threatening to burn the houses of the King's loyal subjects. Last week they were very brisk upon the talk of the Pretender's invasion, but now we are

something quieter. Our Town for its compass has not
been inferior to any for Mobs and Disloyalty, but we
are in hopes things will be better—a great deal of
damage has been done us. We have been very patient
under all these affronts, but hope these matters will
be Rectify'd. We are in expectation of a troop to
keep the Rebels in awe. We have been so alarmed
with the Pretender that we have made no return yet
of these matters above; but know the chief actors
almost to a man."

An Old-fashioned Schoolmaster.

THE school at Meerbrook, being one of our old endowed
schools, has been held by some well educated men.
A Mr. Royle is remembered as having gone thither
from Upperhulme every morning as master, with his
university gown flying in the wind. The Rev. James
Turner, father of the last Vicar of Meerbrook of that
name, was also schoolmaster. It is said that when
angry he used a formidable ebony ferule with such
vigour that the scream of the unhappy boy brought
his wife to the rescue of the culprit. To soothe the
master she administered an effective remedy in the
shape of "a cup of warm ale." It is even said that
she kept this "warming on the hob." Wise woman!
This master wrote the epitaph on a good wife in
Leek old churchyard :—

> She was, but words are wanting to say what ;
> Think what a wife should be, and she was that.

British Position on Gun.

N a letter dated October 16th, 1878, to the *Staffordshire Advertiser,* the Rev. W. Beresford, Vicar of St. Luke's, Leek (at that time curate of St. Chad's, Stafford), wrote :—Written history tells of the brave stand made by the ancient British against the invasion of the Romans 1,900 years ago. Perhaps the hills of our county bear traces of the struggle. Gun, a very bold hill, rises from the Churnet Valley, north of Leek, and runs due north for a couple of miles. Its southern end is steep on all sides, and higher than any of the hills around, except those on the east. Indeed it seems as if Nature had placed Gun here as sentinel over the valley which winds up from the Potteries into the heart of the eastern hills beyond the Roches. Those hills were doubtless a very fastness of ancient British religion and patriotism. The Romans coming into the country by the Watling Street, were probably expected by this very route ; and I venture to think that on examination the top of this southern end of Gun will be found fortified accordingly. It has for some years past been known that a fine old earthenwork ran along the eastern face of the part of the hill in question. I made some notes upon it in 1875 (I think for *The Reliquary*). The embankment with its double foss is in part entire. The other part has been levelled. But enough remains to show us that the original work ran for some 500 or 600 yards, dividing the plateau on the hill top from a morass which occupied a steppe above a very steep ascent from Leekfrith. But beyond the fact that this work ran out at "Park House," nothing could be made of it. Not long ago I observed that a brook broke through the fortification, and, falling down the hill, immediately passed "Lockgate." This name seemed too much like "Lake," or "Watergate," to be unnoticed. I then remembered that there was a solitary spot called "Gun-gate" on the other side of the hill, almost opposite "Lock-gate." Crossing, therefore, over the plateau, I looked for earthwork, and surely enough found that the western side was defended by a long earthwork, like that on the east, and running out at "Gun-gate." A glorious storm cloud was just then coming up from Shropshire over the Potteries. Keeping an eye on that, I hastened to see if the southern brow of the hill above the "Fold" were also defended, and had found what I thought were veritable earthworks, when the van of the storm broke over me, and I had to retreat before it. Since then I have not been able to revisit the spot. Did the Romans come? Local names shall answer. Just below this seeming military position is an ancient road leading towards the eastern hills of which I spoke. On the broad slope of the hill below "Park House" a part of this road, at a point where the plough is said to turn up traces of a battle, is called "Savagees"—or probably "Savage hays." May not one paraphase this as "the fields of fierce struggle?" A little further to the east it is "Hostage Lane."

In a note to the editor of *Olde Leeke,* dated March 12th, 1890, Mr. Beresford says :— Although since the above was written twelve years ago, I have seen nothing to shake my conclusions as to the fact that a struggle did sometime take place on the south-eastern side of Gun, I am now not so sure as to the character and extreme antiquity of the earthworks. For a very similar bank runs up Hellswood from behind the Abbey, starting about 200 yards E.N.E. of the ruins, crossing the foot-path to Meerbrook just below the gate on the eastern side of the Abbey wood, and running along the plantation towards Fold. Leek was a training ground, I believe, for the Roundhead horse in Cromwell's time, and these banks may have had something to do with them, or they may have been huge ditches to shut off the open commons both on Gun and Hellswood from the better land below. Still, the old impression may be the correct one, that Gun and Hellswood on the one hand, separated as they are by " Le Frith," or truce land, from the Hen Cloud on the other (the latter being certainly an ancient British position), were military positions when the Romans and Saxons came thus far, but could get, or would get, no further up into the hills. The importance of Gun depended on the wide views which the hill commands.

A Miscarriage of Justice.

THE courtesy of Mr. Rupert Simms, of Newcastle-under-Lyme, enables us to give the following sketch of a miscarriage of justice that occurred in Leek about 1830. The writer was C. Hulbert, author of the *History of the County of Salop*, and numerous other works, and is extracted from his *Seventy Years of an Eventful Life* :—

"Having sent one of my young men, William Millward, to Burslem, he engaged an excellent place of sale, situate in the Market Place—opened and displayed his goods to the astonishment of the natives ; he had printed catalogues with him. A Mr. Edge was then Inspector of Hawkers, and supposing from a view of the catalogue that there was not any man in the kingdom who could really be the *bona fide* publisher of so varied and extensive a collection, he lodged an information against the young man, took him instantly before the magistrates of Leek, 12 miles distant, where upon the plea that the young man's story and the catalogues were false, he was convicted in the penalty of ten pounds, taken into custody, the property seized—and as he had no money, he was to be committed to prison until the sale of the effects had realized the penalty and expenses. At that time letters were from two to three days in their transit from Burslem to Shrewsbury.

Remaining comfortably at home, and enjoying a party taking tea at my house, the postman brought me a letter from William, stating his condition and that I must immediately come to his relief. My little carriage was then under the hand of the coach-builder. I left the tea table in haste, saw him, related my story; by four o'clock in the morning the repairs were completed, and I was on my way to Burslem, by way of Newcastle. Approaching to that town I met William Millward.

'Oh! I am glad to see you at liberty; jump up into the carriage and return with me.'

'Oh! no, sir, I dare not; they will take me to prison; the constables were taking me there, when a mob of hundreds of people assailed the officers and nearly killed them, set me at liberty, and I ran for my life.'

This grieved me, as I knew our cause was good, and would instantly be proved on my arrival at Burslem, which I did about ten o'clock. Proceeding to the Market Place, I found it filled with my advocates, in great agitation. As soon as they saw me they made the welkin ring with their huzzas.

'Are you right, Mr. Hulbert?' they enquired.

'Quite right,' I replied.

'Shall we break open the room in which your goods are destrained, and punish the rascals in possession?'

'Oh! no, I thank you very kindly.' Standing up in my carriage, I addressed them, and explained the law, that, as a manufacturer, I had a right to remove and sell my own publications, in any part of the kingdom except London, without a license, and that such was my stock. The huzzas and rejoicings were instantly resumed—a party accompanied me to the Leopard Inn, from whence I addressed letters to Lord Clive, Gen. Lord Hill, Panton Corbett, Esq., M.P., and Mr. Donne, Secretary of the Hackney Coach Office, London. I believe each of the noblemen, with my ever-dear friend Mr. Corbett, waited upon Mr. Donne with my catalogue, declaring their conviction, and from personal knowledge, that I was the publisher of every book and engraving; adding their testimony to my character and respectability. The letters referred to I sent by zealous friends to the post office, first apprising the Inspector of what I had done. After refreshing myself and horse, in company with Mr. Powell, of Burslem, formerly of Stanton-upon-Hincheath, I set out to see the magistrates at Leek— the roads I found to be very hilly, so we advanced slowly. On my arrival at Leek, I waited on the Magistrates' Clerk, who informed me that the magistrate who convicted the young man was a Mr. Trafford, and that he lived in Derbyshire, a distance of eight or ten miles. Finding my horse refreshed, I again set out for the Justice's. It was summer time; we arrived at his house, a solitary residence, about eleven o'clock. There was a light in one lower room—the kitchen. I knocked at the door—no one answered; I repeated my knockings, when a servant trembling with fear, in great agitation enquired my business. I related it briefly, adding, 'I have travelled already from Shrewsbury without changing my horse.'

The servant replied, ' Mr. Trafford is in bed.'

' Well, if he is, take up my card while I remain here.'

He did so, and returned with the kind answer, that ' If I would excuse it, Mr. Trafford would see me in his bedroom.' He received me very politely, and assured me that he never signed a conviction so much against his will—that he was inclined to believe William Millward's and Mr. Powell's testimony ; but that Edge the Inspector assured him it was impossible that any one man could be author, printer, and publisher of such a number of expensive works. ' I will, however, instantly write to Edge to liberate your young man and restore your goods.'

We returned to Leek, and reached there about two o'clock in the morning, very much to the joy of the inmates of the inn, who had warmly espoused my cause. I had then travelled about 72 miles. In the morning, by seven o'clock, I waited on the Magistrates' Clerk ; I showed him the note Mr. Trafford had written. He looked at me with some astonishment and pleasure, saying, " Like Edge, I doubted very much the correctness of your catalogue, or that any one man could be author, printer, and proprietor of so many publications. Come to Leek, and I will do all in my power to promote your views and interest ; your energy on this occasion convinces me that your statements are perfectly correct.'

We returned to Burslem, delivered the note to the confused, penitent Inspector, who released the goods, acknowledged his error, became my warmest friend, and in two days letters arrived from the noblemen mentioned

and Mr. Corbett, detailing the success of their application ; and from Mr. Donne, stating his conviction of my
correctness, and that he had ordered Edge to release the
goods and the young man ; and that he would take care
that I should never be again molested.   Here I succeeded well—I never was so popular.   I rewarded my
zealous friends, and presented the beaten officers each
with a gratuity, and my pardon."

Energetic Treatment.

THERE is a place called Leek (no, not in Wales, O
you mad dog!) and near this is a place, the name
whereof shall be presently seen.   Here, medical science
is very advanced indeed.   Read this paragraph from
a Staffordshire journal [*Sentinel*]:—

"Last week a large black dog was seen in the
neighbourhood of Ashenhurst, near Leek.   He went
into the farmyard there, and was seen to bite *two
other boys*, both of which have since gone mad, and
had to be destroyed."

We commend the facts to the attention of the
authorities.   There is no doubt that prompt treatment
is desirable in dangerous cases, and this is very
prompt.—*Punch*, December 23rd, 1871.

Roman Catholicism in Leek.

EARLY in the present century Roman Catholicism had no abiding place in Leek, and the few Catholics who were here either met in secret or journeyed elsewhere for spiritual communion and guidance. The internment, however, of French prisoners, which began with the end of the Peace of Amiens in 1803, and was renewed in 1809 and again in 1812, during the Napoleonic era, caused frequent gatherings to take place. Sometimes services were held in the garret of the house of Mr. Ward, a solicitor resident in King Street, but more frequently in a room in Pickwood Road, now occupied by Mr. Mark as a printing office. Whilst these gatherings were being held, an outer guard prevented intrusion and discovery, and it is not too much to say that such a condition of affairs occasioned much irritation amongst the Frenchmen, and the Mulvaneys, the Flanagans, and other Irishmen in the town. Father Gerard, a French priest, was the first to minister in Leek, and he did duty from Cobridge, at that time the mother Church of the North Staffordshire district. He was succeeded by the Rev. (afterwards Canon) Alfred Jeffries, who came over at intervals from the old chapel

ST. MARY'S.

at Cheadle, and generally stayed with Mr. Henry Bermingham, of London Road. Father Jeffries set to work
to gather money for the building of a chapel, and owing
to his untiring exertions, the old chapel in Fountain
Street was erected in 1828, by Mr. John Higgs, of
Cheadle. The Rev. Samuel Whittaker, of Lisbon (who
was related to the Challinors, the great timber merchants
of Liverpool), followed Father Jeffries ; and in turn was
succeeded by the Rev. Bernard Francis Ivers, who
accepted Leek as his first mission, and who afterwards
was made a Canon, and died at St. Peter's, Birmingham,
about ten years ago. Father Ivers was priest here at
the accession of her Majesty, and several years later
was succeeded by the Rev. F. O'Farrell, who was
educated at Maynooth and Rome, and came here from
Bloxwich. After a residence of about five years Father
O'Farrell was replaced by the Rev. Francis Fairfax, who
stayed only twelve months, and then removed to Leamington, and thence to Oulton, near Stone. Father
Michael Power followed the Rev. F. Fairfax, beginning
here a career of usefulness which has since been seen
to the greatest advantage at Bilston, where the rev.
gentleman is still located. In the spring of 1860, the
Rev. Joseph Francis Anderson was removed from the
heavy mission of St. Chad's, Birmingham, to Leek, and
he entered upon his new sphere of labour with the
greatest enthusiasm. How Father Anderson was mainly
instrumental in establishing the Convent ; how he gave
up his residence in Fountain Street for the Sisters of
the Institute of the Blessed Virgin Mary ; how he begged
money and land for the new chapel in King Street,
which was built from Mr. William Sugden's plans in

1863-4, and opened on May 1st in the latter year; how he opened the schools in 1870 and placed them under Government control in 1877; how ardently he longed for the enlargement and proper furnishing of the chapel; and how well he lived and was loved, and how tragically he died on May 15th, 1884—are all matters comparatively fresh in the memory of our readers, and are the consecutive and connecting links which bind the thorny, persecuting past to the hearty recognition and regard of the present.

The handsome church of St. Mary's which now adorns Compton was opened on May 12th, 1887, and was built mainly by the munificence of Mr. John H. Sperling, of Norwich, father of the Rev. A. M. Sperling, the present priest.

Banks and Bankers.

The Old Savings Bank.

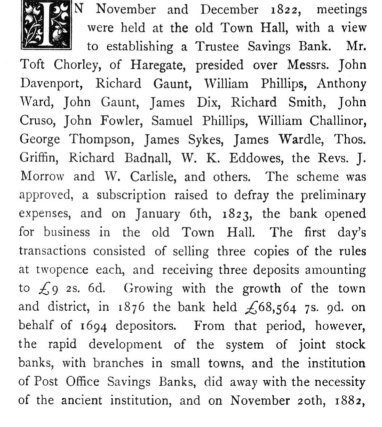

IN November and December 1822, meetings were held at the old Town Hall, with a view to establishing a Trustee Savings Bank. Mr. Toft Chorley, of Haregate, presided over Messrs. John Davenport, Richard Gaunt, William Phillips, Anthony Ward, John Gaunt, James Dix, Richard Smith, John Cruso, John Fowler, Samuel Phillips, William Challinor, George Thompson, James Sykes, James Wardle, Thos. Griffin, Richard Badnall, W. K. Eddowes, the Revs. J. Morrow and W. Carlisle, and others. The scheme was approved, a subscription raised to defray the preliminary expenses, and on January 6th, 1823, the bank opened for business in the old Town Hall. The first day's transactions consisted of selling three copies of the rules at twopence each, and receiving three deposits amounting to £9 2s. 6d. Growing with the growth of the town and district, in 1876 the bank held £68,564 7s. 9d. on behalf of 1694 depositors. From that period, however, the rapid development of the system of joint stock banks, with branches in small towns, and the institution of Post Office Savings Banks, did away with the necessity of the ancient institution, and on November 20th, 1882, the establishment was closed after sixty years of excellent work, the deposits in hand, amounting to £35,745 6s. 5d., being transferred to the Post Office and other savings banks.

BADNALL, ELLIS & CO.

The first private bank was that of Messrs. Badnall, Ellis & Co., who in 1826 carried on business in the Market Place, in the shop now occupied by Mr. Henry Eddowes, and are believed to have commenced business about 1823. The partners were Richard Badnall, of Highfield, and his son of the same name, of Ashenhurst, silk manufacturers; Captain Ellis, probably from Leamington; Henry Cruso and Francis Gibbon Spilsbury, silk manufacturers, machine makers, &c. The bank was called the Leek Commercial Bank, probably in contradistinction to the Savings Bank, and ceased to do business about 1827.

FOWLER, GAUNT, & CO.

Shortly afterwards Messrs. Fowler, Gaunt & Co. began business, in premises on the north-eastern corner of the Market Place. Their transactions were not of colossal magnitude, and in 1847 they came to an end, to the satisfaction of Mrs. Fowler, of Horton Hall, who warmly welcomed a release from responsibility.

MANCHESTER AND LIVERPOOL DISTRICT.

On April 30th, 1829, the prospectus was issued of the Manchester and Liverpool District Banking Company, and on August 29th following, a meeting was held at Leek to consider the desirableness of having a local branch. Mr. Thomas Carr, senr., took the chair, and

Mr. William Challinor, senr., and Mr. Samuel B. Whittles, were elected members of the local committee. It was not, however, until 1833 that a sub-branch was opened for a few hours every Wednesday, in the premises in the Sheep Market now occupied by Mr. W. E. Gwynne, draper. Mr. A. C. Reid was the first manager, and in 1836 he was succeeded by Mr. William Milner, who afterwards became prominently identified with the staple trade of the town. Mr. Milner says, "the principal value of the Leek branch during my time was the reception of deposits, of which a large amount came from the country district around Leek, and it was surprising how much money was held to the credit of people, who, to look at, you would scarcely consider worth a penny."

Mr. Milner left the bank in 1839 and was succeeded by Mr. William Debank Hand, during whose management it was decided to revert to the arrangement of having the branch open only one day a week as a sub-branch to Hanley. A friendly domicile was provided in the house in Church Street where the first Earl of Macclesfield was born, an illustration of which will be found on page 167. Business, however, increased so fast that in 1855 a return was made to daily opening, and Mr. William Carse was placed in charge, in premises in Custard (now Stanley) Street, now occupied by Messrs. Johnson & Son, chemists, and subsequently (1860) to the premises in Derby Street. In 1861, Mr. John Cruso became local director, a post which he held until his death in 1867. Mr. John Baker followed Mr. Carse in 1862, and two years later he was succeeded by Mr. William Buchan, who died in 1874. Mr. Alfred

Roebuck Whyatt then took the management, and upon his death in 1885, Mr. T. J. Smith was removed from Cheadle to fill the vacancy. Whilst the building which now ornaments Derby Street was being erected (1881-3), and for three years previously, the business was removed to Gaunt House opposite, and on October 24th, 1883, the new bank opened its doors.

COMMERCIAL.

A branch of this bank was opened in Leek in 1834, in the premises next to Challinors' yard in Derby Street, Mr. Anthony Ward being the local director. So rosy was the start and bright the prospect, that at midsummer in 1836 the shares were at 70 to 80 per cent. premium. The Leek shareholders, as an evidence of their confidence and appreciation, presented to Mr. Ward a valuable silver epergne. Almost from that moment, however, the the price of the shares fell fast, and in two years they were at 15 per cent. discount. The crash came about the middle of 1840, and involved in heavy loss not only Mr. Ward, but many others, the shareholders losing all their capital, about £300,000. Mr. Ward's physical power was unequal to the strain, and he died on May 31st, 1840, aged 54 years, just twenty-five days before the bank stopped payment.

JENNINGS'S.

Mr. Francis William Jennings opened a bank in 1855, in the house in Stockwell Street now occupied by Mr. Fallon, and near to Cruso's yard. He came to Leek as a book-keeper, and before commencing business as a banker was a commission agent and silk broker.

He sold his banking business in 1877 to Parr's Banking Company, and died on January 10th, 1880.

PARR'S.

Since acquiring the business established by Mr. Jennings, Parr's Bank has largely increased its connection, and it has now handsome quarters in St. Edward Street, opposite the end of the Sheep Market. Mr. James Swindells has been manager since the purchase was made.

MIDLAND.

It is, perhaps, worth recording that the Midland Bank opened a branch in a room at the Black Swan Inn, Sheep Market, in 1877, and kept it open for about a fortnight.

Abridged from "The Banks and Bankers of Leek," by Mr. T. J. Smith, published in the *Leek Times* in March 1891, and subsequently in pamphlet form for private circulation only.

The Trafford Tombstone.

T page 84 in Mr. Sleigh's *History of Leek* will be found the following account of the above monument. I have not altered the ancient spelling. The Hearne referred to, who wrote the account, is the same man who used to say—

> Pox on't, quoth Time to Thomas Hearne,
> Whatever I forget you learn.

(*Oriel*, p. 256, and Fuller's *History of Abbeys*, p. 285).

A small upright stone against the vicarage wall to the memory of William Trafford, of Swythamley, Esq. "the Royalist," (who ob. 10th December, 1797, æt 93) has been the subject of so many fond legends that we have to fall back on Hearne's curious discourses (8vo. ed. 1771, vol. 1, p. 262) for a true interpretation of the origin of the singular crest thereon carved :—

"Ye aunceyentest armorial device I know or have read, is yt of Trafords of T. in Lankashyre, whose (crest) is a labouring man with a flayle in his hande threshinge and thir written motto 'Now thus,' which they seye came by this occasion; that hee and other gentylmen opposing themselves against some Normans who came to invade them, thys Traford did them some horte and kept the passage against them. But that at length the Normans having passyd the ryver

came sodenly uppon hym, and then hee disguysing
hymselfe went into hys barne and was threshynge when
they enteryd, yet beyng knowen by some them and

Wᵐ. Trafford.
of Swithamley Esq:
died Dec: 10ᵗʰ 1697.
Aged 93.

demaunded why hee soe abased hymselfe, answeryd
'*Now thus.*'"

One of the descendants of this ancient family, T.
Trafford, of Trafford, appeared at a Preston Guild fancy

ball "wearing a singular tight dress of party-colours, white and red, with an old English ruff and flail, inscribed, in allusion to the family story, 'Now thus!'"— which dress elicited much admiration.

In John Speed's *History of England*, published in 1627, page 783, is the following statement:—"When afterwards King Henry set his affection upon the Lady Anne Bullen, a Phenix indeed in his Princely eye, and another Hester for Englands salvation, both in herself and royall Bud succeeding as the Heavens and World doe witnesse to this day. She was the daughter of Sir Thomas Bullen Viscount Rochford, Earle of Wiltshire, and Lady Elizabeth, daughter of Thomas Howard Duke of Norfolk. This Earle Thomas her Father was the sonne of Sir William Bullen, whose wife was Lady Margaret, the second daughter and coheire of Thomae Butler, Earle of Ormond, and the said Sir William was the sonne of Sir Godfrey Bullen Lord Mayor of London, who lyeth buryed in S. Laurence Church in the Jewry, pictured in his winding sheet upon a plate of Brasse, and about his gravestone upon a border of Brasse, in many places these words are written *Now thus, Now thus, Now thus,* whose charity was extended upon the poore Householders of that Citie, in distributing among them a thousand pounds. His Lady was Anne eldest daughter and coheire unto Thomas Lord Hoo and Hastings, and his discent out of the House of the Bullens, an ancient Family in the County of Norfolke, accursed therefore be the pen, that slanderously bringeth this Rose from a defiled Bed, whose Serpents mouth to uphold his God the Pope, hath spewed out his poison of untruths and made his tongue a sharpe sword against the Lords annointed. let him therefore receive his portion with the serpent of deceit, and his reward with Sathan the Father of Lyes."

From a consideration of the above extract from Speed, I think we may fairly infer there was some family connection between the Traffords and Bullens. In 1290 A.D., nearly 350 years before King Charles I.'s reign, when Speed's *History* was written, there was a family of Bolene possessing all Pownall, near Wilmslow —anciently called Le Bolyn—which they acquired by grant from the old Cheshire family of Fitton (see Earwaker's *East Cheshire*, vol. 1, page 45). The Traffords have for centuries past, and still have, an interest in Bollin fee (anciently "Le Bolyn"). Sir John Percival, Lord Mayor of London in Henry VII.'s time, the founder of the Macclesfield Grammar School, was born somewhere in the neighbourhood of Macclesfield, and he married Thomasine, a daughter of Sir Geoffrey Bullen, a descendant I believe of the Sir Geoffrey Bullen before mentioned. The surname of Bullen has been spelled a variety of ways—Bolene, Bolyn, Bullen, Bollin, etc. Although Speed says they were a Norfolk family, they may have migrated from Cheshire and taken their name from their Lordship Bolyn (see Earwaker's *East Cheshire*, vol. 2, page 513).

It is by no means improbable that a Trafford married a Bullen or *vice versa*, or that the "Bolene" or Bolyn who had the grant from Fitton was a Trafford and adopted the local name of Bolene from his manor, or the river, now Bollin, formerly Bolyn, otherwise how do we account for Sir Geofrey's motto, *Now thus?*

In Ormerod's *History of Cheshire*, by Helby, vol. 1, page 588, there is the following note on the subject of this Trafford Crest and the tradition respecting it :— " It is observable with respect to this story, which coincides with the vulgar tradition, that the Traffords were settled before the Conquest, in a situation resembling that here described ; and if extracts from 'the Blacke Booke of Trafford' may be credited, Rafe, son of Rafe Trafford, and Robert his Son, had a pardon and protection granted them by Hamon de Mascie, shortly after the Conquest, with the lands and body of one Wulfernote, a Saxon rebel.   Harl. MSS. 2077, p. 292.   Coupling these circumstances with the story above mentioned, it is not improbable that the crest may be founded on some faint tradition of a struggle with that portion of the Norman army which entered these parts under the Earl of Chester, who may be alluded to under the garb, the badge of his descendants ; but whatever the origin of the story may be, the crest was only regularly granted to the family by Laurence Dalton Norroy, about the middle of the sixteenth century.   See Flower's *Visitat Lancast.* 1567."

It may be remarked that we are not aware of any other family in England with a similar crest.   The old Yorkshire family of Pilkington (who have recently married into the old Staffordshire family of Swinnerton, formerly of Butterton Hall, near Newcastle) have for a crest a husbandman with a scythe and the motto *Now thus, Now thus.*   The tradition respecting it is given as follows in Burke's *Landed Gentry :—* In *Fuller's Worthies,* the family of Pilkington is spoken of as a right ancient family, gentlemen of repute in the county of Lancaster

before the Conquest, and also by Gwillim in his *Heraldry*
as a knightly family of great antiquity, taking name from
Pilkington, in Lancashire. At the battle of Hastings,
Leonard Pilkington, lord of Pilkington Tower (the
mounds of the castle still existing denote the site) had
a command under Harold, on whose defeat at Hastings
he fled from the field of battle, and when hotly pur-
sued, put on the clothes of a mower, and so escaped.
From this circumstance he took his crest—" A mower,
of parti-colours, *gu.* and *arg.*" He subsequently joined
the Crusades in 1106, and assumed the arms still borne
by his descendants—A cross, patonce, voided, *gu.* The
crest. A mower, with his scythe in front, habited as
follows :—A high-crowned hat with flap, the crown, party
per pale, flap the same—counter changed, coat buttoned
to the middle, with his scythe in bend, *ppr.* habited
throughout quarterly and counter-changed, *arg.* and *gules.*
Motto—" *Pilkyngton Pailedowne*," " *The master mows the
meadows*," and over the crest, " *Now thus, now thus.*"

THOMAS COOPER, of Congleton.

1663, Apl. 2. William Trafford de Swythernley,
esq : æt 47 was shot (?) at ye beginning of the Warres.
Did oppose Captn. Venables of Leeke for beating up
a Drum for ye Parlt. and ye Drummer's name was
Samuel Endon of Rudyerd. *Huntbach*, 1. 55.

O'er Macclesfield forest old Reynard did fly,
By Tragnell and Runcorn and unto Langly ;
By Shalcross and Greswark and unto Swythamly :
At his brush close did follow the hounds in full cry.
Squire Frith of Bank Hall.

History of Printing.

HE oldest printer of whom any trace can be found was a Francis Hilliard, who appears to have left Bristol and settled in Leek about 1760. He commenced business in the shop at the corner of Derby Street and Market Place, in which, earlier in the century, Michael Johnson, father of the great lexicographer, served his apprenticeship to Joseph Needham, a bookseller. Hilliard brought with him a rather limited selection of type, including a series of heavy Roman founts, some of which continued in use until they came into the possession of Mr. Thomas Grace in 1888, when they were sent to a type foundry to be re-cast into more modern characters. The press he used was of a very primitive type even for those days, and was far behind the one used by Caxton two centuries before, when he immortalised Westminster Abbey by practising printing in its almonry. The machine was worked by a windlass, and it was only possible to take fifty impressions an hour. With more or less success, the father of Leek printers stayed at the historical shop for some time, and then migrated to Scolding Bank, a narrow passage between Overton's Bank and the Fields. At this time he was parish clerk, and filled up his time with bookbinding, paper-hanging, and bill-posting. Then William Michael, his son, appeared on the scene, and about 1820 the firm became Hilliard and Son, and in 1834 the son took sole possession. The distinct lines which now separate one business from another did not then exist, and in addition to printing, bookbinding, bookselling, paper-hanging, bill-posting, and quack medicine vending, William Michael was an auctioneer. An old printer, formerly in his employ, told the writer twenty-five years ago that he had frequently set up the type for a bill, printed the required number, posted them on the walls, and on the day of sale held the goods up whilst his master described and sold them. A good all-round man truly.

The Hilliards kept the field until the advent in 1828 of Mr. George Nall, from Bakewell, who set up his press first in Spout Street and then in the Sheep Market, where he introduced copperplate printing. Prior to coming to Leek, Mr. Nall was in partnership at Derby with Mr. Bemrose, and, therefore, may be said to have assisted at the founding of the large business now carried on in that town and London by the present firm of Messrs. Bemrose and Sons. In this connection it may be of interest to state that Mr. Nall's son printed the first edition (1862) of Mr. John Sleigh's *History of Leek*, and Mr. Bemrose's sons the second edition (1883).

Then followed Mr. Edward Hallowes (who served his indenture with Mr. Nall and is still in business in

Stockwell Street), James Rider (also a former apprentice), George Nall and Son, Robert Nall, and William Clemesha. Since 1865, when the last-named came to the town, printers have increased proportionately faster than the population, with the result that competition is keen as compared with the "good old times" when the art was comparatively unknown in country towns and its professors were few.

The first printing machine of modern make was brought to Leek about 1866 by Mr. William Clemesha, soon after he had purchased, in 1865, the Custard Street business from Mr. Robert Nall, who went to Natal in search of health and found a grave. The motive power was hand labour, and 500 an hour was considered fast work. Now there are about a dozen machines in the town, driven by steam or gas, and averaging upwards of 1,000 per hour.

The Lay of a Moorland Minstrel.

T is not an unusual circumstance now-a-days to find the Leek Commissioners brought to book for their sins of omission or commission, but this is done respectfully and with due regard to the proprieties. Thirty years ago, however, there was a rough outspokenness on the part of their critics that would scarcely be appreciated now, and when the newly-fledged legislators, born of the Act of 1855, began to regulate the markets and fairs a misguided agricultural "poet" eased his mind and startled his friends by writing the following lines :—

There's an ancient town existing between Morridge and
    Mop Cop,
And when the coaches they did run, in it they used
    to stop.
The town was then conducted by men of ancient skill,
They never asked for Parliament to bring them in a
    bill.
One constable good order kept, no other Act did pass,
But now his place it is filled up with mules and a
    jackass.
The fairs were then held in the town ; each one did
    stand at ease ;
There were no rogues to lock them up, each other did
    they please.
The farmers took their horses there and showed them
    in the street,

And foreign dealers they did come, those farmers for
   to meet ;
A brisk and lively trade went on—they freely bought
   and sold—
And then each other's health they drank, while they
   bag'd up their gold.
There was no nuisance in that town—each street was
   free and clear ;
No one did stop the farmers then, nor ask what they
   did there.
But now those happy days are gone, those ancient men
   are dust,
And some that now sit at the Board, are men we
   cannot trust—
No honest deed they ever do—no good in them you'd
   find—
For five they are shortsighted, and six of them are
   blind—
But nine of them are honest men, they see their way
   quite clear ;
So there's more rogues then, than honest men—you'll
   find them everywhere.
The farmers do that town support with bread and beef
   and beer :
What would those fops and blind men do, if farmers
   went not there ?
And yet their lives they would them take—just for a
   little gain—
They have not gotten common sense—because they
   have no brain.
The greatest nuisance there can be at each street end
   doth stand,
Who does on fair and market days the farmer's brass
   demand,
And if he does not give them all on him they will lay
   hold
And serve him with a summons then and take from
   him his gold.
They will not stick at little things—its true what I
   declare—
They'll take the book in their right hands, all but the
   truth they'll swear.

If a farmer takes his horses there and trots them
  through the street,
That stinking nuisance he will see, some rogue he's
  sure to meet ;
He'll swear he offers it for sale—if not one word is
  spoke—
He's not afraid to swear a lie, unless one should him
  choke.
A farmer's life's in danger now, when he to that town
  does go—
They'll force him in a pig-yard his horses for to show.
They say they have a Smithfield, but I say that's a lie,
Its nothing but a pig yard a bit bigger than a sty.
I have a horse on sale myself, but there I'll never go,
I'll never mix with mule and ass, no horse with them
  I'll show.
If farmers now would all unite and all be of one mind,
A first-rate place to hold a fair, for them I soon would
  find ;
If they would all be of one heart and from that town
  would keep,
And take their horses all elsewhere, likewise their cows
  and sheep—
Their board would soon be very bare, they'd have but
  little meat ;
If farmers they would keep away, each other they might
  eat.
So now I challenge all that Board and all their learned
  men
If any can me contradict, let him take up his pen ;
And if he does write back in rhyme, he'll have to use
  his brain,
And then I'll show him how its done—I'll soon write
  back again.

A Leek Poet.

I N 1820 a weekly periodical, entitled "The Bookworm, a Literary Journal of Staffordshire," made its appearance, but, alas, only lived a quarter of a year. It was published at Stafford, and a volume in boards, with a title page and editor's address, afterwards sold. This is now very rare. One reason attributed to its non-success was the "great depression, especially among the mercantile and manufacturing classes." The contents were chiefly made up of reviews of new books, papers on chemistry, selections, correspondence, anecdotes, and original poetry. Under the latter head, in No. 7, appears a poem called "The Farewell," by "C., Leek," whom we hope in time, the great healer, found a solace for his pain.

> Too lovely Lady, fare thee well !
>   But deign to give, e'er yet we sever,
> Some token in my breast to dwell,
>   Some trifle—then adieu for ever !
>
> Yet think not that I e'er can need
>   Aught to remind my soul of thee ;
> In mem'ry's page I still shall read
>   Thy charms, alas ! too well for me.
>
> But 'tis a sweet, a soothing duty,
>   When ev'ning sleeps, and none are near ;
> On the dear gift of absent beauty
>   To breathe a sigh, to drop a tear.
>
> Then oh ! let this my solace be,
>   A solace easy to impart—
> One lock of hair will serve for me :
>   With thee I leave a broken heart.

Old Water Mills.

ENRY 8: 30 ° and 31 °. Account of John Foxe, bailiff of town of Leke:—Rents of Customary tenants £15 12 10, with 61s/1 from lands and tents. in Mylne-strete. Two water mills etc. Edwd. Fitton, Knt: dep. steward or lordship of Leke. Edward earl of Derby, chief-steward (another account of Mich. Wentworth, "farmer and collector of rents there.") *Exchequer, Ministers' accts. no.* 137 *and* 5. *p.* 56.

> His knaves thro' our forest Ralph Kingsley dispersed :
> Bow-bearer in chief to Earl Randal the first.
>
> Old Tarporley Hunting Song.

14 °. Eliz : Trinity-term. Whereas the tenants of Leke and Delacras *(sic)* and rectory of Leke exhibited their bill of complaint, shewing that sir Ralph Bagnall is *seized thereof etc.* That the Crown reserved to itself a yearly rent of £105 11 7½, now in arrear £446 3 9, which we ought to have paid ; nevertheless they are summoned to this Court to pay said debt. That sir Ralph had conveyed divers lands to his brother sir Nicholas. Plaintiffs pray that these lands might be extended and seized into the Queen's hands, and that they might have them in lease till they have levied

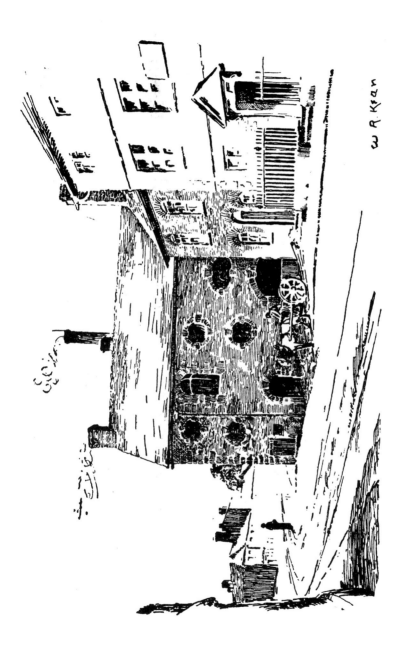

the said debt—Ordered that a Commission shall be
awarded. *Ex. Decrees and orders* 4, *pp.* 200, 9, 10, 74,
etc.

10 ° C 1. Thos : Ruddiard of Rudyerd, esquier,
v Charles Randle Ashenhurst of Ashenhurst, esquier,
Two water corn mills in manor of Leeke and in
Dewlincres *(sic)* granted by Ed. 6. to sir Ralph Bagenhall
at a fee-farm rent ; and by B. to Ralph R—plaintiff's
father—Tenants and inhts. of Leeke ought to grind
their corn &c at sd. mills, paying 16th pt. thereof and
no person ought to erect any other mill there ; but
Defendant has erected a horse mill, &c. *Ex. bills and
answers, no.* 70.

The Church Missionary Association.

THE Leek Ladies' Church Missionary Branch Associa-
tion was founded in 1824, but from motives of economy
it was not until 1826 that a report was printed.
Branches at Longnor and Flash had become affiliated
to Leek, and, according to the report, the committee
could not "to the satisfaction of all parties, withhold,
at least, an occasional report." In 1826 the officials
of the branch were :—Treasurer, Mrs. Smith ; Secretary,
Miss H. Cruso ; Committee, Mrs. Turner, Miss Boothe,
Miss Carr, Mrs. Place, Miss Smith, Misses Turner, and
Miss Walwyn.

In 1824 the sum remitted to London was £50 ;
1825, £57 2s. 6d. ; 1826, £76 6s. 3d.

A Notable Incident.

JEAN Baptiste Françoise Mien, a resident in Leek for nearly 70 years, was taken prisoner at St. Domingo in 1803, together with his master, General Brunet. With a number of others he was interned at Leek on October 3rd, 1804, and married and settled down. During the famine which aggravated the horrors of the French Revolution, his parents, who had lived at Ris, a village on the road to Fontainebleu, managed to conceal a quantity of flour in wine casks stowed away in their cellars; and young Mein, though then only seven years old, was often employed in carrying by night a large loaf to his mother's brother, a M. Carrière, who lived in Paris, some fifteen miles distant. It was on one of these occasions that, mounted on his uncle's left shoulder, he was taken to see the King's execution in the Place Louis XV., on the 21st January, 1793. He has (says "Notes and Queries") a lively recollection of the awful scene, and graphically describes how that when the unhappy monarch wished to make an " oration " to the dense mob surrounding the scaffold, the inhuman drum-major raised his staff of office as a signal for the drums to beat, and amid the deafening *roulement* the knife fell.   His mother, a midwife, from her freedom of speech or some other cause, became obnoxious to the government, and was consigned during the Reign of Terror to the conciergerie. Our friend perfectly well remembers going with his father to see her in prison, and thence, as he alleges, before Robespierre at his own house, "somewhere between the Rue Rivoli and the Rue St. Honore," where the Dictator, whom he describes as a fine-looking man, sat at a long table. This worthy lady had a "desperate tongue," and being somewhat of a politician managed to convince Robespierre that her life was necessary to the State, and was consequently allowed to return home in peace with her husband and child. But one of the moving causes he conceives, of the arbiter's unwonted clemency was the boy's presence, since during the whole of the interview he never ceased stroking his (the child's) head, muttering to himself, "Pauvre petit garçon; pauvre petit garçon!" Strangely enough, Mien's first visit to Paris after his imprisonment was in 1814, when the re-interment of Louis XVI, and Marie Antoinnette was taking place at St. Denis, after the remains had been dug up in the garden of Descloseux, where, as he affirms, the skull of the King was found placed between the legs of the skeleton.

Our hero died at Leek, on July 15th, 1870, aged 83 years and 11 months.

Stanlowe Hall.

YOU could hardly have a nicer walk than that from Leek to Stanlowe; or, if you be a bit of a cripple, from Wall Grange station up Ladderedge to the old hall at the top. Stanlowe lies just beyond the smithy at Ladderedge. There is an old pool near the gate, and an almost forsaken drive runs up from the high road opposite the end of the road leading up from Wall Grange station. You see the dark front of the hall from the highway, and as you mount up the drive, a steep one, you notice first of all, the lowe on the left which gives the place its name. At the top of it, a field away from the drive, is a curious erection consisting of three flights of rough unmortared stone stairs leading to one point. Mount them and a glorious view towards Endon on the one hand and Cheddleton on the other spreads out before you. From these two points the old family long associated and still connected with Stanlowe Hall seem to have come. From Endon the Bulkeleys (or Bull-cloughs), from Cheddleton an heiress of the Sherrards, the great people of that place, joining together in a marriage between Bulkeley and the Stanlow produced the race

who built the old hall behind you.   The three arms
of the stone erection on which you stand point to these
several quarters, Endon, Cheddleton, and Stanlowe, as if
expressive of the union of the three ancient races once
living hereabouts.

How fine the old hall behind you looks, seen
through its surrounding trees ! But first notice the lowe
or grave-hill, on which you stand. See how the ground
seems to have been built up of big stones, doubtless
covering the skeletons of some notable Saxons of ancient
days, and showing the origin of the name—Stonelowe—
the grave among the stones.

One lingers as long as the rude wind will let one
before turning towards the house, the views are so tempt-
ing.   But the attractions of an old Elizabethan house
are strong ; and as one's friend discourses of the terrible
fight between an old Bullclough and a Lockwood, which
took place by the road-side at the top of Ladderedge in
the Wars of the Roses, before, however, the Bullcloughs
came to Stanlowe, we saunter towards the hall.

Modern farm buildings somewhat disfigure the foreground, but one does not look at them, for now from
the stile, the house is well in view.   It has a double
gable, joined by a battlemented curtained wall, behind
which stood men-at-arms in troublous times to defend
the narrow entrance between those high walls which protect the front.   An inscription tells you that the house
has been "restored ;" that is, we suppose, that the vile
wing on the left, which looks as if it had been imported
from Warslow or Longnor, was then added.   But beware
of the dog which springs out of a horse-block by the
imposing gate posts which lend dignity to the approach

to the front door. Look there to the right. That gable has had some time a noble bay window; and on the left what an elegant series of small square mullioned lights lit the hall place within! How noble, too, is the doorway! But shut your eyes to the inscription of 1866 above it, and see only the house as it was left by Cromwellian owners. Except for "restoration" it seems almost unchanged. It must have been built by the first Bulkeley who settled at Stanlowe, and in the days when England seemed to break forth into new life and vigour under grand Queen Bess.

The house has long been occupied by a tenant farmer; but never lady of high degree in old time could be more courteous or kindly than its present mistress. She shews us the hall, now divided by wainscote into several rooms; the kitchen to the right; the parlour, an old room in a new (and bad) external setting, with a fine oak mantelpiece; the stairs leading up to large chambers above; the cellar, now full of water; the draw-well, 92 feet deep; the bowling green at the back (rather a rolling green, however, from its inclination), and a curious narrow little dungeon in the back wall of the house. But we must not linger, for our hostess is a busy housewife, and it is harvest time; so with a hasty glance round the high walled garden, we take leave.

The following extracts from the Leek Old Church register may be of interest:—

1667—Buried Lady Bulkeley of Stanlow.

1671—Sampson Bulkeley gave 8d. towards a collection for the rescue of the English taken slaves by the Turks.

1675—Buried Thomas Bulkeley of Stanlow, gent., Aug. 21.
    Aug. 16th.   John Bulkeley of Stanlow and
    Elizabeth Webb of Stone, where there married.

1677—Baptised Thomas their son.

1702—Thomas Sleigh of Leek, gent, married to Sarah
    Bulkeley at Rocester by Vicar of Leek.   (*Query :*
    A runaway match).

                                —BLACK BEAR.

THE LEEK VASE.   *(See page 95)*.

An Ancient Quarrel.

OLUME number 10 of the William Salt Society, throws strong light on the history of the Moorlands in the reign of Edward II. It may be known to some few of our readers that a quarrel broke out in 1275 between the great and little landowners of the Moorlands, in which the Abbot of Dieu-la-Cresse and the lord of Alton on the one side were ranged against the combined gentry of the hills on the other. The Abbot seems to have taken an illegal toll of persons passing through his lands. This offended Rudyerd of Rudyerd on the north, Beresford of Beresford (who seems to have had great forest rights in Malbonck forest on the top and east of Morridge), Meverell of Throwley, Okeover of Okeover towards Ashbourne, and, above all, Cheddleton of Cheddleton on the south. The latter, who, by the bye, was trying to get back the advowson of Cheddleton from the Abbey, seems to have been especially aggrieved, for, as the publication says:—"The jury states that William de Chetelton, William Shirard (Scarratt), Richard and Thomas his brothers, William de Butley, Thomas son of Ralph de Rudyerd and John his brother, are common malefactors and disturbers of the peace, and that near the feast of St. Margaret, 17

E.II. (1324) they had beaten William Maunche, the
servant of the Abbot of Deulacres, at Lek (Leek).
And the Sheriff was ordered to attach them. Afterwards the said William de Chetelton made fine for that
as well as for the other transgressions as appears below,
&c. And John de Rudyerd afterward appeared and
made fine with the King for two marks, for which
Adam de Beresford, Ralph Burghiloun, William Beresford, and Richard del Boure were sureties and stood
bail also for his good behaviour."

The fact that William Beresford lived at Broncote
near Upperhulme on the edge of his father's forest,
and that Tittesworth anciently belonged to the Rudyerds,
may shew that the present quarrel between Rudyerd and
Dieu-la-Cresse was as to a right of way between Rudyerd and Tittesworth.

This, however, was neither the first nor the second
quarrel of the series. Half a century the ill-feeling had
gone on ; and, three years before, " The jury presented
that William de Chetelton, the Lord of Chetelton, is a
common malefactor and disturber of the peace, and a
maintainer of false quarrels, and that he collected unknown malefactors, and rode armed about the country
to the terror of the people, and that he was of the
society of the said James and John sons of William
de Stafford, and had insulted the Abbot of Deulacres
at Deulacres in 1321, so that the Abbot dare not leave
the doors of the abbey. And the jury of Totmonslow
presented that the said W. de Chetilton, Nicholas de
Longford, Knight, John de Twyford, Knight, with others
unknown, in the month of August, 1323, entered the
park of Thomas de Furnival of Alton and took one

of his beasts. The Sheriff was therefore ordered to attach them ; and Vivian de Staunton, William de Chetwynde, Vivian de Chetwynde, John de Ipstones, James son of William de Stafforde and Adam de Beresford afterwards came forward and made fine for the said William de Chetilton at £20, and stood bail for his good behaviour in future under pain of forfeiture of all things that could be forfeited to the King."

The same year the lord of Alton is arraigned for the misconduct of his troopers. He kept them, he said, to help the King, and they had only stolen sixteen pigs from Meverell of Throwley and corn from others because they were hungry.

The record, which chiefly details the exploits of young men,—their elders appearing only to bail them off—throws a strong light on the condition of the country when the Abbey was standing and when Cheddleton Hall frowned over the road from beside the church. Clearly, since this part of the country was against Furnival, it was also, at least passively, against King Edward II. It was, in short, even then beginning to espouse the Lancastrian cause, and to array itself on the side which was afterwards known by a Red Rose. —Black Bear.

The Last Steward of Dieulacresse.

N illustration of the way in which the Reformation corrected the ideas of Englishmen, and brought them back again to what they had been in the earlier ages of the Church of England, is supplied by the old wills which are treasured up in the Probate Court at Lichfield. We give extracts from two, that of William Damport, or Davenport, the last steward of Leek Abbey, and that of another person living in Derbyshire; both are specimens of their time.

In 1552, William Davenport of the Frith, in the county of Stafford, bequeaths his "soul to the Lord God, and ladye S. Marie, and all the holie companie of heaven, and his bodie to be buryed, if it might be, in the Church of Leke." In the other will, made in 1596, the testator "renders his soule into the handes of Almightie God, my onely maker and redeemer, trusting to be saved onely by the meritte of Jesus Christ my onely Saviour; and my bodie to be buried at the discretion of my executors. Such worldly goods as it hath pleased Almightie God in His goodness to bestow upon me, I give and bequeath," &c.

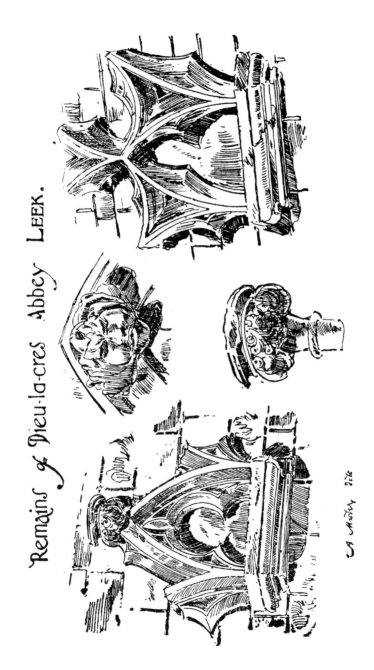

Remains of Dieu-la-cres Abbey   LEEK.

These extracts shew that the Reformation was not
a changing but a strengthening and purifying of the
church and people of England.

William Davenport's will is very hard to read.
We looked with much curiosity to see whether he had
secured to his own use any of the plate of the
Abbey. There was in it a word which looked much
like "Gold" something or other, but it proved to be
simply "holde shepe." His brass and pewter were
worth only 3s.; and his total fortune, with the exception of a cottage or two and a few bits of land,
amounted to xx*l.* viii*s.* vi*d.*; so that, like most poor
men of the time, he got very little out of the con-
fiscation of the Abbey property, which made rich men
—for a time—richer still.

THE ABBEY GROUNDS.

On this fair plane tradition says,
A structure stood in ancient days,
Whose walls immense and lantern'd brow,
Smil'd over all the vale below;
In cells immur'd full often here,
The good have uttered many a prayer,
And here the sad devoted monk,
Has under dismal penance sunk,
By sheer devotion sternly driven
Thus to befit himself for heaven.
How many beads have here been told,
By strangers shelter'd from the cold;
I think I see the pilgrim kneel
In prayer before his evening meal.
I think I see the incense rise,
When offering holy sacrifice.
From here no more soft music floats;
All 's hushed, except the ring-dove's notes.

Only one crumbling column stands
Left by the greedy spoiler's hands—
The only vestige that remains
Upon the consecrated plains.
And simply by the name alone
Of "Dieulacres" the spot is known.

The "Mayor" of Leek.

AMONGST the archives of Messrs. Challinors and Shaw, there was recently found the following quaint invitation :—

[COPY.]

Sir,—Haveing the Honour to be Mayor of Leek I shall have my ffeast at the Cock on Tuesday the 2d. day of Janry next Where I hope for the favour of your Company to Dine—Am Sir

Yr very hble Servt.

JNO. SNEYD.

Bishton 16th Decr. 1758.

Probably the Venison Feast, now merged into the Commissioners' banquet, was a survival of the "Mayor's" feast referred to in this old note of invitation. In many places "mock corporations" are still in existence, and a few years ago a partially successful effort was made to revive the ancient custom in Leek. Mr. R. S. Milner was the first "mayor," and Mr. T. H. Bishton was appointed "recorder."

The Cock referred to, was an old inn now converted into the shops occupied by Mr. S. Howes, Mr. M. Carding, and Mr. N. Gosling.

"Alienation" of Town Lands.

FROM the extracts here given from a report published in 1849, it would appear that in the first half of the present century something like criminal negligence characterised the management of the land and houses belonging to the freeholders of Leek. The report is the work of James Alsop, Joshua Brough, Charles Carr, William Challinor, Nathan Davenport, and Robert Hammersley, and is characterised by not a little straightforward speaking, albeit the term "alienated" is rather euphemistical.

The messuages, lands, and tenements commonly called the Leek Town Lands, forming the subject of this report, are situate in Back-o'-th'-Street [Belle Vue], Kiln Lane, Nab Hill, Westwood Heath, Woodcroft Heath, and Leek Moor. Unfortunately, of the time when this property (the allotment on Leek Moor of course excepted), fell into the hands of the freeholders, and by what means it was acquired, no record has been preserved. In, or about, the year 1720, an attempt was made, apparently by two of the principal tenants, to seize upon part of the lands; and to defend and secure the rights of the freeholders, recourse was had to legal proceedings.   If the evidence on which this defence was founded could be recovered (and not impossibly it still somewhere exists in a documentary form) much light would probably be thrown on the earlier history of the connection.   In a lease, dated 1724, this property is stated to have been in the possession of the freeholders "from the time beyond memory."   Its earliest written records to which your committee have had access, are contained in the "Leek Freeholders' Account Book," an interesting and well preserved old volume wherein the accounts are kept, and meagre notices occur of the annual or occasional meetings of the freeholders and trustees from 1711 to 1845.

The principal items of expenditure are these : for highways, paving, and soughing, £2,154 18s. 7d. ; suit for defence of the title of the freeholders, £58 14s. 6d. ; other law charges, £337 12s. 9d. ; purchase of land, etc., etc., for widening streets, £205 4s. 4d. ; "Market House and Lock-up," [Old Town Hall] £808 17s. 5½d. ; land at the bottom of Derby Street, and alterations, now used as a Cattle Market, £343 19s. 3d. ; fire engine, repairs of, etc., £119 11s. 3d. ; repairs of the organ in the Parish Church, and part salary of the organist, £353 1s. 0d. ; charges on the allotment, Leek Moor, £63 5s. 9d. ; compensation to tenants for improvements, £121 0s. 0d. ; beadle, salary, and clothing, £76 3s. 1d. ; property tax, £41 14s. 0d. ; repairs, £70 14s. 9d. ; receiver of rents, £63 10s. 0d.   The more early meetings of the freeholders to audit the accounts were evidently very agreeable re-unions : and after paying for "cleaning the spout," or putting up

"Miln Gates," or other small matters it would take a local antiquary fully to explain, and then handing over the lion's share of the rents to the "Supravisors of the Highways," or to "Thomas Hollinshead, Esq., for money laid out in the defence of the premises," some half-crown or four-and-sixpence, it may be, would be found left to be spent for the good of the house, and for the refreshing and bracing up to its proper tone of the public spirit of the assembled freeholders: the Green Dragon [the Swan], it seems, was one of the houses patronized on these occasions.

The rent account is illustrative of the extraordinary rise in the value of land which took place during the last and early part of the present century. From 1711 to 1716, the rents of Woodcroft Heath and Westwood Heath respectively stood at 8s. and £1 6s. 8d. per annum. In 1723, they had advanced to £1, and £8; in 1778, to £12, and £20; and, on referring to the statement, it will be seen, that the former lot, from 1825 to 1830, brought in £31, and the latter, from 1821 to 1828, £56, annually. In 1711, and for some years subsequently, the total amount of the rents, was £2 15s 6d.; at the present time it is £99 19s.

The mode of distributing the funds arising from the Town Lands is, in great measure, discretionary with the freeholders, one condition being observed—that of promoting the public weal. In the lease already referred to, these funds are expressed as having been immemorially "imployed by the direction of the freeholders for the repair of the highwayes within the sd Town, or for some publick use tending to ye joynt benefitt of the sd freeholders." In the session of 1805,

an Act was passed for inclosing certain Commons and
Waste Lands "within the townships of Leek, Lowe,
Leek Frith, and Tittesworth, containing in the whole,
by estimation, three thousand acres, or thereabouts."

The trustees appointed under this Act were ordered
to meet on the 24th of June in each year to "settle"
the accounts. Then follows a list of the lands, etc.,
from which an income continued to be derived. From
this list it appears that the total acreage was 34a. or. 26p.
and the rental £90 19s. od. After stating that the
balance in hand in June was £122 9s. 11d., the
committee state that "they regret exceedingly to an-
nounce that in the course of their enquiries they have
ascertained that a large portion—nearly *one-fourth*—
of the Town Lands has become alienated." Then
follows a list of the "lots of which the freeholders
have been deprived." The chief causes of deprivation
are given as "No rent paid since 1819." The "alienated" property included about forty houses in Belle Vue,
together with six acres of gardens and fields, including
two acres at Nab Hill. "To this total," the committee
report, "must be added four acres more of Nab
Hill, which were lost long previously, making the
superficial extent of the loss sustained by the freeholders
altogether to exceed *ten acres*." The committee then
remark :—" Much blame is laid on, and is unquestionably
due to, the late receiver of rents; but he is not the
only party who is fairly open to censure. Unmistakeable
indications of great negligence are manifest at an earlier
period than that of his appointment to office. The
committee have met with a memorandum (1801) inti-
mating that "the small rents have been usually collected

once in three or four years;" and to the great irregu-
larity thus incidentally noticed, they mainly ascribe the
loss of so many of the small tenements, and the
pecuniary sacrifices at which others of them have been
retained. Attempts have been made to recover part
of this property, but without success. With respect to
the Nab Hill, there is, to say the least, much of
mystery connected with its disappearance. Two-thirds
of this field of six acres have long ceased to form
part of the Town Lands; but at what time this took
place, or under what circumstances, the committee have,
as yet, been unable to make out. If it be enquired
by what means can loss be prevented in future; your
committee reply, that in their opinion the remedy is
simple and easy of application. For trustees, let men
be chosen who would regard their office as something
more than an honorary distinction; such as would
take the pains to make themselves acquainted with
their duty, and be ready, in case of emergency, to act
with decision. For this end, also, the committee suggest
for consideration, the expediency of circulating among
the freeholders a plan and descriptive sketch of the
property, as they believe there are few persons in that
body to whom its extent and locality are known. But
the best and surest means of prevention may be found
in the freeholders themselves. Let them not begrudge
a few minutes a year in attendance at the general
meeting; let them exert an intelligent, though not
captious or ungenerous, vigilance over the proceedings
of the executive, and an effectual check will be put
upon further waste. It is a mortifying reflection, that
for want of a little public spirit, the freeholders of

Leek have incurred the loss of a property—it is to be feared irrecoverably,—which, at a moderate rental, and without the charge of a penny for the buildings standing thereon, would bring in at least from £30 to £40 annually towards the improvement of the town."

Leek's only Gentleman.

ILLIAM CONDLYFFE, who died on March 9th, 1867, aged 70, claimed to be the " only gentleman " in the town, and if the possession of singularly eccentric manners and the wearing of garments of an old-time type were necessary to make his title clear, few would be disposed to question his right to the self-claimed distinction. Certainly he was the last male member of a distinguished family, and as he died a bachelor and his sisters are dead, the family is now extinct and lives only in the names of the Alms-houses near the Cemetery. He never loved the Commissioners, and he never missed an opportunity of expressing in forcible Saxon the opinion that that august body did not contain a single gentleman of noble extraction or rank to give either substance or solidity to their accidental importance. Referring to the rates laid in 1855 he termed them " impositions levied on the town by a set of new sprung tyrants." He held them, indeed, in great contempt, and his remains were interred in Meerbrook churchyard, outside their jurisdiction.

Writing to his son on the 9th of June, 1783, the grandfather of the subject of our sketch, in sending a remittance of five guineas, said " I hope you will be as careful as may be and beg you will be frugal and diligent in your business, for cash is very scarce here and people can hardly get a common maintenance even on oatmeal, for that is our usual daily bread. We pay for it eighteen-pence per peck. Butter is 8d. or 9d. a pound, and every other kind of eatables accordingly."

The First Sunday School.

HE Leek Methodist Sunday School was commenced in 1797 in Mount Pleasant Chapel,
and was mainly originated by Charles Ball.
The Scholars numbered 40, but in a short time they
rose to 300, and in 1835 numbered 1,029, inclusive
of 43 at Bradnop. The first teachers were Charles
Ball, William Hammersley, William Gibson, Samuel Joul,
William Vigrass, William Goodwin, James Wardle, and
Joseph Heywood.

The first anniversary sermon was preached on
December 15th, 1799, by Mr. Jeremiah Brettle, the
following hymns being sung by the school children :—
" Hymn to be sung at coming into the chapel ' Great
God to thee our hearts we raise'; a select piece to
be sung before sermon, 'Come let us join the host
above'; hymn to be sung before collection, ' Jesus,
great source of truth and grace'; hymn to be sung
after the collection, ' Parent of all we bless thy name.' "
(*Vide* circular printed by Hilliard.) The collection
realised £8, and a private subscription of £1 8s. was
also received. The disbursements amounted to £9 8s. 4d.,
inclusive of the following items : Preacher's expenses
from Macclesfield, 6s. ; balance due to treasurer, 4/2 ;

bad copper, 2/8; teaching children to sing, 10/6; and pens, ink, and paper, 19/6.

From 1801 to 1812 the anniversary sermons were preached in the Parish Church, by the Rev. Richard Bentley, vicar, except in the first-mentioned year, when the preacher was the Rev. — Horne. The vicar was a very kind friend to the school, and would have done anything for its general good. No time was wrong for him to preach. He used to say: "Well, Mr. Cutting, you know what to do if you cannot get a preacher: have the old one." In those days there was a strong feeling of opposition to the school, and several ministers consented to preach and afterwards declined to do so. The last time the sermon was preached in the Parish Church was in 1812, and from that time to the present the sermons have been preached under Wesleyan auspices. Mr. Richard Cutting was superintendent from 1808 until his death in 1856, and Mr. James Wardle was treasurer from 1808 until 1862, when he died. The first Church Sunday School was established in 1813.

It may be interesting to note that the disbursements in the year ending 1888, in connection with the four Wesleyan Sunday Schools now existing, amounted to considerably over £500. The Wesleyans have also Sunday schools at Flash, Gradbach, Newstone, Calton, Winkhill, Danebridge, Rushton, Gratton, Endon, Ladderedge, Cheddleton, Wetley Rocks, Bradnop, Upperhulme, Harper's Gate, and Fernyhill.

Iband=loom Uleaving.

N January 1st, 1839, Mr. Joseph Fletcher, secretary to the Hand-loom Inquiry Commission, held an inquiry into the condition of the hand-loom weavers of Leek, and from a blue-book (kindly placed at our disposal by Mr. William Allen) we are able to give extracts from the interesting report and evidence :—

Leek, which contains about 5,000 inhabitants, has long been the seat of the manufacture of broad silks of the best quality, and of plain ribbons by hand ; upon the latter of which the manufacture by power has gradually encroached. There are yet about 150 broad-looms and 180 engine-looms in the town ; but only half of the former and a third of the latter are now fully employed. About thirty of the broad looms have the jacquard machinery attached ; but the small figures are produced by the alternate pressure of a number of treadles. The ribbon looms are employed chiefly in making plain black sarcenets, and scarcely any satins.

Steam-power, however, has taken both the work and the workmen from this department, and now makes all the galloons. The number of steam engine looms is about 100. Those of

Messrs.	Carr	...	...	...	...	... 20
,,	Glendinning and Gaunt...		...			10
,,	Worthington ...		...	...		... 10
,,	Wreford ...		...	...	...	50
,,	Ward ...		...	...	...	... 10

100

There are no power-looms making broad silks, though some are being erected. The power-weaving of ribbons, ferrets, and galloons, in those looms, is part of the whole system of silk manufacture in the Leek factories, which embraces also the throwing and spinning of silk, and the twisting of it into sewing-silk, braids, etc.

The principal occupation of the hand-loom weavers is in the production of black, checked, or figured silk neck-handkerchiefs, and a few gros-de-naples and figured gown-pieces of the first quality; the best plain black ribbons, and silk serges of superior qualities. They manu-facture chiefly for the best home market, and all the principal employers conduct their business on the same principles; each firm throwing their own silk, weaving or twisting it, and disposing of their goods by their own agents to the retailer, or occasionally to the warehouse-man. All have their own style of business and their own country connection. The beautiful raven black, which the dyers of Leek alone can give (perhaps on account of the qualities of the Churnet water, which runs by the town), forms some bond upon the black ribbon trade; although these dyers work also for Manchester, London, etc. The sewing-silks, twists, and buttons, are alone designed for exportation, either by the manufacturers or through merchants.

The hand-loom work is given out to "undertakers" warped and round. They are owners of a varying number of looms, and employ journeymen and apprentices, to the former of whom they pay the warehouse price, after deducting for loom rent, etc. The hand ribbon looms yet employed are chiefly worked by the female members of the undertakers' families, the power-factories having taken all the journeymen away from them ; and there are no apprentices being brought up to this branch of the trade. Apprentices are taken into the broad trade, generally for seven years, commencing between the ages of eleven and fourteen.

The prices are all by the piece; handkerchiefs being paid for by the dozen, other broad silks by the yard, and ribbons by the piece of 36 yards. The following are the lists of Messrs. Ellis, Russell, and Co., from which those of other employers do not materially differ : —Black sarcenet ribbons—widths : 2, 7½d. ; 4, 9½d. ; 6, 11½d. ; 8, 1/1½ ; 11, 1/4 ; 12, 1/7 ; 14, 1/11 ; 16, 2/3 ; 18, 2/7 ; 20, 2/10 ; 24 and 30, 3/6 and 4/6 per piece of 36 yards. Plain black bandanas—32in., 5/- ; 34in., 5/6 ; 36in., 6/6 per dozen. Black Barcelonia, 3 threads—26in., 4/6 ; 28in., 4/6 ; 30in., 5/- ; 34in., 5/6 ; 36in., 6/6 ; 38in., 7/6 per dozen. Black Brussels, 4 threads—32in., 6/ ; 34in., 7/- ; 36in., 8/- ; 38in., 9/- per dozen. Fancy handkerchiefs—From 6/- per dozen to 16/- per dozen, varying according to quality and pattern.

The broad-silk weavers, in 1834, endeavoured to get a formal agreement among the masters to a list of prices, and several abortive strikes took place. The prices in the hand-engine loom have necessarily declined before the power competition, to the injury of the undertakers or first hands, but not of the journeyhand class, who are now working the power-looms themselves.

One of the principal masters supposes the nett weekly earnings of the power engine loom weavers to average 16/- per week, but the relieving officer of the union estimates it at much less. The hand engine loom trade is so disorganized by the withdrawal of all regular journeymen, that there are only the loom owner's own earnings and those of his family to be estimated. On 12 dys. of black sarcenets, the manufacturer above alluded to thinks about 11/- might be earned; or 10/6 if fire and light be deducted.

The earnings of the broad looms weekly, at the warehouse prices, are estimated by the same gentleman at about 25/- per week on handkerchiefs, and from 16/- to 18/- on figured goods; from which filling and fire and light have to be deducted. But the weavers whom I examined represent the average as much less.

There are about 40 undertakers in the broad trade; a considerable number of journeyhands; a few women, the wives of journeyhands; and a few apprentices. The undertakers appear to be a class superior in habits and condition to those of almost any other place; but those of the journeyhands are low; their wives are commonly piecers and doublers in the factories, wind for the sewing silk manufacturers, or are mill overlookers. They work commonly by the piece, but a woman's weekly wages are reckoned at 5/- to 5/6, except for doubling, which is very badly paid. The children early get employment in the factories, even at six or seven years of age; the silk mills being exempt from any limitation as to their age. Their wages increase from 1/- per week, when first admitted, up to 2/6 when about 13 years of age. Some are employed at quill-winding for the weavers.

The houses of the undertakers are many of them convenient and substantial buildings, consisting of four apartments on the ground and first floors, with workshop above. One of my witnesses pays £10 rent, 4/- street gas tax, 2/6 for highways, 12/- poor's rate, 9d. Easter dues, and 4d. church rate per annum, besides 6/8 water money. It is the journeyman class who are obviously more expressly the object of inquiry, on account of their poverty ; and of these the most important body is the steam factory weavers. The relieving officer testifies that, during the fifteen months that the union has been formed, he has had no weavers on his books except through sickness, and these were among the poor journey-men, who live perhaps in £5 cottages. They have generally had families, and, though their homes betokened great poverty, they were clean, as also were their persons and dress, and those of their children. The town is notable for its cleanliness.

Embezzlement of silk at the factories prevails to an enormous extent, and has lately much increased. Re-ceivers are readily found. There are, however, few dissolute people. The greater number not only send their children to Sunday schools, but go to places of worship themselves. Of the young men, many subscribe to the Mechanics' Institute, especially for the winter, while in summer they are generally busy at cricket.

Except a small endowed school there is no public day-school, and nearly all the instruction which the children receive is at the Sunday schools. In the Wesleyan Sunday schools there are upwards of 1,000 children.

The hand engine loom undertakers recommend a tax on machinery, and the broad loom weavers desire a repeal of the corn-laws.

The Old Workhouses.

THE old Workhouse, or House of Industry, in Brook Street, formerly called Workhouse Street, was erected in 1768, in lieu of the old one in Derby Street, which was converted into three dwellings. In 1834, the average number of paupers was 54 in the house, who were maintained and clothed at a cost of 3s. 6d. per head per week. The amount of poor rates collected in the year 1775 was £404; in 1790, £462; 1810, £1,353; 1820, £1,870; 1825, £1,647; 1830, £2,013; and in 1833, £2,274, but out of the latter sum £248 15s. was paid to the country rates. About ten rates of fourpence in the pound on buildings, and sixpence on land, were collected yearly; and the assessment was laid on about half the rack rental. In 1883 there were 1368 houses in the township, the number in 1811 being only 841.

Tokens and Half=pennies.

 URING the recent alterations at the Roe Buck Hotel, a workman found in the cellar a small coin about the size of a sixpence. Supposing it to be an old half-sovereign he showed it with some glee to his friends, and he was not a little disappointed to find that it was only a Leek token, which above two hundred years ago passed current in the town as a half-penny. The coin is rather rough in manufacture, is scarcely round, and very thin. On the obverse is "John Gent," with the grocer's arms, and on the reverse "In Leeke, his half-peny, I.G. 1666." In general appearance it resembles and is the same size as one shown to us by Mr. Richard Clowes, of Leek, which bears the date of 1670, and of which we give below a representation.

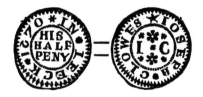

In Mr. Sleigh's "History of Leek," mention is made of a similar coin to the above and of the same date, but as having been issued by "Samuel Clowes;" and Boyne gives an account of a third issued in 1667 by "John Wood, in Leek, His halfe-peny."

Thanks to the courtesy of Professor Sheldon, C.C., and Chairman of the Leek Board of Guardians, we are able to give a *fac-simile* of a newly-discovered Leek token. The coin is of thin, highly tempered brass, and

is much corroded. So far as we have been able to gather the discovery is an important one, as in no local or county authority have we found any reference to a heart-shaped Leek half-penny.

In 1793, a commercial half-penny was issued, of which the following is a *fac-simile*; the inscription within the outer ring being shown upon the edge of the reverse :—

In the following year another was issued of quite a different pattern, and an exceedingly well-executed coin, as may be gathered from the following woodcut of the obverse:—

The reverses of the half-pennies of 1793-4 are the same, except that the inscription "Payable at Leek, Staffordshire," gives place to a cross-milled edge.

These coins, though generally welcomed as a means of readier exchange, were received by some with disfavour, whilst a few absolutely declined to accept them. Amongst the latter was Mr. John Fowler, of Horton Hall. Writing about the time the coins were issued, a rhyming silk manufacturer, who disapproved of Mr. Fowler's refusal, said :—

Pray, friend John! why set thy face
Against the coinage of this place,
It surely argues want of sense,
Because thou'st nought to do with pence.
Hannah sells, receives, and keeps the till :—
(All's cream and grist that goes to Hannah's mill ;
Potatoes, cabbage, and all sorts of trash
Are here converted into cash :—)
This good dame Hannah, as we suppose,
That leads poor Jacky by the nose !
Do all things, John, for good of trade,
Because thy bread and butter's made ; *
Cut and served up with heavy thumbs :—
So, eat thy loaf, and give Hannah th' crumbs.

* Mr. Fowler's father amassed a fortune, as a mercer, at Wolverhampton.

"Died to Live and Lived to Die."

NDER the north wall of the new portion of the Old Churchyard, lie the mortal remains of one James Trafford, who would appear to have been a dyer by trade if the above-quoted epigram has any claim to wit. The inscription, which is partly grass-grown over, runs as follows:—"In memory of James Trafford, who departed this life September 17, 1861, aged 56."

> A loving friend, a husband dear,
> A tender partner lieth here,
> Who died to live and lived to die
> In hopes of bliss and endless joy.

Eleven years previously, Trafford had buried his daughter Harriet, aged 16, and he seems to have found comfort and consolation in the following quatrain:—

> Refrain your tears and weep no more,
> Because your daughter is gone before;
> In love she lived, in peace she died—
> Her life was asked, but God denied.

In 1855, the death of his son George gave Trafford another chance of demonstrating what a dab hand he was at poetry of a grave character, for he makes the the young man, who died at the age of twenty-three, responsible for the following lugubrious farewell to the world:—

> Read this and weep, but not for me:
> My time was long in misery;
> My life was short—my grief the less,
> Blame not my haste to happiness.

Ballhaye Hall.

BALLHAYE HALL is a large stone mansion, the old seat of the Davenport family, its name being, like many others in the neighbourhood, of French origin, viz., *la Belle Haye* (the fair desmesne). I have before me a very interesting indenture of 6th February, 7 of Elizabeth, whereby Sir Ralph Bagnall, for considerations therein recited, grants to Henry Davenport in fee all that messuage or tenement with appertenances called Ballhaye, situated in the hamlet of Leek, Lowe, and Tettesworth, then in possession of the said Henry Davenport and others, with all lands, etc. —*testes* :—John Sneyd, Wm. and Thos. Smyth, John Hygynbotham, Wm. Ward, Nich. Montgomery.

Among others there is an interesting document extant relating to rent charges, etc., bearing the names of Christopher Hatton, the famous favourite of Queen Elizabeth, and Francis Needham, who then resided at Spout Hall, Leek. The Davenports above mentioned were a branch of the old Cheshire Davenport family, whose coat was surmounted by the honourable crest a thief's head in a halter, granted to them as rangers of

Macclesfield forest and shewing their right of execution of deer stealers. The present mansion was built about 100 years ago by Dr. Davenport Hulme, who inherited the estate from his uncle, with stone taken from the bed of the Dane brook.

Dr. Hulme married the widow of Samuel Unwin of Sutton-in-Ashfield, and afterwards, owing to family differences, the estate came into Chancery. In 1853, by an order of the Court, it was sold by auction and bought by Messrs. Joshua and John Brough, the representatives in the female line of the Davenports and Hulmes, and is at present in the possession of Mr. W. S. Brough.

The Park is beautifully situated, and still contains some very fine beeches, hornbeams, and flowering limes. There are four trees still standing on the high ground overlooking Foxlowe. It is related that eight others have disappeared from the same spot, and that the whole were known as the " twelve apostles." There is also an old story of a strongly chalybeate spring near the carriage road. From the Park there are fine views of the Roaches, and from the western windows of the Hall the sunset over Gun, seen across the lake, is a beautiful sight.

In the " Beauties of England and Wales," there is a very pretty drawing by J. P. Neale, engraved in steel by Schury, of the Hall and Park with the Roaches in the background. This is perhaps more interesting as Dr. Hulme in 1813 or thereabouts, planted the Hencloud, which was also his property. On still nights a very sweet and clear echo may be heard from the Hall when the bells of the Parish Church are rung.

Ball Haye
Hall

J.R.Keen

The road through the Park and the lodge were constructed in 1854, and the Parsonage of St. Luke's Church was built in 1856.

There is a very good etching of the Hall by Mackaness, in the series of plates published in 1885.

H. H. B.

BALLHAYE JACK.

The will of this historic and well remembered personage is sealed (as is his father's given below) with a large seal of arms quarterly. By it Mr. Davenport left directions for the due discharge of all his debts, and then to his wife £100; to Isaac Cope, of Leek, surgeon, £50; to Joseph Mellor, merchant, £50; and to Lucy, daughter of Isaac Cope, £50. All his real and personal estate he left to Isaac Cope and Joseph Mellor in trust to reduce the whole to one yearly income, half of which was to be paid to his widow, and one-fourth each to Lucy Cope, and to the education of his nephew, James, son of his sister Sarah Hulme, who was to finish his education at Cambridge rather than Oxford, and to assume the testator's name and arms. He desired to be buried in as quiet a manner as possible with his ancestors in Leek churchyard. The will is dated 1785, and witnessed by William Challinor, Thomas Phillips, and George Cope.

John Davenport, of Ballhaye, the elder, in 1782 left all to his wife Sarah for her life. Then the property was to pay a guinea to his son John and his son's John's wife, Hannah, to buy them rings. To Henry his son £20. To son James £20, and £20 to son John. To his daughter Sarah Hulme £20; to daughter Mary Pedley £20; to her son John £20; the rest to his wife. Sons Henry and James, executors. Sealed with a fine seal of arms quarterly. Signed with "the mark of John Davenport, he having through infirmity lost the use of his right hand so as to prevent his writing his name."

Leek in 1817.

IN 1817, Leek contained thirteen streets and lanes; three large inns and several ale-houses; two Sunday schools (Church and Methodist); 952 houses, containing 972 families; 2,023 males, 2,390 females—4,413. In addition to the Church, there were three other places of worship, for Calvinists, Quakers, and Methodists.

A Longnor Centenarian.

THE following is an extract from the deaths in the *Westminster Magazine* of 1780, and has reference doubtless to the great grandfather of Mr. Isaac Fidler, of Longnor :—" Near Buxton, Derbyshire, Samuel Fidler, aged 105. He walked from his own house to Buxton within three days of his death, which is upwards of five miles."

Panel from Alton — A.M.

The Bowling Green.

RALLY, at any rate, a general belief prevails that the bowling green near to the ruins of Dieu-la-cresse Abbey was made by the monks, and it seems strange that its history has apparently escaped the researches of local antiquaries. The yew trees near the green are evidently centuries old, and as they seem to have been placed as a shelter to the green, it is just possible that the monks indulged in this pleasant and health-giving recreation.

About sixty years ago, the green was the scene of an exciting match. A local lawyer had matched the late Mr. William Goostrey, for ten pounds aside, against a crack Manchester bowler, the green being so peculiar in its construction, that the stranger was given a start of seven out of twenty-one. The night before the match someone, obviously a supporter of the Manchester player, stole one of Mr. Goostrey's bowls, the theft handicapping him apparently out of the contest. Annoyed that such an unfair advantage should have been taken, the Leek player's hand forgot its cunning until his opponent had made his score fifteen to *nil*, but then his marvellous knowledge of the green asserted itself, and getting the "jack" he ran out an easy winner. The missing bowl was afterwards discovered in the Churnet.

Of the old bowling green at Bagnall, an esteemed correspondent writes :—" Mr. Salt, the ' oldest inhabitant,' who is now crossing the shady side of this ' vale of tears ' (in a battered top hat, and supported by a pair of stalwart crutches), is fond of narrating how the patriotic parishioners of Bagnall red-lettered the conclusion of the peace after the battle of Waterloo by a ' peace celebration' dinner, and how, at the age of five, he witnessed them disporting themselves after it on the village bowling green. Mr. Twyford's grandfather played in a match here (about 1815) of the Leek and Moorlands Club *versus* a Potteries team, but can't say which won. ' Ah, well ! it was a famous victory ! ' "

The green is being restored to more than its pristine loveliness by an enterprising Leek man—Mr. John Keats, of Bagnall Hall—to the designs of Messrs. Sugden. A fine belt of shrubbery will encircle the green, which will be returfed in the most approved manner, and graced by a tall flag-staff and a low stone pavilion.

Topography, Population and Trade.

WE extract the following from White's "General History and Description of Staffordshire," published in 1834: Leek, the largest market town in the Hundred of Totmonslow, and one of the handsomest in the county, has long been engaged in the silk manufacture, and covers the summit and declivities of a pleasant eminence, above the river Churnet, and nearly in the centre of a deep but spacious valley, of a circular figure, the acclivities of which rise rapidly on every side to the distance of six or seven miles, and form one of nature's proudest and most stupendous amphitheatres, the foreground of which consists of fertile pastures, enlivened by several rivulets, the Cauldon canal, and many thriving plantations; whilst the more distant hills, rising tier above tier, partake of the general heathy character of the Moorlands, and are crowned on the north-east side by a long range of lofty perpendicular rocks and crags, called the Leek Roches. The town is distant 10 miles N.E. by E. of Burslem, 10 miles S.W. of Longnor, 14 miles S.E. of Macclesfield, 10 miles N. of Cheadle, and 154 N.W. by W.

of London. Its parish is a very extensive and highly picturesque district, which has increased its population since the year 1801, from 6,819 to 10,780 souls, and is divided into ten townships, of which the following is an enumeration, showing the annual value of the lands and buildings as assessed for the property tax in 1815, and the population of each in the year 1831 :—

Township.	Annual Value.	Population.
Leek and Lowe	£10,041	6372
Bradnop	2,946	467
Endon with		487
Longsdon and	6,294	398
Stanley		118
Heaton	2,076	402
Leek-Frith	4,958	873
Onecote	3,330	456
Rudyard and Cawdry	1,245	117
Rushton James	1,228	304
Rushton Spencer	1,690	337
Tittesworth	1,975	447

The silk manufacture in the town has long been in a flourishing state, and has of late years been so considerably extended, that several very extensive mills have been erected for twisting and doubling the silk ; and the population of the town now amounts to nearly 7,000 souls, though in 1821 it only amounted to 4,855 ; in 1811, to 3,703 ; and in 1801, to 3,489, The articles in silk and mohair, for which the town is chiefly celebrated, are sewing silks, twist, buttons, ribbons, ferrets, galloons, handkerchiefs, shawls, sarcenet, and broad silk. An immense quantity of Florentine buttons, consisting of wood, bone, or iron moulds, covered with worsted stuff, are also manufactured here, and give employment to many hundred women and children in

the surrounding villages, who are employed in sewing
the cloth upon the moulds.   In the silk trade many
large fortunes have been made by the late and present
manufacturers; and some of their weavers and other
workmen have been enabled, by industry and economy,
to build convenient houses for their own occupation;
but, unfortunately, a large number of the operatives
here lack that providence and sobriety which are so
much wanted in all other manufacturing towns.

The Price of Gas.

IN 1825, an Act of Parliament was obtained for lighting,
watching and improving the town of Leek, under the
control of a body of Commissioners, who were empowered to levy rates on the inhabitants to the amount
of £400 per annum; but for many years the expenditure
exceeded the receipts, so that by 1833 they had been
obliged to borrow £600 on mortgage.   They paid £2
each per annum for 103 street lamps, and £7 yearly
for lighting the church clock dial, to Mr. West, of
Durham, the constructor, principal proprietor, and lessee
of the gasworks, which were established in 1826, by
46 proprietors, in 200 shares of £26 each.   In 1833,
the gas was sold at 12s. 6d. per thousand cubic feet.

Singular Conversion.

BOUT the year 1824, Reuben Jackson, shoe-maker, West Street, was one of the worst characters in Leek, and he and his ferocious bull dog were well known at every bear and bull baiting and wakes for many miles round. Jackson, who was a strong, powerful man, had no objection to enter into a quarrel or a fight, and relied in a great measure upon his dog, which would worry anything he set him upon, to finish off his opponents. One night, the late Mr. George Bull, the most successful local preacher the Leek Wesleyan circuit ever knew, had engaged to preach in a cottage near to Jackson's house, but the congregation overflowed the limited house-room, and Mr. Bull delivered his address from the door-step. Jackson was attracted to the spot, not to listen to the preacher, whose blunt eloquence had won many bad characters to better lives, but with a view to inflict injury and annoyance upon him. Remarking to some of the bystanders, "My dog has pinned many a bull, and he shall pin another to-night," he set his dog at Mr. Bull, but to his utter amazement, the discrimin-ating animal pinned his master by the hand and tore his coat. Utterly defeated he hurried into his own cottage, and there succeeded in ridding himself of the infuriated dog. The next day, wondering what had caused the dog to act in such a remarkable manner, he went to Ipstones, picked a quarrel with a man, and then set the animal upon him. The dog at once attacked the man, and would have torn him to pieces if Jackson had not beaten him off. "I was then convinced," said Jackson some years afterwards at a lovefeast at Cheddleton Chapel, "that there was something in religion, and that God would not let my dog worry Mr. Bull. I at once gave up my wicked courses, parted with my dog, and cried to God, for Christ's sake, to pardon all my sins." Jackson kept the coat for twenty years, and frequently showed it to his friends as the means by which he found salvation. He afterwards successfully worked hard to save others, and died happily at Rocester, where he was a Primitive Methodist local preacher and class leader.

Dates of Parish Registers.

Leek	23rd April, 1634
Horton	1st October, 1653
Cheddleton	4th October, 1696
Rushton	1st October, 1700
Ipstones	1727
Endon	2nd March, 1730
Meerbrook	2nd April, 1738
Onecote	12th July, 1755

Ancient Place=names.

PITT in his "Topographical History of Staffordshire," published in 1817 by J. Smith, of Newcastle-under-Lyme, gives the following interesting list of the ancient and modern names of places in the district of Leek.

Anestanefelt	Alstonefield
Bidolph	Biddulph
Caldone ...	Caldon or Cauldon
Cedda, Cedla...	Cheadle
Cheltetone	Cheddleton
Chrochesdene or Crochestone	Croxden
Cuneshala	Consall
Denston	Denstone
Dulverne ...	Dilhorne
Enedien	Endon
Fernelege...	Farley
Hetone	Heaton
Hortone ...	Horton
Lec ...	Leek
Longenalrie	Longnor
Madevelt	Mayfield
Risetone ...	Rushton
Rudierd	Rudyard
Sceon	Sheen
Tene	Tean
Wareslie ...	Warslow

The First Figured Ribbon Weaver.

THOMAS HORTON, a Coventry man, who had served with the 87th in America, was the first weaver of figured ribbons in Leek, and worked for Mr. Thomas Sutton about the beginning of the present century.

"Nosey" Bowcock.

EADLE, Bang-beggar, and Pinner was the high-sounding title of an old-time guardian of the peace. Long before Leek blossomed into the possession of law clerks, clerks, superintendents, inspectors, and sergeants, the safety of the town was placed in the hands of a high constable, constable, and a third bearing the title set forth above. They were appointed annually at the Court Leet and Court Baron held by the lord of the manor, and were paid by him for their services. When these ancient courts ceased to be held in Leek is not quite clear, but the date of extinction is about 1840.

George Bowcock, known as "Nosey," in deference to a very prominent nasal organ, ornamented with all the signs of a bad fracture, was the last beadle, bang-beggar, and pinner who was appointed. He was an old pensioner, and lived in Pickwood Road, in those days a most respectable thoroughfare. He was tall and thin, and irascible. Children called him "Nosey" at the peril of their bones, for woe betided anyone whom he caught in the act. He had an affection for drink, and was often made the victim of practical jokes, especially by the wild doctors of the period. He died at the age of sixty-two, and was buried in the old churchyard by the Rev. R. H. Goodacre, the then curate, on May 23rd, 1846. Our sketch is from an old painting in the possession of Mr. William Allen, solicitor.

"NOSEY"
BOWCOCK

W. R. Kean del[?]

Congregationalism.

N the middle of the 17th century there lived and laboured the Rev. Joseph Machin, the Puritan minister of the Parish Church, Ashbourne, who was accustomed to preach the gospel in the Moorlands of Staffordshire. He was a gentle, loving, and faithful servant of Jesus Christ. In 1654 he removed to Astbury, Cheshire, and resided in the parsonage with the Rev. John Moxon, who joined with him in preaching there and at Rushton in this county, on alternate Sundays. About the same time Mr. Machin set up a monthly lecture at his own expense, by the most eminent ministers, in several towns including Stafford, Uttoxeter, and Leek, and in doing this he was sowing good seed which was to spring up after many days.

But evil times were impending, for in 1662, after Charles II.'s restoration, was passed the Act of Uniformity. Two thousand ministers could not conform to this and had to quit the Church of England, and henceforth became known as Nonconformists. Of this this number were Mr. Moxon and Mr. Machin.

Then in 1665 another Act was passed to harass
the Nonconformists, entitled the Oxford or Five-mile Act,
and the results of these oppressive measures were that
great numbers suffered the most extreme hardships in
being fined, or plundered, or driven from their families,
or imprisoned, and in other ways. Early in the struggle,
Mr. Machin, with whom we just now are specially
concerned, retired to Whitley and died in 1664, at the
age of 40. But the light he had kindled in this
neighbourhood was not quite extinguished. We find
from an indenture dated 1683, two years before the
death of Charles II, that there stood two dwelling-
houses on the Derby Street site, one occupied by
Catherine Grosvenor, the other by Randle Silitoe. This
property had recently been purchased from Thomas
Rudyerd, Esq., lord of the manor. But let us pass
on five years, to the Revolution of 1688, soon after
which was passed the famous Act of Toleration, which
relieved Dissenters from the penalties previously inflicted,
and permitted them to worship God according to the
dictates of their consciences. Availing themselves of
this greater freedom, it was about this time that
the Dissenters of Leek began to gather together as
a congregation. Most likely the occupiers of the two
cottages were of the number, or at least were friendly
towards them. Anyhow in a few years the property
was used for religious service, was rented and licensed
for that purpose by the first minister, the Rev. Josiah
Hargreaves, who was resident in the year 1695. It
was converted by him into a meeting house, and he
purchased it in the year 1716, as we learn from an
indenture of that date, and in 1732 made the property

over to trustees. The first trustees were the Rev.
Hugh Worthington, of Dean Row, in the county of
Chester; the Rev. Thomas Culcheth, of Macclesfield;
the Rev. Thomas Irlam, of Congleton; Richard Godwin,
of Thorncliffe, and John Bradley, of Rudyard Hall,
both in the parish of Leek.

Mr. Hargreaves had removed to St. Ives in 1725,
seven years previously, and it was not until the year
1730, that we have mention made of any other minister.
But in that year there came a young man to Leek,
Mr. Hugh Worthington, jun. (whose father was a
minister of a church at Dean Row, Cheshire), and he
entered upon his pastoral duties here, but stayed only
five years.

From this point we have no definite information
for a number of years, but we learn from " Historical
Sketches of Nonconformity in Cheshire," that Dr. Edward
Harwood, for some time prior to 1765, preached on
alternate Sabbaths at Wheelock, near Sandbach, and at
Leek. He was followed by the Rev. Benjamin Ratcliffe
who also preached at Leek on alternate Sundays and
was minister in 1773; but in 1775 a new lease was
made out, and new trustees appointed, among whom
was Samuel Bradley of the Fold, who is described as
a yeoman, and as eldest son and heir of John Bradley,
late of Rudyard, deceased, whose name appeared in the
first deed. There were also several of the Godwins
on this trust—a respectable Thorncliffe family, one of
whom was a minister. At the time this second deed
was issued, viz., in 1775, the Rev. Evan Lewis was
minister here; and in another deed, dated 29th September, 1818—43 years afterwards—the said Evan Lewis

VIEW IN DERBY STREET
LEEK. O. Mosley del.

is described as living at Coton Cottage, in the parish of Milwich, in this county.

In the year 1780 the first old chapel was taken down and rebuilt. A minister's house also was erected in the adjoining garden, and a small endowment fund was raised. At that date, however, the Rev. Evan Lewis had retired, and the Rev. James Evans was minister. Several years afterwards, perhaps about 1790, the congregation were the victims of a Church and King mob, who took the seats and fittings from the Chapel and burnt them in the Market Place. The senseless cry of " The Church in danger," had roused the feelings of the populace against Dissenters, and that was the way in which they were allowed, if not encouraged, to express them.

How long Mr. Evans remained in Leek, is not known, but it must have been about the close of the last century, or the beginning of this, that Jonathan Scott, usually called Captain Scott, because of his having been in the army, was an occasional " supply," and did great good. Mr. Scott was a most zealous preacher, and was regarded as the Cheshire Whitfield. He was ordained to the office of Evangelist, but though he chiefly devoted his energies to Cheshire he visited Leek as just stated.

At the time of Scott's death, in 1807, the Rev. Robert Smith was here as a minister, but he removed to Nantwich, and was succeeded by the Rev. Stephen Johnson, who laboured zealously, but whose stay was short. The Rev. James Morrow was elected minister in 1812 or 1813, and continued to officiate until his death in 1836. It was during his pastorate, viz., in

1830, that a number of Mr. Morrow's hearers left
Derby Street Chapel, and worshipped in a large room
in the Black's Head Inn yard. Various "supplies"
preached until the Rev. Wm. P. Bourne, student of
Highbury College, London, was elected by the newly-
formed church as their pastor. The congregation increasing, a new chapel (now the Temperance Hall) was
built in Union Street at a cost of £1,300. This was
in 1833, and the Ashton family and the Brough family
took a special interest in the undertaking. In consequence of ill-health Mr. Bourne was soon compelled
to the deep regret of his attached flock to resign his
charge and to remove to the south of England. He
settled at Teignmouth, Devon, where he died in
1840.

His successor was the Rev. Robert Goshawk, also
of Highbury College. On the death of Mr. Morrow,
and about the time that Mr. Goshawk became pastor
of the secession church, service was continued for some
months in Derby Street Chapel, but eventually the
premises were given up to the trustees, a majority of
whom were then worshippers in Union Street Chapel.
And thus a six years' division was healed, and the
two chapels were held by the same congregation. The
Derby Street Chapel was not open for divine services
on Sunday, excepting in connection with the Sunday
school which assembled there, until the erection of new
schools in Union Street, adjoining the chapel, in 1845,
at a cost of £450; but week-night services were held
in the gallery part of the building, which was floored
off for the purpose, until the whole pile was taken
down in 1862.

Early in the year 1856, Mr. Goshawk relinquished his connection with the church, and the Rev. Josiah Hankinson, a student of the Lancashire Independent College, filled the vacancy. In 1862 the corner stone of the present handsome church was laid by Mr. John Brough, and it was opened for service on December 22nd, 1863. Its total cost was about £5,000.

The old chapel stood a considerable distance back from Derby Street, and had a small graveyard in front. Between it and the Roe Buck Inn was the minister's house, and before Russell Street was opened, it was flanked on that side by a field. A schoolroom for the use of Mr. Morrow, who kept a private academy, had been built in front of the chapel gallery: it was supported by iron pillars and covered a portion of the graveyard. The little graveyard is covered by the north-west corner of the Church. Beneath the right-hand entrance porch is the grave of Mr. and Mrs. Morrow. And a memorial tablet, on which are engraved the names of all who were interred beneath, excepting such as had no memorial stones, has been placed on the right-hand vestibule, from which it will be seen that Mrs. Morrow was the last interment.

Abridged from an anniversary sermon, preached in 1890, by the Rev. Josiah Hankinson.

Rudyard Lake.

HE late Dr. Garner, F.L.S., was of opinion that a hundred years ago, the site occupied by Rudyard Lake was a valley through which ran a small rivulet. An engineer conceived the idea of forming the lake, and accordingly dammed up the rivulet. The water, however, was not sufficient, so he went to the watershed at Axe Edge, and made a large culvert, through which he carried a portion of the water which naturally would have flowed into the western sea. This diversion caused the stolen water to flow into the Churnet, and thence by means of the Dove and Trent into the Humber.

In Rudyard Vale, in the neighbourhood of Horton, there is a capacious reservoir, made by the proprietors of the Grand Trunk Canal, to provide an unfailing supply of water for the upper part of their navigation. This reservoir is about a mile and three quarters in length, and more than one-eighth of a mile in breadth, and its depth is about fifteen feet above their guage. It contains when full 2,420,000 entire yards of water, or sufficient to supply their canal 100 miles in length,

or to fill a lock three yards deep 10,000 times; it is
consequently a sufficient supply in a dry season.—Pitt's
Staffordshire.

THE REGATTA.

The local poet of the period, advertised the regatta,
which took place in 1856, in the following fashion:—

Good people all, both great and small, come listen for
    awhile,
I'll sing to you a verse or two, that's sure to make
    you smile,
It's of the grand regatta and the glorious fun and lark,
That will take place upon the lake, in famous Rudyard
    Park.
Chorus—
Then haste away without delay if you wish to have
    a lark,
Make no delay but haste away and visit Rudyard Park.

On the Twenty-first of April young men and maidens
    gay,
To see the lark in Rudyard Park, some thousands
    trudge away.
From Burslem, Leek, and Congleton, devoid of care or
    pain,
From Macclesfield and Manchester they come upon
    the train.

To commence the sport at one o'clock they make the
    valleys ring,
The Artillery cannons will be fired by bombardier King,
And then there'll be a rowing match, believe me what
    I write,
To see the boats skim through the lake will fill you
    with delight.

The bands they will so merrily play, and ladies they
    will sing,
Some will waltz all round the park and dance the
    Highland fling,

The Manchester regatta men are going to be there,
And the little iron steamer, too, the Countess of
Ellesmere.

There'll be a steeple chase, and barrow race, and games
of every sort,
The May pole will be trimmed with flowers to carry
on the sport,
There'll be firing at the targets and while the boats
do run,
There'll be a jolly sack race, that will cause both mirth
and fun.

There never was such sport and fun or such a jolly
lark,
As will take place upon the lake this day in Rudyard
Park,
For every game that you can name, as ever yet was
known,
Will be played in Rudyard Park on Easter Monday
afternoon.

The Society of Friends.

 UAKERS are ancient in their connection with Leek. In 1654, according to the Friends' minute book, the town was visited by Richard Hirkook, who "met with very rough treatment." Thomas Hammersley, who is supposed to have been a Leek man, appears to have been prominently connected with them at this period, and in the year above-mentioned he was allowed to serve as foreman upon a jury without taking the oath, the judge afterwards complimenting him upon the "upright verdict" he had brought in (George Fox's *Journal*). In the following year the Quakers were persecuted for publishing to the Leek people "the excellency and spirituality of the true Gospel-worship," one Richard Dale, seventy years of age, being imprisoned for three weeks, and one William Yardley, for nineteen. In 1661, Henry Boman was prosecuted by James Sheldon, of Alstonefield, for not paying tithes, and was kept in gaol for nearly fourteen months.

The present meeting-house, of which we give a representation, was built in 1694, and a burial ground attached. During the visit of the Young Pretender in 1745, the building was "broak open in the night and

FRIENDS' MEETING-HOUSE.

turn'd into a stable, throwing the seats in a heap."
The soldiers also broke open two closets, but were
disappointed in their search for money. On the other
hand, Mr. Toft, of Haregate, a Quaker, who is believed
to have written the account of the outrage, insisted
upon the Scotchmen piling their arms at his front-door,
whilst he entertained them with boiled beef and
vegetables.

It was in this burial-ground that Margaret Lucas, the
preacher, who wrote an account of her "Convincement
and Call to the Ministry" (published in London in 1797)
was buried in 1769. The curious little book is prefixed
with "the testimony of the friends of the Quarterly
Meeting of Staffordshire, held by adjournment at Leek,
the third of the fifth month, 1770," and states that she
was educated in the national worship, and strictly
conformed to its external rites and ceremonies, but
afterwards joined the Society of Friends.

Curious Highway Cases.

N July 14th, 1835, a curious case was tried
at Mayfield. Isaac Hesford, collector at the
Leek Edge toll-gate, was summoned for
charging the Rev. E. J. Moulton, of Leek, father of
Dr. Moulton, President of Wesleyan Conference, 1890,
the sum of threepence, as double toll, when he was
proceeding to discharge his ministerial duties of the
Sabbath day, and had claimed exemption on that
ground. Mr. Flint, of Uttoxeter, appeared for the
complainant, and Mr. F. Cruso, of Leek, for the
defendant. After hearing both sides, the magistrates
decided that the claim to exemption was fully established, and decided accordingly, ordering the lessee to
pay costs.

Ten years later, the keeper of the Waterhouses
toll-bar was summoned for refusing to allow Mr. John
Nadin, a local preacher of Hartington, to pass through
the gate without paying toll, when driving to his Sunday
preaching appointment. The magistrates upheld the
preacher's claim to exemption. Mr. William Challinor
appeared for Nadin, and was thanked by the Local
Preachers' meeting for the marked ability he had shown,
and for his generosity in making no charge for his
services.

Ibolidaps.

BOUT five hundred years ago, it is probable that tents were erected in the Old Church-yard, and that the memory of the patron saint was kept green by a fast, followed next day by a feast. Gradually, however, the fast was forgotten and only the feast remembered, and the Wakes was "characterised by merrymaking and often disgraced by indulgence and riot." Shakespeare discredits one of his characters by saying that " he haunts wakes, fairs, and bear baitings,"—an eloquent testimony to the way in which the festival was observed during the Elizabethan era. In Leek, too, the occasion has fallen off its saintly pedestal. Those whose memories are good for fifty years will remember the yearly incursions of country and Pottery cousins; how they swarmed into the town in carts of every description. No thought was paid as to how many persons the horse could draw: how many the vehicle would hold was the only considera-tion. It was, indeed, from their visits that the term a " Pottery load" became a synonym for a cruelly over-laden horse. Arrived at Leek, which is said to be "out o' th' noise," these fearful "sisters, cousins, and aunts" and brothers, nephews, and uncles ate and drank neither wisely nor well—only too much, and then made the night hideous with shouts and screams as they "rattled o'er the stony streets" on their way home. Since then, however, a change for the better has taken place, and although the high level of five centuries back is not reached—although there is little evidence of saintly reverence or devotion,—the festive season is more soberly and rationally observed, and signs are not wanting that the Wakes is hurrying along the road so fortunately fatal to bull-baiting and bear-baiting.

Club-day, too, a day formerly devoted to the celebration of the anniversaries of friendly societies, is declining in popularity, and is now observed as a children's festival.

Leek to Daventry in 1838.

MR. F. A. NUNNS, a son of the nurseryman who, early in the present century, had a shop in Leek Market Place and cultivated "Nunn's Gardens," writes of a journey from Leek to Coventry in 1838:—"We had to drive to Whitmore, the nearest railway station to Leek, and thence by train to Birmingham and Rugby. We travelled second class. The windows of the carriages were not glazed, and on the journey by rail, we had to put up an umbrella to keep off the rain. The third class carriages were 'stand-ups,' not unlike the cattle trucks of the present time."

Westwood Hall.

OHN DAVENPORT, who was born in Derby Street, on September 9th, 1765, purchased Westwood in 1813 from the Hon. William Booth-Grey, who lived there for some time. The estate remained in the family until 1868, when it was

Tower of Westwood, Hall.

acquired by Mr. John Robinson, the mansion having been re-built in 1851. The hall is considered to be an exceptionally fine specimen of modern Elizabethan architecture, and is situated on a well-wooded eminence high above the Churnet, and amidst lovely scenery.

Moorland Traditions.

HE wild and lonely moorlands about Leek abound with weird traditions and superstitions. The headless horseman dashes over stock and stone, and snatches up any unfortunate wight who may chance to come belated in his way; when, after a wild chase over hill and dale, the victim is left almost lifeless at his own door. Then there is the ghastly story of the man-eating family, whose crimes are discovered at last by a wandering pedlar who seeks shelter for the night at the lonely house in the waste. The pedlar is accosted in the doorway by the youngest child of the house, who remarks admiring his fat hands, and exclaims "What nice pies they will make!" The pedlar takes to flight without another word, but the men of the house pursue him with bloodhounds, and the pedlar only escapes by crawling up to his neck in water under a bridge. Men and hounds are close about him above and below, but the dogs are foiled by the running water, and at daylight the chase is given up, and the pedlar crawls away, half dead, to bring the officers of justice upon the scene. The wretched ghouls expiated their crimes on the jibbet,

and the house was levelled to the ground, but still at
night the men and hounds are heard to urge their
dreadful chase, and woe betide the poor soul that
meets them! It may be said that official records of
any such trial and condemnations are wanting. But it
must not be hastily concluded, therefore, that the story
is altogether baseless. A more humorous story is
that of the old woman who was a witch and used to
traverse the country under the form of a hare. So
well known were the old dame's vagaries, that it was
the custom of the neighbouring farmers to bribe the
old witch's husband to turn her out before their dogs.
Puss always afforded an excellent course, but when
hard pressed she would suddenly disappear. But one
day as she was dashing over a stone wall the foremost
dog got a grip at her, and drew out a mouthful of
hair; but on the other side of the wall nothing was
to be seen but an old woman ruefully rubbing a
wounded patch on her pate, and eyeing men and dogs
with such malignant glance that all slunk hastily away.
—*All the Year Round.*

Marsden of Cowhaye.

JANE, the wife of Anthony Marsden, of Cowhaye (and
daughter of Thomas Gilman, of Bradnop) had, twice
twenty-four children by her one husband. One of them,
the Rev. Thomas Marsden, rector of Llanfrathen, in
Wales, published in 1848, the "Poet's Orchard."

Beggars' Way Field.

FROM the diary of a late resident we glean that Mr. W. Phillips purchased Beggars' Way Field from Messrs. Farm and Hilditch, paying what was then called a very high price, namely, £500. When he had improved it, he let it to a James Bestwick, when it was made to pay five per cent on the purchase. Mr. Philips also said that his father purchased the "Turk's Head" publichouse, with the field, then called "Turk's Field," (wherein he erected his residence) and a field opposite the railway station, for £1,000, from a family named Buxton of Ashbourne. The publichouse he afterwards sold to one Robert Leason for £300.

Another Tragical Event on Gun.

THE farm of Wetwood lies on the east side of Gun, and was once the property of the Hulme family. In the month of November, 1763, Mrs. Ann Hulme, second wife of Mr. John Hulme, of Wetwood, was returning home on horseback over Gun, having a basket containing pitchers. When going through a gate, but a few fields from her home, the pitchers rattled, the horse took fright and started off, when her dress caught on the gate, dragged her off the horse, and she was killed. She was a clever horsewoman, and had her dress not caught on the gate, she would have preserved her seat. She was interred in Leek Parish Churchyard on the 17th November, 1763, being 46 years of age.

Dr. W. F. Moulton.

ILLIAM FIDDIAN MOULTON, M.A., D.D.,
President of the Wesleyan Conference 1890-91,
was born at 15, Ballhaye Street, on March
14th, 1835, in the house formerly occupied by Miss
Brough, and nearly opposite to Queen Street. His father
was the Rev. James Ebenezer Moulton, who was third
minister at Leek in 1833-34-35 ; and his great grandfather was Thomas Bakewell, one of Wesley's first
preachers, who wrote the hymn, " Hail, Thou once
despised Jesus." Dr. Moulton was educated at Wood-

house Grove School, near Leeds—one of the Connexional schools for ministers' sons. At the Grove young Moulton soon won distinction as a scholar, and he is one of his old school's brighest ornaments. In 1851, when only 16 years of age, he matriculated at the London University, graduating as B.A., in 1854, with honours in mathematics, and in 1856 he took the M.A. degree, with the gold medal for mathematics and natural philosophy. In 1858 he entered the Wesleyan ministry, and was appointed assistant classical tutor at the Richmond Branch of the Theological Institution, and six years later the senior tutor in classics and Hebrew. For 16 years he was at Richmond College, and during those years some 500 ministers passed in and out before him. He was elected into the Legal Hundred in 1872, the earliest date possible, having only travelled the necessary fourteen years. In 1874 he was designated by the Conference to the headmastership of the Leys School, Cambridge, receiving during the same year the honorary degree of D.D. from Edinburgh University. Dr. Moulton was soon recognised as a power in Cambridge life, not merely in Wesleyan circles, but in the University, and the University did credit to itself as well as honour to Dr. Moulton by conferring on him in 1877 the honorary degree of M.A. He has rendered signal service to all Christian churches and to the nation at large by his valuable labours as a member of the New Testament Revision Committee. He is also the author of several standard theological and other works.

ⱦopulation Statistics.

UNTIL 1851 the local census returns were for the township of Leek and Lowe, Tittesworth being separately enumerated. The figures for the first half of the present century were :—

	1801.	*1811.*	*1821.*	*1831.*	*1841.*	*1851.*
Leek and Lowe.	3489	3703	4855	6374	7233	8602
Tittesworth ..	274	273	288	447	438	606
	3763	3976	5143	6821	7671	9208

In 1855 the return was based upon the radius of 1,500 yards from the Market Place, prescribed by the Leek Improvement Act, which was obtained in that year, and subsequent returns give the following figures :

	1861.	*1871.*	*1881.*	*1891.**
Leek	10,174	11,331	12,865	14,100

* Estimated.

Capture of Smith O'ⱦrien.

THE capture of Smith O'Brien was effected by a mail guard, named Hulme, a native of White Chimnies, near Leek. He received the reward of £500, and resigned his situation on the Great Southern and Western Irish Railway, and returned to Leek.

A French View of Leek.

WE extract the following from Moreri's *Historical Dictionary* (1716) :—" LEEK : ville d'Angleterre, avec marché, dans le compté de Staff : á 154 milles Anglois de Londres. C'est la principale ville des Pays-marècageux, rénommée par une-espèce d'*excellente biere* qu'on y fait, et que les Anglois appelent *Ale;* et par le bons edifices qu'on y voit."

[LEEK, a town in England, with a market, in the county of Stafford, 154 English miles from London. This is the principal town of the Moorlands, renowned for a kind of *excellent beer* which is made there, and which the English call *ale*, and by good edifices which are seen there.]

The Fynney Lane Estate.

THE father of the late Mr. William Phillips purchased the Fynney Lane Estate from one Ferdinando Bullock, residing in the south, for £23 pounds per acre. The acreage was 183, and the purchase money £4,109, exclusive of £600 paid for the timber. The tenant paid 17s. per acre. Soon after the purchase Mr. Bullock was killed whilst out hunting.

Obituary of Notable People.

LSOP, JAMES, silk manufacturer, aged 62, 1868.

Anderson, Rev. Father, 60, 1884.

Andrew, Joshua, 74, 1891.

Ashenhurst, John, of Ashenhurst, 1597.

Ball, Charles, founder of Leek Sunday Schools, 1823.

Ball, Martha, 100, 1825.

Barlow, Benjamin, organist, 60, 1873.

Barnes, Rev. Jeremiah, 75, 1883.

Beresford, Anthony, 102, 1874.

Best, John, of Horton, 104.

Bosley, Thomas, of Longsdon, 110, 1590.

Bowcock, Corporal Samuel (a Waterloo hero), 82, 1858.

Bowcock, " Nosey " (George), 62, 1846.

Bradley, Joseph, old soldier, 97, 1879.

Brealey, Thomas, land agent, 70, 1870.

Brindley, Dr. James, 39, 1841.

Brindley, James, canal engineer, 55, 1772.

Brookes, Mary, of Horton, 119, 1787.

Brough, Benjamin, old soldier, 58, 1880.

Brough, John, 73, 1882.

Brough, Joshua, silk manufacturer, 83, 1885.

Burrows, Peter, last driver of Defiance coach, 1853.

Bull, George, grocer and local preacher, 77, 1872.
Caldwell, Dr. Richard, 1585.
Carr, Thomas, silk manufacturer, 58, 1867.
Carr, Thomas, senr., silk manufacturer, 81, 1844.
Chadwick, Dr. Charles, 1836.
Chorley, Joshua, 1837.
Condlyffe, William, gentleman, 70, 1867.
Cooper, Dr. Richard, 70, 1872.
Cruso, John, solicitor, 77, 1867.
Cumberlidge, William, murdered at Foxlow, 1854.
Cutting, Richard, silk manufacturer, 84, 1856.
Daintry, Rev. John, vicar, 58, 1751.
Davenport, Dr. Peter Walthall, 36, 1813.
Davenport, Uriah, ringer for 70 years, 91, 1860
Deacon, Rev. George Edward, vicar, 77, 1886.
Fergyson, Robert, auctioneer and ironmonger, 67, 1866.
Flint, Dr. Charles, 74, 1864.
Fynney, Mountford, 68, 1881.
Fynney, William, of Fynney, 110, 1584.
Gaunt, Matthew, 78, 1873.
Gaunt, Richard, 1844.
Gee, David, silk manufacturer, 88, 1876.
Gent, Ellen, 104, 1737.
Gibson, Silas, 94, 1887.
Goodwin, Stephen, silk manufacturer, 55, 1888.
Griffin, Thomas, high constable, 1839.
Grosvenor, Dr. Thomas Fenton, 73, 1831.
Grosvenor, Dr. William, 101, 1765.
Hacker, John Heathcote, solicitor, 1870.
Hale, widow, 100, 1854.
Hammersley, William, 64, 1835.
Hanby, Thomas, father of Leek Methodism, 64, 1796.

Heath, George, the Moorland poet, 25, 1869.
Heathcote, Rev. Thomas Henry, vicar, 77, 1860.
Heapy, William, shot at Burslem, 1842.
Howard John, old soldier, 85, 1879.
Hulme, Dr. J. Davenport, 75, 1848.
Hulme, William, 100, 1538.
Jennings, Francis William, banker, 69, 1880.
Jones, John, schoolmaster, 79, 1833.
Jones-Byrom, Commander W. H., 36, 1867.
Killmister, Abraham K. ("Tom Oakleigh"), solicitor, 1858.
Lockett, Elizabeth, 100, 1748.
Lovatt, John, silk manufacturer, 48, 1864.
Lucas, Margaret, Quakeress, 68, 1769.
Macclesfield, first Earl of, 66, 1732.
Magnier, Peter Louis, French prisoner, 92, 1874.
Mien, Jean Baptiste François, 83, 1870.
Mills, Elizabeth, 100, 1858.
Millward, Samuel, silk manufacturer, 47, 1837.
Naden, John, gibbetted on Gun, 1731.
Nall, George, printer and postmaster, 69, 1870.
Nall, Robert, at Verulam, 37, 1871.
Needham, Robert, of Rudyard Hall, 80, 1887.
Nicholson, Joshua, founder of Institute, 73, 1885.
Phillips, William, of the Fields, 85, 1871.
Redfern, Thomas, solicitor, 64, 1864.
Rider, George, parish clerk, 91, 1863.
Robins, Dr. James, 56, 1856.
Rogers, Ann, 100, 1850.
Russell, John, senr., silk manufacturer, 71, 1871.
Shallcross, Mary, 100, 1852.
Smith, William (" Buttermilk "), 1866.
Sneyd, Rev. John, 74, 1873.

Sykes, Joseph, master of Grammar School, 56, 1888.
Trafford, William ("Now thus"), 1697.
Turnock, Edward, of Rushton, 105, 1753.
Tuyl, Miss Maria Van, 80, 1877.
Vaudrey, Rev. J. H., curate, 34, 1869.
Walker, Charles, local preacher, 73, 1871.
Ward, Anthony, silk manufacturer, 54, 1840.
Ward, John, silk manufacturer, 68, 1890
Wardle, Ellen, of Butterton, 104, 1837.
Wardle, James, 85, 1862.
Woodward Ellen, of Leekfrith, 10c, 1864.
Worthington, Andrew Jukes, silk manufacturer, 62, 1872.

Chronological Table.

1085   Leek a royal possession, afterwards given to Hugh Lupus.

1208   Leek charter signed by King John.

1209   Earliest trace of Ipstones.

1214   Dieu-la-cresse Abbey erected.

1215   Richard Patricius vicar of Leek.

1246   Consall estate granted to Sir Wm. de Chettelton.

1297   Town and Church destroyed by fire.

1299   Destructive Hurricane, lasting a month.

1310   Ashcombe belonged to the Sneyds.

1313   Original charter enrolled.

1318   Edward II. at Leek.

1334   Edward III. gave Rushton-spencer to Sir Roger Swinnerton.

1485   Button-making carried on.

1539   Dieu-la-cresse surrendered to the King.

1552   Manor granted to Rauffe Bagenalle.

1558   Last Abbot of Dieu-la-cresse made his will.

1559   Tithes of Leek given by Queen Elizabeth to Sir Rauffe Bagenalle.

1562   The Smiths bought Kniveden.

1574 Date on Cheddleton tower.
1585 Dr. Richard Caldwell died.
1597 Manor, fairs, and markets bought by Thos. Rudyerd.
1600 Cheddleton Church sold.
1612 Horton Church sold.
1626 Date on Roe Buck Hotel.
1627 Leek Old Hall (Red Lion) erected.
1629 May Fair and Pie Powder Court established.
1640 Ralph Sneyd, M.P. for Staffordshire.
1643 Town garrisoned during Civil War.
1658 Publication of banns of marriage at Market Cross discontinued.
1666 First Earl of Macclesfield born.
1668 Parish Church chimes and clock fixed.
1670 Date on Cheddleton porch.
1673 "The third market in the county."—*Blome.*
1680 Date of Lilly's prophecy.
1685 Introduction of silk weaving.
 „ Revocation of Edict of Nantes.
1694 Friends' Meeting House built.
1696 Ash's Almshouses opened.
1697 "Now thus" died.
1699 Deaths thrice the births through Black Plague.
1711 Earliest record of Town Lands Trustees.
1713 Margaret Lucas came to Leek.
1714 Vicarage rebuilt.
1715 Meeting-house wrecked and furniture burnt in Market Place by a mob.
1716 Leek famous for good ale.
1717 Extraordinary floods.
1718 First Earl of Macclesfield became Lord Chancellor.
1723 Lord Macclesfield bought manor of Leek.

1723 Grammar School founded.

„ Public reception of Lord Chancellor Macclesfield.

„ Robert Harrison of Leek, under-sheriff of Stafford-shire.

1725 First Earl of Macclesfield fined £30,000.

1731 John Naden committed for trial.

1732 First Earl of Macclesfield died.

1735 Thomas Loxdale, vicar, resigned.

1738 John Naden condemned to death and executed.

1741 Simon Sherrat starved to death on Morridge.

1742 James Brindley, the engineer, came to Leek.

1745 Young Pretender at Leek.

1753 Date of Horton Church bells.

„ Onecote Church foundation stone laid.

1755 Earthquake at Leek.

„ Onecote Church opened.

1757 Church damaged by violent wind.

1758 Naylor's Dole bequeathed.

1760 Printing introduced by Francis Hilliard.

1765 James Brindley, the engineer, left Leek.

„ John Davenport born at Leek.

1768 Old Workhouse in Brook Street erected.

1769 Margaret Lucas interred in Quakers' burying ground.

1772 Date of Rushton James Enclosure Act.

„ First organist at Old Church appointed.

„ James Brindley died.

„ John Wesley first at Leek.

„ St. Edward's Church first organ opened.

1774 John Wesley's second visit.

1776 Date of Rushton Spencer Enclosure Act.

„ Roman coins, "more than would have filled the largest whisket," found two miles south of Leek.

1777 Dr. Johnson at Leek.

„ Earthquake at Leek and Rushton.

1782 John Wesley's third visit.

1783 „ „ fourth visit.

1785 Warslow and Elkstones Churches consecrated.

1787 Mary Brookes, of Horton, died, aged 119.

1788 John Wesley's last visit.

1790 Ipstones Church re-built.

1791 Congregational Chapel seats burnt in Market Place by a mob.

„ First subscription library formed.

1793 Rudyard Lake made to feed Trent and Mersey Canal.

1794 Yeomanry troop formed.

1796 Great hailstorm.

„ Thomas Hanby, father of Leek Methodism, died, aged 64.

1797 First Sunday school established by Wesleyans.

1800 Figured ribbons first woven.

„ Leek canal finished.

1805 Date of Leek Enclosure Act.

1806 Old market cross removed to Cornhill.

„ William Badnall left £1,000 to Leek poor.

„ Old Town Hall built : cost £808 17s. 5½d.

1810 Mount Pleasant opened.

1813 Great fire at Swythamley.

„ John Davenport bought Westwood.

1814 Great snowstorm.

1815 Date of Horton Enclosure Act.

„ Wakeman drowned in Churnet.

„ West Street school opened.

1816 Loyal Volunteers enrolled.

1816　St. Edward's restored.

1817　Blanketeers marched through the town.

1819　Highfield Hall built by Richard Badnall.

1820　Two cannon balls found in old Basford lane.

1821　Bible Society formed.

1822　Wesleyan Missionary Society established.

1823　Badnall, Ellis, and Co.'s bank started.

,,　　Charles Ball, founder of Sunday schools died.

,,　　Old Savings Bank opened.

1825　First Improvement Act granted.

,,　　Two cannon balls found in old Basford lane.

1826　Beverley baloon fell on Gun to the consternation
　　　of natives.

,,　　Gas first used.

,,　　Great snowstorm.

1827　Badnall, Ellis, and Co.'s bank closed.

1828　Ashenhurst bought by the Phillipses.

,,　　Ballhaye Street Chapel opened.

,,　　First Roman Catholic Chapel erected.

,,　　Sir Walter Scott at Leek.

1829　Manchester and Liverpool District Bank opened.

,,　　Old Cattle Market bought by Town Lands Trustees.

,,　　Steam first used.

1830　Great fire at Wreford's mill.

,,　　Last interment in Quakers' burial ground.

1831　Bull baited at Longnor.

,,　　Catholic bazaar.

,,　　First cheese fair.

1832　Church clock lit with gas.

,,　　Edward Buller, M.P., first elected.

,,　　John Davenport first elected M.P. for Stoke-upon-
　　　Trent.

1832 Joseph Mellor sentenced to death at Staffordshire Assizes for stealing bread and cheese at Leek.

1834 Old Congregational Chapel opened.

1835 Bees swarmed on shoulders and neck of servant girl.

„ Highway robberies at Pack Saddle Hollow.

1836 One thousand Leek teetotallers dined together.

„ Suicide of a Spaniard at Red Lion.

1837 Charles Carus Wilson imprisoned for three months.

„ First meeting of Leek Board of Guardians.

„ Forty-nine per cent. signed marriage register with a cross.

„ Great thunderstorm.

„ Hay sold at 10 guineas per ton.

„ Heavy snowstorm in May.

„ Mechanics' Institute established.

„ Oddfellowship (M.U.) established.

„ Samuel Millward, who kept a pack of harriers, died.

„ Silk mill at Cheddleton.

1838 George Allen, George Davenport, and Samuel Harrison drowned in Rudyard Lake.

„ Great thunderstorm : Old Church damaged.

1839 Hand-loom Weaving Parliamentary Inquiry.

„ Hurricane.

„ Thomas Griffin, head constable of Leek, accidentally killed.

1840 Ballhaye bought in at 8,500 guineas.

„ Commercial Bank broke.

1842 Chartists marched into the town, and William Heapy shot at Burslem.

„ Charles Adderley, M.P., first elected.

„ Leek Yeomanry re-enrolled.

1843 National school opened.

1844 Brumby, a Leek schoolmaster, published a system of stenography.

„ Cricket club established.

„ George Heath, Moorland Poet, born.

1845 Commissioners bought gasworks.

„ Gas 12/6 per 1000 cubic feet.

1846 Last of the Joliffes died in Mill Street, aged 85. Sir Symon Degge writing in 1662, said, Jolley, " Lord of Leeke, half of Chedleton, Carswall, Prestwood, Botham's and a pawn in Ashenhurst's estate." His fortune was equal to a million sterling of modern currency. The Staffordshire estates were sold in 1765.

„ Staffordshire Agricultural Society's first show at Leek.

1847 Fowler, Gaunt, and Co.'s bank closed.

„ St. Luke's foundation stone laid.

1848   do.   consecrated.

1849 Churnet Valley line opened.

„ Inquiry as to Town Lands.

1851 Cock-low barrow opened.

„ Westwood Hall re-built.

1853 Public baths opened.

1854 William Cumberlidge killed at Fox Low.

1855 Improvement Act granted.

„ Staffordshire Agricultural Society's second show at Leek.

1856 Lord Macclesfield's water rights bought for £11,000.

„ Regatta at Rudyard.

„ Rev. Robert Goshawk resigned.

„ Richard Cutting died.

„ St. Edward's nave roof restored.

1857 Brunswick Chapel opened.
,,   Cemetery provided.
,,   Old market cross removed to Cemetery.
1859 "Cap Sunday" discontinued.
1860 Volunteers enrolled.
1861 St. Luke's organ opened.
1863 Congregational Church opened.
1864 Cheddleton Church restored.
1865 Roman Catholic Chapel in King Street erected.
1866 First printing machine.
,,   Smith murdered at Whiston Eaves.
1867 Leek to Stoke line opened.
,,   Old Church new chancel opened.
,,   St. Edward's re-opened.
1868 John Robinson bought Westwood.
1869 George Heath, Moorland Poet, died.
,,   W. May drowned in Rudyard Lake.
1870 Cottage Hospital erected.
,,   Dieu-la-cresse offered for sale.
,,   First paper established : "The Leek Times."
,,   Hyde and Stretch drowned in Rudyard Lake.
1871 Ragged School opened.
1872 Duke and Duchess of Teck at Leek.
,,   Nine hours' system adopted.
,,   Old Town Hall sold.
1873 Neal Dow at Leek.
1874 Fatal boiler explosion at Upperhulme.
,,   New chimes at Old Church.
1877 Ipstones Church re-opened.
,,   Jennings's bank closed.
,,   Midland Branch Bank opened and closed.
1878 St. Edward's new organ opened.

1878   Staffordshire Agricultural Society's third show at Leek.

1880   Harry Tichborne Davenport, M.P., first elected.

„   William Young Craig, M.P., elected.

1882   Old Savings Bank closed.

1883   New bank in Derby street opened.

1884   Town Hall purchased for £5,000.

„   Nicholson Institute opened.

1885   Charles Crompton, Q.C., first M.P. for Leek division.

1886   Ten per cent. signed marriage license with a cross.

1887   St. Mary's Church opened.

1891   Great snowstorm (May 16th).

Index.